PENGUIN BOOKS

THE BOOK OF BABEL

Nigel Lewis was born in 1948 and educated at Midhurst Grammar School and Magdalene College, Cambridge. He is the author of a verse translation of *The Soldier's Tale* and, more recently, a history of the Slapton Sands tragedy in the run-up to D-Day, *Channel Firing*. He lives in north London with his wife, Susan, and their two sons.

The Book of Babel

WORDS AND THE WAY WE SEE THINGS

NIGEL LEWIS

PENGUIN BOOKS

PENGUIN BOOKS

Published by the Penguin Group
Penguin Books Ltd, 27 Wrights Lane, London W8 5TZ, England
Penguin Books USA Inc., 375 Hudson Street, New York, New York 10014, USA
Penguin Books Australia Ltd, Ringwood, Victoria, Australia
Penguin Books Canada Ltd, 10 Alcorn Avenue, Toronto, Ontario, Canada M4V 3B2
Penguin Books (NZ) Ltd, 182–190 Wairau Road, Auckland 10, New Zealand

Penguin Books Ltd, Registered Offices: Harmondsworth, Middlesex, England

First published by Viking 1994
Published in Penguin Books 1995
1 3 5 7 9 10 8 6 4 2

Printed in England by Clays Ltd, St Ives plc

To Benedict and Mark

Metaphor is the dreamwork of language and, like all dreamwork, its interpretation reflects as much on the interpreter as the originator . . . So too understanding a metaphor is as much a creative endeavor as making a metaphor, and as little guided by rules
    – Donald Davidson, *What Metaphors Mean*, 1981

Even for our grandparents a 'House', a 'Well', a familiar tower, their very dress, their cloak, was infinitely more, infinitely more intimate: almost everything a vessel in which they found and stored humanity . . . The animated, experienced things that share our lives are coming to an end and cannot be replaced. We are perhaps the last to have still known such things
    – Rainer Maria Rilke to his Polish translator, 1925

CONTENTS

PART ONE Dreamwork of Language 1

I HORSEHAIR 3
Blamyra 3 *Panache* 10 *'Like Cauliflowers . . .'* 13 *Frizzy Hair* 17
Chevaux de Frise 21 *Haywire* 26 *Black and Blue* 26 *A Head of Hair* 29
Grifo and Mota 31

II SPRING DAY 36
Butter-Birds 36 *Eggs in the Mirror* 38 *The Halfwit in the Hedgerow* 43
Gaulish 48 *Spots and Dots* 49 *Buds and Buttons* 52

III DAY SPRING 54
Death of the Dawn 54 *Goodly Light* 58 *Orient* 60 *The Returning
Bird* 61 *Alektor* 62 *Day Clean* 62 *The Hesperides* 64 *Gold* 66
Akkisukpok 69 *The Sunshine Breakfast* 70 *Orange* 71

IV PLOUGHING THE SEA 79
Words like Wheat 79 *Ploughing the Sea* 81 *Pioneer and Clown* 83
Pigs . . . 84 *. . . and Ploughs* 90 *Slugs and Snails* 93 *Woodpecker* 94
The White 97 *Little Nails* 99 *Spike* 99 *Cicada* 101 *Spray* 103
Garbo 105 *Judas's Bran* 108 *Flour and Flower* 112 *Malaka* 113

V BIRDS OF A FEATHER 115
Wine in a Cup 115 *Blackamoor's Teeth* 120 *Porcelain* 121 *Perna* 124
Pearls before Swine 127 *Birds of a Feather* 129 *'Of Ireland . . .'* 132
Canard 136 *Foam-Born* 139 *Star of the Sea* 147

PART TWO Lexicon 155

Bibliography 307

Dreamwork of Language

PART ONE

Dreamwork & Language

I HORSEHAIR

Blamyra

A spring day by the sea. A crisp breeze is blowing. There are waves on the sea and clouds in the sky. Sheep and spring lambs are grazing in a field.

All around us in this scene are categories which the intellect recognizes but the imagination overrides, and in the boundaries between them – the shoreline separating land and sea, the horizon where land and sea end and the sky begins – are the makings of metaphors.

The word metaphor, used of words, is itself a metaphor. It means, literally, a 'carrying over'. In modern Greek it still carries its literal as well as figurative meaning. The adjective *metaphoroikos* refers to any means of physical transport. *Metaphoréas*, 'a carrier', may refer to the national airline or to a railway porter.

In metaphor, words are 'carried over' boundaries, or 'transferred', to reappear in new contexts. The 'carrying' is done with varying degrees of conscious awareness. Our awareness of the presence of metaphor similarly varies. On the one hand we have the striking and often self-consciously 'flowery' metaphors of rhetoric, that ancient art in which metaphor was long ago recognized as the most important figure of speech. At the other extreme are words which have appeared for so long in their 'new' contexts and become so impacted in them that we tend to use them unawares, and take them for granted where they are. The 'eye' of a needle or the 'teeth' of a saw are examples of these 'dead metaphors'.

Janet Martin Soskice in her *Metaphor and Religious Language* states an important truth about language use when she writes in criticism of another scholar: 'To be "consciously alert" to all dead metaphor

would more likely be a sign of madness than of intellectual rigour.'
I would take that insight further. Metaphors are made in the
unconscious, and something in the metaphor-making process itself is
resistant to conscious examination and analysis. In the study of
metaphor, as in the study of other manifestations of the unconscious
mind, reason must operate in a world where reason does not rule.
Instead, a kind of mad logic holds sway. Not for nothing has
metaphor been called 'the dreamwork of language', although I should
add that that is only one of many definitions of metaphor (125 have
been counted). Many of those definitions conflict; none of them is
considered comprehensive.

Varro, the Roman etymologist of the first century BC, expressed a
form of the 'carrying over' of metaphor in a simple analogy. 'Often',
he wrote, 'the roots of a tree which is close to the line of the property
have gone out under the neighbour's cornfield.' Varro's tree was
language. Words too have roots. Metaphorical transference can occur
not only within languages, but between them. If we take Varro's 'line
of the property' to refer to the complex and fluctuating boundaries
between languages, for example, then a word apparently indigenous
to one's own land or language may in fact be a loan-word, originally
nourished by someone else's. A word may even become an expatriate,
dying out in the language of its origin but thriving in another.
Burrowing under the borderlines, like roots, words in Varro's image
are inveterate trespassers.

For the doctrinaire rationalist, this trespassing is an infernal nuisance.
For him, metaphors are 'category mistakes', semantic spanners deep in
the works of language. The philosopher Hobbes wrote of what he
called 'proper words'. From this strict rationalist perspective,
metaphors are instances of catachresis, 'improper use of words; application of a term to a thing which it does not properly denote', as the
Oxford Dictionary defines it. The trouble with that definition is that
metaphorical catachresis is not only a universal phenomenon in
language but that language as we know it is inconceivable without it.
Not even the act of rational thinking is free from it, for 'language', as
William Empson wrote (in *The Structure of Complex Words*), 'is full of
sleeping metaphors, and the words for mental processes are all derived
from older words for physical processes'. Where would philosophy

4

and psychology be without 'psyche', the concept of mind? Yet 'psyche' is a metaphor: it was originally associated with breathing.

Here in the field by the sea the imagination goes to work in other fields, trespassing between categories. The seeing eye of our seaside observer picks out the white patches of foam churned up at the waves' crests and scudding along the sea's surface, and he notes their resemblance to the energetic white horses (or kids, or lambs) in the field where he is standing. The perceived connection is helped along by, and helps along, the idea of the sea as another field, a stretch of land.

Today the sea isn't as craggily inhospitable as it can be, but in the crisp breeze it is slightly rough and wild, like uncultivated moorland, *blamyra*, as the Norwegians once called the Atlantic, 'the blue moor', and *dra over blamyra*, 'crossing the blue moor' for travelling to North America.

The sky, too, is a 'blue moor'. Perception of the sky and the clouds parallels perception of the sea and the sea-foam. Sky, sea, and land are perceived in terms of one another. There is much duplication of metaphor. In language, the sea's blue and white, and the sky's, tend to be perceived as being at one, as they are in the Greek flag, the *keeonolevkás*, the blue-and-white – the colour-combination in which Greek fishing boats, caïques, are often painted, and upon which James Joyce insisted for the binding of the first edition of *Ulysses*.

It is perhaps because of that blueness that the name for the sky in many European languages (French, Spanish, Italian) is also the word for 'heaven'. Even in German, *Himmel*. Through the smoked glass of the English language, however, the sky is seen in terms of cloud. That, in fact, is what the Old Norse word *sky* meant, a cloud. In English it replaced the Anglo-Saxon *welkin*, also cloud. English seems to be unique in this substitution of cloud for heaven, and if etymology is any guide, there is nothing new about English obsession with the weather.

Often the sky is perceived in terms of the sea. In the 1840s, in his *Modern Painters*, John Ruskin wrote of skies in which clouds were 'slipped over each other like the scales of a fish', and of banks of cloud exactly resembling 'sea-sand ribbed by the tide', which when separated produced 'the mottled or mackerel skies' ('wrinkled' my two-year-old son called them). 'Mother-of-pearl' is another long-standing description for certain configurations of cloud.

Ruskin loved delicate distinctions. The skies he liked best resembled nothing on earth at all. 'The appearance of the delicate ray far in the sky, threading its way among the thin, transparent clouds, while all around the sun is transparent fire', was for him 'the most beautiful phenomenon of all'. He was a collector of skyscapes from nature, a connoisseur and classifier of clouds. Some cloud-formations touched by light – the pearls of his collection – were extremely spiritual and evocative of the finer feelings. Others suggested the peasantry and the market square, like those 'vulgarly known as "mares' tails"', or the 'large, irregular fields of equal size, masses like flocks of sheep'.

Our observer, who happens himself to be a 'vulgar' peasant, may lack Ruskin's refinement, but he has the virtue of directness. If he is French, he will say of this sky filled with fleecy clouds simply that it is *moutonné*, 'sheeped', as a bibliophile might say of a book that it's 'foxed'. And looking out to sea, the whitecaps too are simply *moutons*, sheep. (French, incidentally, seems to show a preference for sheep. French leapfrog is *saut-mouton*, and a motorway flyover too is a 'leap-sheep'.)

In the English phrase, these frisky waves are 'white horses', 'mares' tails' of a kind, while, if our observant peasant is Spanish, they are likely to be *cabrillas*, 'little goats' (Spanish has a word, *cabrilleo*, for the action of the waves lapping to form the 'little goats', or kids).

Varro wrote of the Aegean Sea that it was 'named from the islands, because in this sea the craggy islands in the open water are called "goats" [*aeges*], from their likeness to she-goats'. One of Varro's editors comments: 'very dubious etymology'. So it is. It was less the islands that resembled goats than the skittish white water round their coasts . . .

Ruskin wrote of cloudy skies he called 'capricious'. The modern understanding of 'capricious' to mean whimsical, unpredictable – the sense in which Ruskin (and Shakespeare) used the word – is shaped by a mistaken etymology connecting 'caprice' with the Latin *caper*, or *capra*, he- or she-goat: the windblown clouds, supposedly, are skittish goats.

But language is itself capricious: the supposed goat in 'caprice' was originally a hedgehog. The word is from the Italian *capo*, head, and *riccio*, hedgehog, and originally meant 'horror', in which the hair is said to stand erect like spines. The writer Samuel Beckett wore his hair capriciously *en brosse*. An eccentric in a London pub once handed him an impromptu ode beginning 'Hail, O hedgehog-headed . . .'

Riccio, like the French and Spanish words for 'hedgehog', *hérisson* and *erizo*, also means by transference the spiny husk of the chestnut and, as an adjective, curly. So capricious could translate as 'curly-headed'. Clouds, although not capricious in the hedgehog sense, are often metaphorically perceived as hair, just as the sea is.

Ruskin sees a redeeming spirituality in his vulgar 'mares' tails' when he calls them 'excessively fine, silky, parallel fibres' – like angel-hair, perhaps: Ruskin's skies are forced heavens full of angels. We are scarcely aware of the metaphorical basis in 'cirrus' clouds – *cirrus* in Latin was a curl, a ringlet, a lock of hair. Locks may likewise be 'hyacinthine' – after the convoluted curliness of the hyacinth's petals.

Moutonner in French has the sense to frizz or curl the hair, and seems to give an insight into an ancient metaphor, Homer's recurrent epithet, 'the curly-headed sea'. The crisp breeze frizzes the sea's surface. Crisps, from the Latin *crispus*, are also curls; potato crisps are curly. A sheep's fleece is crispate, and in modern Greek those curly (and capricious) white waves are *arnákia*, lambs.

So the sea, like the sky, can be *moutonné*. Homer probably had in mind not the hyacinthine head of a human being, but the fleecy head of a lamb: unless it was the *aeges*, the goats, mentioned many centuries later by Varro.

It hardly matters, though, whether they are goats, lambs, sheep, kids, or horses. The metaphors essentially resolve into one metaphor, in which, to concentrate on the whitecaps, white water first provokes the suggestion of white, curly hair, and then, in turn, the image of a white animal grazing in a field. The metaphorical leap is between water and hair. The animal-imagery then follows fairly tamely, as a by-product as it were of the underlying metaphor.

It is my contention, moreover, that the hair metaphor underlies and effectively 'controls' a great deal else in language. The animal-imagery for waves doesn't occur in isolation, but within a bloc of

7

metaphors having hair as the common 'genetic' factor, a family so large, so intermarried, so complex and often devious in its relationships, so false sometimes in its friendships, as to suggest that the image of hair is a key metaphoric vehicle common to all languages.

The family's sheer size, its ancestry, the doubt attaching to many of its real or supposed branches, must make us wary of attempting a comprehensive family tree.

Let us consider for a moment, for example, only the 'hair' metaphors as they relate to water. Having identified this powerful unconscious undertow beneath the surface of our simple 'white horses' we will, if we are not careful, be swept into deep waters where discussion becomes uncontained and effectively drowns.

Discussion of language has a dismaying tendency to spill over in almost any direction and at almost any point, but especially into myth, on the one hand, and literary criticism on the other. It is by way of being a general principle of this book that if this tendency must sometimes be followed, most of the time it must be checked. If it is not, we will soon find ourselves wrestling, for example, with the question of Neptune's beard, why mermaids have flowing locks, and the mysterious connection between the River Ganges and the flowing hair of a goddess: 'The Ganges . . . flowing from the foot of Vishnu and through Siva's hair . . .' We might equally scour literature for passages like that one, from *A Passage to India*, or this one from T. S. Eliot, whose J. Alfred Prufrock saw mermaids riding seaward on the waves

> Combing the white hair of the waves blown back
> When the wind blows the water white and black.

. . . Still worse, we might flounder in attempts, inevitably doomed, to link this aspect of language with evolutionary theories proposing man's relative hairlessness (except on his head, the only part of his body above the water when he swims) as evidence for his aquatic origins.

We see where enquiry of that kind might lead. Do aquatic origins conceivably underlie evidence for a tendency to 'see' swirling water in terms of filaments, like hair? Do they underlie also the linguistic line of succession leading from the Sanskrit *bala*, hair, through Tibetan and Romany to the Welsh *bala*, a stream?

Remembering that metaphor is a *carrier* let me try to supply a little more of the theoretical background as to how that carrying actually works. In the technical terms employed by I. A. Richards, the 'vehicle' of this core metaphor is the notion of hair, while the thing or meaning that is carried, the 'tenor', may be any one of a wide variety of phenomena; the identity of the tenor depends on the context in which the metaphor is employed.

If I were to use the Russian word *ikrá* in a Russian fish-market, for example, I would doubtless be taken to be referring to a sturgeon's roe, which is what it means. On a football field, however, *ikrá* would more probably refer to that part of the leg for which the English metaphor is the 'calf' (which a large raw sturgeon's roe resembles, and which *ikrá* also means).

This may seem simple and straightforward enough; in fact, when one considers it, it is an extraordinarily sophisticated process revealing an extraordinary physical intimacy with the world. And it is a universal process as old as our knowledge of language itself. As far back as we go, we will find metaphor. Nor is that all, however. *Ikrá* may seem to be an isolated instance, a spot of imaginative Russian 'local colour'. But when we look deeper into metaphor we discover that there is a considerable family of metaphors comparing parts of the leg – 'ham' and 'calf' for example – to meat. To the native speaker, these are dead metaphors; to the non-native, they are vividly alive.

These 'universal metaphors', as they have been called, are not merely ornamental ways of saying things more colourfully. They are, in Ezra Pound's distinction, 'interpretative', instances of catachresis in the specialized sense with which writers on metaphor use the word; that is, they supply a name where a name would otherwise be lacking – the 'stem' of a glass, the 'brow' or the 'foot' of a hill. In none of these instances is the metaphorical leap as great as it is in 'white horses'. The greater the leap, the more one is likely to be aware of the presence of the metaphor; and, a second rough rule of thumb, the greater the leap the more likely different languages are to land in a different location, the less their metaphors are likely to concur. When they do concur, however, when they are not idiosyncratic or random fancies, but apparently 'universal', it begins to be reasonable to suppose that there may be a cognitive significance in the fact of their concurrence.

This book subscribes to what has been called 'the strong metaphor' theory whereby metaphor, so often treated as the product of 'fancy', is considered to be at the psychological deep core of perception. Briefly, according to 'strong metaphor' and its adherents, metaphors not only arise out of perception but are formative of it. By this argument, catachresis – the perception of similarity and consequent crossing of category-divisions – becomes a vital tool in perception, as well as its most obvious and vivid manifestation in language. These semantic 'improprieties' are a key way in which perceptions are located, fixed, and perpetuated. Intentionality and will play little or no part in this process. We do not choose universal metaphors – they choose us. They are refined and perpetuated in poetry and literature, and they play a crucial role in prejudice, too, for metaphor, which we may think of as a kind of metaphysical glue, an affirmation of magical unity, may also be divisive, stressing particularity and difference in the face of essential similarity, as well as similarity in the face of difference. A dead metaphor is the fossil of a once lively perception. To borrow Empson's phrase, however, some that seem dead may merely be 'sleeping', as with the age-old metaphorical rhetoric of racial hatred. Metaphors are 'carriers'. Human beings are carriers of metaphors.

Those watery 'white horses' have been with us for many thousands of years. Their persistence is not that of a random fancy which happens to have stuck. There is a certain inevitability about them. They derive from an interpretative metaphor that is based upon the image of hair, and of which the notion 'hair' is the vehicle. This underlying metaphor is deeply imprinted in language. It is so extraordinarily prevalent and persistent that we may even begin to feel trapped by it, and to wonder whether language finally permits any perception of whitecaps on the sea other than in terms of hair, heads, and horses.

Panache

A horse that is white (or grey) is in German *Schimmel*, which is otherwise (and more usually) mould or mildew. Not a very dashing concept of a white horse. In one language, then, a white horse is a wave. In another, it is equated with mould.

Latin American Spanish for a white horse is *palomino*, which in Spain itself means a young pigeon. More commonly, however, pigeon, or dove, is *paloma*, and *palomas*, figuratively, are an alternative version of 'little goats', white horses on the sea. So a Spaniard saying that there were little pigeons, *palominos*, on the sea, would seem to a Mexican to be saying that there were white horses. A shared whiteness, which seems to be discreetly hinted at in the word's root, makes the doves for the purposes of metaphor conceptually interchangeable with horses.

German for a white horse in the sense of wave is *Schaumkrone*, 'foam crown', an apparently static or 'frozen' word-picture seeming to anticipate by centuries the famous photograph of a splashing drop of milk forming a perfect crown, and seeming, too, to be a quite different way of conceiving the sea. With a little reflection, though, we realize that it not only comes from the same linguistic stable as the white horses, but is effectively identical with them.

In a letter to David Garnett in 1912 Frieda Weekley (later the wife of D. H. Lawrence) wrote of Italian soldiers as having 'such hats, a foam of cockfeathers on them'. Lawrence, who was with her, underlined the *foam*, and wrote in the margin 'Good God!' But Frieda was the daughter of a German officer. Her English was never fluent. She was thinking of the German *Feldwebel*, the sergeant-major, and figuratively the *Feldwebel* is the 'head', the *Schaumkrone*, on a bock of beer, after the supposed resemblance of beer-foam to the plume of feathers atop the helmet of the old German army uniform. French has the same concept. A shandy is *un demi panaché*, or simply *un panaché*, 'a feathered [or plumed] half [of beer]', after the feathery foam on the shandy's surface.

In English, these feathers and foam crowns are crests. The *Oxford Dictionary*'s list of the meanings of 'crest' gives first, 'A comb, a tuft of feathers or the like, upon an animal's head', and second, 'An erect plume of feathers, horse-hair, etc. [we are back to horses], fixed on the top of a helmet or head-dress'. With the third meaning we reach the heraldic sense of 'crest'. It is only when we get to meaning 7.c that we find the sense in which the word is most commonly used today, 'The curling foamy ridge of a wave', and the date of its first known recorded usage in English in that sense, 1440.

The *Schaumkrone*, then, is only a crest with that word's heraldic history more obviously intact, waving, a focus for all eyes, above the tumultuous battlefield of the water below. It is only horsehair all over again, in a slightly different disguise.

So the words break out of the careful categories of etymology into a broad field of perception where the rule seems to be a kind of unconscious geometry closely attentive to form and finding common ground between otherwise disparate phenomena.

In this common ground cabbages and kings, things we may regard as ridiculous in such close conjunction with things and qualities we regard as sublime, may happily coexist. The supposedly sublime, indeed, may boil down to being a metaphorical, or metaphysical, abstraction or extension from the supposedly commonplace.

Panache, for example, a plume, is also an abstract quality, fairly defined, I think, by Somerset Maugham in his story 'Appearance and Reality' as seeming to signify 'dignity and bravado, display and heroism, vainglory and pride'. Vaingloriousness may seem ridiculous and strutting to us today, but it was once the prerogative and mark of a crest-wearing knight-at-arms or a gentleman bearing a coat of arms.

Panache is an admiring word for blind courage, hot-headed reckless-ness, a magnificent, disdainful contempt – it approximates to the Italian *sprezzatura*, the quality of contempt which Castiglione, in *The Courtier*, considered essential in a gentleman. (I won't pursue the connections which *sprezzatura*, like *panache*, seems to bear to fizzy drinks – for example, the German *Spritzer*.)

Maugham himself bears out this extended sense of *panache* with two examples from the field of battle into which consideration of the metaphorical significance of hair will soon lead us further. 'It was *le panache*', wrote Maugham, 'that made the French gentlemen at Fontenoy say to the officers of King George II, fire first, gentlemen; it was *le panache* that wrung from Cambronne's bawdy lips at Waterloo the phrase: the guard dies but never surrenders.'

Panache is a *rising above*, like the chivalrous knight on his *cheval*, rising above the battle; like the plume waving above his helmet; like the foam on his glass of shandy; and like the *Schaumkrone*, the crest of the wave. Figuratively, *panache* is a rising above circumstances.

We shall have occasion to look again at heraldry, but in passing we note here that two of the ten or so traditional lines of partition on shields and coats of arms are '*Wavy* or *undy*, which is supposed to have been taken from water, and *nebuly*, which is supposed to be derived from clouds' (A. C. Fox-Davies, *A Complete Guide to Heraldry*). These lines of partition – boundaries – themselves represent a metaphorical crossing of boundaries. Here, this time in emblematic form on a shield, are our white horses all over again.

Where do we expect to find a knight, though, if not on a foaming white steed? The image seems to be deeply buried in what we may as well call 'the collective unconscious'. The etymologist Ernest Weekley (Frieda's first husband) argued, contrary to convention, that the popular association of 'nightmare' with horses was probably right. 'There must have been a time', he wrote, 'when to Western Europeans the mounted horse was as startling and trampling an apparition as it was to the Mexicans when they encountered the Spanish con-quistadores. The "bogyman" of the Greek peasant child is still the centaur. The dreaded Scottish *kelpie*, or water-monster, usually appears in equine form, and the names Hengist and Horsa, i.e. stallion and mare [in Old German], of the adventurers who first flew the White Horse banner off the coast of Britain seem to class the animal with the fantastic and terrifying beasts of heraldry.'

Here D. H. Lawrence would probably have agreed with his rival for Frieda. Just before his death the author of *St Mawr*, about an untamed stallion, wrote *Apocalypse*, which abounds in horses (the horsemen of the Apocalypse). 'Horses, always horses! How the horse dominated the mind of the early races,' Lawrence wrote. 'Far back, far back in our dark soul the horses prances.'

Far back, too, in our dark language.

'Like Cauliflowers . . .'

The writer G. K. Chesterton claimed all his life to be 'haunted' by an 'analogous kinship' which he could 'never locate' between, of all things, cabbages and the sea. Invariably, the one reminded him of the other. Revealing this sense of kinship in *A Shilling for My Thoughts* he reveals another which we may find still harder to 'locate' – between his own sensibility and that of the 'mob' with which he proclaims himself 'on a level'.

I mention this 'blokish' populism, with its accompanying polemic against the 'bookish', because it distorts the perceptions which, for a shilling, Chesterton would share with us and have us share with him. He writes, for example, of the use of language by those he calls 'rustics', that they 'do not talk bookishly about clouds or stones, or pigs or slugs, or horses or anything you please. They talk piggishly about pigs; and sluggishly, I suppose, about slugs; and are refreshingly horsy about horses. They speak in a stony way of stones; they speak in a cloudy way of clouds; and this is surely the right way.'

These are the 'thingy' peasant words like muddy Wellington boots to be found in Joseph Wright's great dictionary (published from 1898 to 1905) of the English dialects. But it is also language confined to barracks, the language of unimaginative dullards, and as we have already begun to see, it is precisely not the rustic way with language. On the contrary, if rustics are refreshingly horsy about horses, they are even more refreshingly horsy about waves or clouds, and as for semantic piggishness the evidence when we come to consider it will be that they are refreshingly piggish about almost anything you please.

If anyone is cloudy about clouds, it is rather the bookish Ruskin, while the blokish Chesterton is himself refreshingly cabbagey, not about cabbages, however, but about the sea. His 'analogous kinship' is based partly on colour (a vexed question) – the green of the leaves – but chiefly on a sense of shared geometry, 'the grand curves of the cabbage that curl over cavernously like waves' and 'that dreamy repetition, as of a pattern, that made two great poets, Aeschylus and Shakespeare, use a word like "multitudinous" of the ocean'.

But Chesterton, like the good bloke he is, readily surrenders his own cabbage analogy to someone else's he finds 'twenty times better'. A country girl from Buckinghamshire, a 'rustic', on seeing the sea for the first time, said it was 'like cauliflowers'; much better than cabbages because 'they show the wave breaking as well as curling, and the efflorescence of the branching foam, blind, bubbling and opaque. Moreover the strong lines of life are suggested.'

The lines, however, are those of vegetable not animal life. Chesterton's sea with its cavernous waves seems to be rougher than our sea of white horses, but at the same time it is less dynamic. Those 'horses' are unruly, in powerful if restrained motion towards the shore, a rhythmic, repetitive motion suggestive of the act of combing the hair, whence the American 'combers' or 'beachcombers' for waves and a further sidelight on Eliot's 'Combing the white hair of the waves' . . . By contrast, the cabbagey or cauliflower sea is static. It gives us an art sea reminiscent of Hockney's *A Bigger Splash* or, better, Hokusai's *The Wave*, where a cavernously ribbed, ragged, conceivably cabbage-leaf-like wave threatens to engulf a small boat on the boiling water below. Hokusai's wave even has a highly convoluted crest, a *Schaumkrone* quite like that of a cabbage leaf and very like the leaf of a lollo or *frisée* lettuce.

This metaphor for the sea in which vegetables are the vehicles seems to be metaphorical miles away from the white-horse one. Yet when it is boiled down its conceptual basis is exactly the same – a sameness only hinted at in Chesterton's choice of the verb 'curl'.

'Cabbage' is from the old French *caboche*, a head, and itself jocularly means 'head' in dialect English. 'Cauliflower' is from 'cole' (cabbage, the German *Kohl*) plus 'flower', and like other things on sale in greengrocers' shops (wallnut for walnut, sparrow-grass for asparagus) there is a faint whiff of popular or folk etymology about that 'cauli-'.

Chesterton doesn't tell us how his Buckinghamshire country girl spoke, but in dialect English cauliflowers were 'curly-flowers', or with other members of the brassica family, like the plant we still call curly-kale, they were 'curley-greens'. Lettuces, too, are still conventionally 'crisp', or curly.

'Cauliflower' survives as a term for a bruiser's ears, but it was once, as a noun, the head of froth on a glass of ale (was that the sense in which the country girl used the word?) and also 'a little clot of hot wick in a candle' (think of the black marks on a cauliflower when it starts to go rotten). As a verb, 'to cauliflower' was to powder wigs, which are notable for their curliness. The white powder turned a wig into a cauliflower, or 'curly-head', whose usual meaning was a curly-headed boy.

Chesterton's sea conceived as cabbages or cauliflowers is only Homer's 'curly-headed sea' from another angle. He called the country girl's image 'pure literature'. But language, or 'name-poetry' (the term which Professor Max Müller used, in the 1860s, for metaphor-making), had pre-empted her 'literature', as it tends to do in all but the most laboured or grotesque extended literary metaphors. Often, indeed, as in the lines of T. S. Eliot I've quoted, literature seems only to be eliciting or extending the sense inherent in a well-established, well-worn linguistic metaphor, and using that reinvigorated metaphor as an imaginative springboard.

Of course a cauliflower is not the same thing as a white horse: but language provides clues to an underlying pattern of perception by which we realize that the Buckinghamshire girl's simile is nothing like as original as, at first sight, it seems.

There is a further point to be made before we leave Chesterton and his country girl. Just as Chesterton in his polemical keenness confuses directness of 'rustic' character with a supposedly unsophisticated direct-ness of 'rustic' perception, so he confuses a supposed metaphorical originality with philosophical insight, even with wisdom. 'The first essential of the merely bookish view of the sea', he writes, 'is that it is boundless, and gives a sentiment of infinity.' It is, he adds, quite certain

... that the cauliflower simile was partly created by exactly the opposite impression, the impression of boundary and barrier. The girl thought of it as a field of vegetables, even as a yard of vegetables. The girl was right. The ocean only suggests infinity when you cannot see it; a sea mist may seem endless, but not a sea. So far from being vague and vanishing, the sea is the one hard straight line of Nature. It is the one plain limit; the only thing that God has made that really looks like a wall.

This is nonsense. The sea is not infinite, but neither is it circumscribed as a field is, and certainly it isn't a yard. The sea-horizon is neither a wall (there is always, anyway, something beyond a wall) nor the only hard straight line of Nature: the desert and the prairies offer similar lines. The sea-horizon isn't limitless, but neither is it straight and narrow. It was, rather, the girl's horizons that were narrow, and her mind, not the sea, that was a yard, a kail-yard from which grew the image of the sea as resembling kail. The wall of that yard, her mind, was the boundary – the necessary 'boundary and barrier' – which her imagination had to cross in order to make the metaphorical leap and connection. The country girl was so imaginative about the sea precisely because she was so ignorant of it.

Her image was of the kind which lexicographers call 'emergency metaphors' – responses to the linguistic emergency that arises when, in ignorance of the true or accepted name or nature of a new phenomenon, and in an attempt to 'place' it, one grasps at a known one. They are obvious examples of catachresis – supplying a name where none is available – and are particularly associated with the speech of children. Every parent will have his or her memory of charming emergency metaphors, such as my own small son's awestruck response to the stormy Atlantic off Cape Finisterre: 'Juice!' The pidgin languages abound in emergency metaphors, which largely accounts for the tendency to treat pidgin-speakers as children (for **Pidgin**, see the Lexicon, page 260). Many metaphors in commonly accepted adult use among native-speakers must have begun life as emergency metaphors, however.

Chesterton's country girl found herself in an emergency. It would certainly have been more conventional if the vehicle 'white horses' had ridden to her rescue instead of 'cauliflowers', but if one temporarily forgets conventional usage and thinks consciously of the image, are cauliflowers in this context really any stranger than horses?

Chesterton's passing reference to 'dreamy repetition, as of a pattern' and to the 'multitudinous ocean' opens up a new line of enquiry. From apparently simple beginnings, it is now that we start to see how complex, subtle, and even mysterious metaphor can be.

Frizzy Hair

In 1990 an American surgeon turned writer, Dr Richard Selzer, decided a word was needed to express all that the image of moonlight on water summons up in our minds. He had already had a go at sunlight on water, and come up with 'aquasol', a made-up word – or neologism – abandoned when he discovered it was already the brand name of a nasal decongestant. With 'path of moonlight on the water' he was more hopeful, and 'narrowed the possibilities down to two: "lunaqua" and "aqualune"'.

Neither is likely to enter the linguistic mainstream – few neologisms do. The language already at Dr Selzer's disposal was more resourceful than he evidently realized, however. He would have fielded more promising candidates if he'd searched both further afield within English and other languages, and, on the other hand, closer to home. Curiously, the family of phenomena to which moonlight on water belongs has preoccupied not only language but Dr Selzer's own discipline, medicine.

Earlier, we found images of curly hair to underlie metaphors for clouds and whitecapped waves. *Moutonner* is both to curl and to frizz. But I take curly, or wavy, hair to be one thing and frizzy hair another. Curls are comparatively gentle curves, while frizzy hair is full of hairpin bends; frizzes are very much finer and more numerous than curls. Frizzy hair is more complicated than wavy hair, and so are metaphors for frizziness.

Frizziness and hair generally take us into territory where perceptual difficulties abound – difficulties amusingly hinted at in the Latin American Spanish *invisible*, a hairpin in Argentina, a hairnet in Mexico.

'Curly' whitecaps or clouds may be distinguished from one another readily enough. But if we move now from 'Combing the white hair of the waves' to Eliot's next line, 'When the wind blows the water white and black', and think now of a sudden gust of breeze making a tremor over the surface of still water, then we have something subtler, a trembling like that of moonlight, an indistinguishably fine and frizzy tangle. Think, even, of an Afro hairstyle, or of 'fuzzy-wuzzy', defined by the *Oxford Dictionary* as 'a nickname for the Sudanese warrior, from his method of dressing his hair':

> Fuzzy-wuzzy was a bear
> Fuzzy-wuzzy had no hair
> So fuzzy-wuzzy wasn't fuzzy
> Was he?

'Fuzzy' is used also of vision or an image that is out of focus. Moonlight eliminates half-tones and spectrally transforms scenes familiar from daylight.

Dr Selzer's supposed path of moonlight on water is in fact a 'lyrical' dressing-up of what we actually see. It seems to lead from the stock formulae of hackneyed verse rather than from freshly observant language. The moon's reflected 'path', usually, is crazy paving. Another American, writing of a wartime experience in which he saw the moon's reflection in the English Channel, called it by the sailor's expression, 'the loom of the moon'. That is already better than 'aqualune' or 'lunaqua'. The near palindrome loom/moon hints at inefficient reflection, and crucially, recalls the wavy rays of light woven on the water's shifting surface, like fibres on a loom.

Quite unconsciously, that former sailor was drawing on a rich and ancient body of association. The word we turn to now is the French verb *friser*. Paul Robert, in his French dictionary, defines it as 'To curl or wave locks of hair [or] tufts of fibre'. Weaving is waving: *friser* encompasses both. Metaphorical usages of the verb and its derivatives can all be seen to refer to one central complex of associated abstract qualities which, without *friser*, it might be difficult to put a name to. 'Frizziness', or 'fuzziness', now starts to seem evocative less of a certain kind of hair than of qualities which frizzy or fuzzy hair is seen to share with other phenomena.

The words in this area appear to be attempts to pinpoint fragile, complex, and evanescent phenomena that baffle precise perception and descriptive embodiment in language. They try to 'see' what can't quite be seen clearly, capture what can't clearly be expressed, perhaps because it is in the essence of the thing to defy exact observation and description. But the words nevertheless manage the job very well, probably as well as it will ever be managed, while at the same time subtly capturing the elusiveness of the thing described.

The reflexive *se friser*, for example, is used of a horse whose raised leg, when it moves, grazes the leg resting on the ground. A horse *qui se frise* – weaves itself? frizzes itself? – produces a tentative criss-cross effect like that of a loom weaving, or frizzy moonlight on water, movement which may momentarily make one think the fault is not with external reality but with one's eyesight.

Friser and its noun, *frise*, give us the English 'frizz'. In English we speak of someone who pursues an erratic path as 'weaving', and in French *frisant* is used of light which 'weaves, skims, shaves'. Paul Robert gives the example *un rayon de soleil frisant*, a 'weaving' or refractive ray of sunlight, the 'split-end' effect, for example, of sunlight seen through undergrowth or eyelashes: 'tender trambeams truckle at the eye', as Gerard Manley Hopkins expressed it in a poem.

Robert tells us that *friser* may be related to *frire*, to fry. Certainly we speak of frying things to a crisp, and there is an English 'frizz', 'to make a sputtering noise in frying', which may, the *Oxford Dictionary* suggests, only be 'fry' with the echoic termination of that double 'Z'. Hot, bubbling fat or (golden) olive-oil is also visually reminiscent of sunlight on disturbed water, however, and the double 'Z' of 'frizz' may be as much suggestive of visual fuzziness as it is echoic.

Light on disturbed water 'dazzles', or 'zigzags', words in which it has been suggested that the 'Z's' are tiny letter-pictures. Ruskin wrote of 'The hieroglyphic use of the zigzag, for water, by the Egyptians'. Turn the 'Z' through ninety degrees and the result is an 'N', 'the zigzag line', according to Hensleigh Wedgwood in 1866, 'which represents the wavy surface of water [and which is] used as the symbol of Aquarius among the signs of the zodiac'. (This is admittedly an archaic 'magical' view of language: I confess, I am under the spell of those 'Z's'.)

It is to this almost indefinable dazzle of disturbed water found, for example, in the 'fizziness' of fizzy drinks, that sufferers from migraine will sometimes refer in order to convey a sense of the dizzying 'aura' of migraine. According to Oliver Sacks in his book *Migraine* the aura might be quite incommunicable to others if there were not external phenomena bearing some resemblance to it, or aspects of it, to which the sufferer could refer:

Good descriptions of the aura are vitally *needed*, because it is a phenomenon of the utmost importance, which can cast a great flood of light not only on migraine, but on the most elemental and fundamental mechanisms of the brain-mind; good descriptions are hard to obtain, because many aura phenomena are exceedingly strange – so strange as to transcend the powers of language; and good descriptions are made rarer still by the presence of something uncanny and fearful, the very thought of which causes the mind to shy.

Language, however, has performed scintillatingly in this very difficult area. A way to grasp a sense of the migraine aura is to look, through language, at how the non-migrainous 'brain-mind' has perceived aspects of reality which are, as it were, inherently migrainous.

We must be careful now not to ride madly off in all directions. Even Dr Sacks's choice of verb there – 'shy' – is interesting. The French adjective, *ombrageux*, 'shadowy', is 'shy, skittish' when used of a horse, 'touchy' when used of a person. Shadow is especially deceptive in moonlight, or in the dappled, camouflage-effect of light through leaves (whose 'strobe' effect on Joan of Arc as she rode through the forest, it has been suggested, may have triggered her visions). In writing now about extreme perceptual difficulty, I run the risk that the reader, too, will shy. Let me tighten the rein.

A shying mind is what one would expect in migraine. The horse shies at shadowy areas in which its field of perception fails, just as in migraine the mind shies at the sinister and scary blind-spots produced by the 'brain-mind', and known to doctors as 'scotomas'. The aura of migraine has much in common with 'the loom of the moon'. Dr Sacks writes: 'Elementary hallucinations which are commonly experienced are rippling, shimmering and undulation in the visual field, which patients may compare to the appearance of wind-blown water, or looking through watered silk.'

Chevaux de Frise

The migraine aura also resembles a mental battlefield, whether an ancient or a modern one, a confusion of arrows crossing the visual field, or head-splitting explosions, spectacular shellbursts, and so on. And it happens that the terminologies of migraine and the military share common ground.

A friend who is a migraine sufferer describes his hallucinations as 'buzzing asterisks' – those pervasive 'Z's' again – and I remember another who would describe her headaches with the (I think) invented word 'zizzing'. Sacks gives us the medical term for those 'asterisks' when he writes of 'the gross zigzag appearance which justifies the term *fortification-spectrum*'. ('Zigzag', a 'reinforced' word, like 'seesaw', is thought to have been used originally of fortifications.)

In a book on migraine published in 1868, George B. Airy named this syndrome 'teichopsia' – which literally translated from the Greek means 'wall-seeing'. It more precisely refers, however, to a castle's crenellations or, for that matter, to the upward zigzags of a ziggurat. (In reference to the migraine aura, an early Anthony Burgess novel set in Gibraltar was called *A Vision of Battlements*.) The twelfth-century mystic Hildegard of Bingen interpreted her visions of crenellations as glimpses of the walls of the City of God. Sacks describes them – as illustrated in Hildegard's own vivid paintings – as 'typically migrainous fortification figures'.

But if these figures may appear to exist in the mind, they also exist in the material world; and if the mental figures are symptomatic of migraine, visual over-exposure to the physical figures may likewise produce a degree of migrainous vertigo, nausea, dazzle-blindness, and headache in someone not normally a migraine sufferer. A day on a sun-dazzled sea, for example, or even among the repetitive multiplicity of battlements in a medieval city, may baffle the visual cortex to produce a 'splitting' headache.

The terminologies of the military and of migraine overlap elsewhere. Another military term, now defunct in its original sense, also denotes a characteristic hallucination of the migraine aura. 'Minute luminous lines', or a 'fine structure of intersecting lines' are known as *chevaux de frise*. That means, literally, 'Friesian horses'. There is a breed of black cart-horse, or war-horse (they were used in the Thirty Years War, 1618–48), called 'Friesian', after the Dutch province of Friesland.

Chevaux de frise is what etymologists rather glumly call a 'jocular' expression. They weren't horses at all but '(any form of) portable wire entanglement', or, as they are defined more precisely, and slightly differently, by Paul Robert, '[Pieces] of wood or iron bristling with stakes, [used] to cut off a camp, to forbid passage'. The original Dutch name for them was *Vriesse ruyters*, Friesian horsemen. Their chief use was to deter cavalry charges.

If we turn to a description of 1708 we get a better picture of the resemblance of *chevaux de frise* to the intersecting lines of the migraine aura: 'Large Joists . . . Ten or Twelve Foot in length, with Six Sides into which are driven a great Number of wooden Pins about Six Foot long, crossing one another, and having their Ends armed with Iron-Points.'

Chevaux de frise looked like frizzy or fuzzy hedgehogs (children's writer Alison Uttley called her hedgehog 'Fuzzy-Peg'). 'Hedgehog' too was once a military term. Littré tells us that it was the name for both a spiked barrier and a type of bomb. Hitler in his last-ditch stand of 1945 designated certain cities, like Breslau, *Igelfestungen*, 'hedgehog-fortress'.★

In *chevaux de frise* we cannot fail to be struck by that *frise* and the coincidence, if that is what it is, whereby French for frizziness is also French for Friesland. Probably a dogmatic structuralist would tend to dismiss this out of hand as an instance of the random 'arbitrariness' of signs. However, the Dutch possessive, *Friesch*, 'of Friesland', irresistibly suggests the German *frisch*, meaning fresh or cold – Friesland is *frisch* because it is coastal flat-land over which a crisp breeze blows from the sea. Then we may start to wonder about 'frizz', 'freeze', and *frisson* – shivering too is a kind of shying: when it freezes, we shiver.

This may sound far-fetched – or as the Spanish say, *traído por los cabellos*, 'dragged by the hair' – but we shall discover shortly that there are sound etymological grounds for connecting the perception of frizzy hair with that of freezing cold; grounds, that is, for believing that in this instance at least language is not behaving arbitrarily, but on the contrary is faithfully shadowing the perceptual reality.

With *frise*, though, we do hit a barrier – a mental if not military *chevaux de frise* – where the mind shies at yet another meaning of the word, as a kind of woollen cloth. It exists in English, too. The Gypsy, in D. H. Lawrence's *The Virgin and the Gipsy* (I have been rereading Lawrence recently), 'wore a sort of shooting-jacket . . . of dark green-and-black frieze'. Some French etymologists have argued that this is from *Frise* meaning Friesland. But can we really be confident that *frise* for a woollen cloth has nothing at all to do with the *frise* of weaving?

We shall be struck too by the closeness of that *chevaux* (horses), to *cheveux* (hair). In the context it is frizzy hair and *frisant* light that we

---

★ In warfare an *Igelstellung* is a 'hedgehog position'.

expect as an image for visual dazzling, not Friesian horses. And in a remarkable unintentional pun, it is frizzy hair that Oliver Sacks mistakenly gives us in *Migraine*, when he alludes not to *chevaux* but to *cheveux de frise*.

Language, too, has a migrainous aura: here, Dr Sacks fell victim to one of its illusions, and the mind shies at the appositeness of his error.* He might have been alerted by the poor grammar of his phrase – 'hair of frizziness'. It should be *cheveux frisés* – hair, as the French say, frizzed into *tire-bouchons*, 'corkscrews'.

Screws, too, are curly or frizzy: migraine sufferers will sometimes compare their hallucinations to the hypnotic turning of a screw, its thread apparently emanating from an inexhaustible source, like moonlight on water. In a paper of 1941, for example, the doctor and migraine sufferer K. S. Lashley compared the pattern of the scintillations he saw to 'the illusion of movement of a revolving screw'.

The 'brain-mind' has raided many other aspects of reality to convey the 'frizzy' effect of *chevaux de frise*. Sacks quotes a nineteenth-century description: 'It may be likened to the effect produced by the rapid gyration of small waterbeetles as they are seen swarming in a cluster on the surface of the water in sunshine . . .' Those waterbeetles might be said to 'fizz' like bubbles just above the surface of soda water, and they recall a passage from Nabokov in which a swarm of small insects in a sunlit clearing is compared to needles sewing the air. We may also remember the medical term for spots swimming before the eyes, which is the Latin *muscae volitantes*, or flitting flies. The same idea is found in idiomatic Spanish (*moscas volantes*) and French (*mouches volantes*).

Patrick Trevor-Roper, in *The World through Blunted Sight*, calls spots before the eyes 'the simplest intruders in the visual field . . . floating wisps', but a cloud of flitting flies, like motes of dust dancing in a beam of sunlight – whether seen in external reality or in the mind's eye – is still complex enough to outwit the powers of precise perception, accurate mental tracking.

---

* Especially (and confusingly) when the 'horses' in *chevaux de frise* actually *can* refer to hair: in English, the phrase once had the transferential sense of eyelashes, fortifications of the eyes.

Dr Sacks describes the hallucinations of migraine by reference to material objects all exhibiting a repetitive, dazzling, eye-outwitting geometry, that multitudinous 'dreamy repetition' which Chesterton saw in cabbages: '. . . some patients may observe, on closing the eyes, a form of visual tumult or delirium, in which latticed, faceted and tessellated motifs predominate – images reminiscent of mosaics, honeycombs, Turkish carpets . . .' That list can be added to almost endlessly. Other examples might be marquetry, mazes, kaleidoscopes, light in a canopy of leaves, rows of figures, fine print, sequins, check and moiré patterns, the flickering screen of a word processor (like the one before me as I write), sewing, knitting, or weaving, or sponges, with their repetitive, honeycomb-like appearance; 'fuzzy' is related to the Low German *fussig*, spongy.

I am tempted to add Japanese script. 'The Japanese are the most bespectacled nation in the world,' wrote John Morris in *Traveller from Tokyo* (1945). 'Without doubt the chief reason for this is the nature of the written language.'

Then there is the chessboard, a fortification figure over whose black-and-white 'crenellated' grid a fiendishly complex war game is played. The king may 'castle', but may not move out of check by castling; the knight's, or horse's, move, is a zigzag. Spanish seems implicitly to recognize the chessboard's relationship with the fortification figures of migraine in *jaqueca*, a headache, and *jaque*, check in chess, while *jaquear* is to put someone in check, or to harass someone in warfare. In heraldry, the crenellated line of partition is known as 'embattled'.

Chess is perpetual harassment, embattlement. Played over the rectilinear grid, a chess game is an intricate mental tangle, a *chevaux de frise* formed of the imaginary interlocking or conflicting 'power lines' of the various pieces. In the same broad context, we discover the Dutch *Vries* to mean both a frieze and 'baize (a checkered stuff)', as my dictionary defines it. A game of chess could be played on a square of *Vries*.

With frieze, freezing, frizzing, and Friesland we reach perpetual check at the tantalizing limits of language. But having introduced 'frieze', I will risk one further tentative point. The French *frise* – frizziness or Friesland – is also a frieze. I thought this must be mere accidental or arbitrary overlapping – but there is evidence to link friezes and frizziness. Nowadays we tend perhaps to think of friezes as representational, but in Norman churches (for example) they are frequently abstract, and possess the same repetitive, eye-defeating qualities found in the migraine aura. Among recurrent motifs are the zigzag and the heraldic *chevron*, a word we associate (yet again) with the military and (yet again) with curly-headed goats (it is from *chèvre*, goat). Chevrons resemble *chevaux de frise*.

The repetitive geometry of these church friezes, the Turkish prayer rugs mentioned by Sacks, and, abundantly, Islamic decorative art (in which the zigzag is a recurrent motif), may be a meditative device to disorient the worshipper and abstract him from the physical world by inducing a mild form of the mystical migraine that Hildegard of Bingen metabolized for herself: flying fortresses, precarious castles in the air, castles in Spain. Entering God's house, we find reproduced on its walls the walls of God's City . . .

Haywire

The origin of this word goes back to the old farm days when bales of hay were tied up with a stiff wire, which, when cut, coiled more or less on itself, with the result that in a short time a pile of wire was accumulated which was almost useless for any practical purpose. Then, when the radio industry first started, some of the earlier sets were known as a 'bunch of haywire', because they were so crisscrossed and confused that nobody had any idea where the wires came from or went to. From that, there developed the use of the expression in connection with a person's mind. This is sometimes used as 'going haywire', meaning to become mentally unbalanced

(C. A. Richards, New York, 1933)

Black and Blue

Returning to the field by the sea, and having looked at the *myra*, the 'moor' of *blamyra*, let's look more closely at the *bla*, the blue. What colour is the sea?

'The veined mingling of violet and green', 'a purple that is almost dark red', 'a green that is almost yellow' – what colour is Chesterton's cabbagey sea? The answer seems self-evident. It is blue, the colour on which Chesterton eventually settles, or green, or grey.

In fact, however, the simple question raises complex ones concerning the psychology, and perhaps physiology, of colour-perception and its embodiment in words. George Steiner writes (in *After Babel*) that languages segment the spectrum in ways which can be startlingly different. Words for colours present 'difficult issues in the neurophysiology and psychology of perception'. A paddle at the edge of these deep waters should suffice to show just how deep they are, and why I choose to acknowledge the difficulties then duck out of them.

Generally, it's said of languages and the peoples and cultures that produce them that they tend to agree on colours at the red or 'hot' end of the spectrum, but often to disagree at the blue or 'cool' end. We shall see that perception of the red end is by no means straightforward, but at least all European languages have a word for red. In some, however, the blue end is altogether absent, or colours we think of as markedly different are resumed in the one word. For both green and grey, for example, Celtic has only *glas*. Romany has no word or words at all for blue, green, or grey. Quite outside Europe, the highly sophisticated language of Japanese has only *aoi* for everything from green to the outer edges of violet. As has been noted, the delicate use of this range of colours in Japanese ceramics makes the absence of verbal shading the more remarkable.

Colours can be used emblematically, or figuratively, to denote, for example, excellence. There is a Red Sea and a Yellow Sea, but no sea is naturally red or yellow. If the colours here are at all descriptive, they describe temporary phenomena which language has permanently associated with the thing described. It has been variously suggested, for example, that the Red Sea is so called because of the reflection of the sunset, or a profusion in it of reddish algae, or of reeds – i.e. 'reed' sea.

When we come to the Black Sea, however, we begin to wonder where to draw the line between the figurative and the descriptive. Let us approach the Black Sea via the Atlantic, *blamyra*, the blue moor. But is the Atlantic really blue? Isn't it, rather, grey, as slate is grey?

27

Then what about 'slate-blue', a common phrase for the colour of northern seas?

Our sense of what is meant by *blamyra* will be further modified if we turn to another Norwegian word, the Old Norse *blamann*, or blue man, for a black man and, especially, a Moor. The sea is a blue moor; a Moor is a blue man. We pause, however, when we turn to Spanish and the etymology of 'Moor': it is probably related to *mora*, a mulberry or the fruit called in English a blackberry, whose juice is deep purple.

Morado, as an adjective, means purple or violet, and as a noun means a bruise, a conventional description for which, in English, is black and blue. How black is a blackberry? How blue is it? What colour is an aubergine, which is sometimes used as an image for black human skin?

Perceptually, it appears that green tends to grey (it's been suggested, for example, that the 'dapple' in a 'dapple-grey' horse once referred to the dappled markings on an apple-green apple), while grey in its turn tends to blue and blue to black. The writer Norman Douglas had difficulty persuading Calabrian peasants that the Mediterranean was blue: to them it had always been a *black* sea. The blue Mediterranean is conceivably black, then; the Black Sea is blue.

Homer's stock epithet for the Aegean was 'wine-dark'. Do we attribute a supposedly black or wine-dark sea simply to a differing cultural consensus on colour? A physiological explanation seems necessary. But if 'wine-dark' (which may only have meant 'sparkling') seems like gobbledegook to us, it is highly specific and nuanced gobbledegook, like an epithet from an interior decorator's catalogue. Homer's blindness doesn't account for that specificity. Somehow, the sea is being seen differently. We wonder whether the ancient world wasn't in effect, in modern terms, colour-blind. The idea that the ability to distinguish colours at the cool end of the spectrum must have evolved within recorded history was put forward by a nineteenth-century German scholar, Hans Magnus. But words too evolve, and they do so, we assume, more rapidly than the physiology of the eye. Language lags behind perception. How far are our colours cultural constructs? Are we only really able to 'see' a colour when a word for it exists?

What did we call magenta before the Battle of Magenta (1859)? What was blue before the word 'blue' evolved? In his 'philosophical inquiry' *On Being Blue*, the American William Gass writes of the origins of 'blue' in the medieval Latin *blavus* 'and the earlier, more classical, *flavus*, for the discolorations of a bruise, so that it sometimes meant yellow, with perhaps a hint of green beneath the skin'.* Bruises are multicoloured. By this explanation the perceived blueness (or black-and-blueness) of bruises came to dominate perception of bruising's other colours.

Another explanation (offered by Philip Howard in his amusing pages on colour in *A Word in Time*), is that *flavus* meant yellow, or bruised, and that by the slip of a scribe's pen it became *blavus*, basis for the German *blau*, the English 'blue'. Misprints and copyist's errors have played their part in the history of language; this one, by this reasoning, must have supplied a semantic need. But the copyist's-error theory still doesn't tell us why blue came to be so named then, and not before.

A Head of Hair

The *capo*, head, of 'capricious', was mistaken for *caper*, goat. Oliver Sacks mistook the *chevaux* of *chevaux de frise* for *cheveux*. Those *chevaux* look markedly like chevrons, and both words remind us of *chef*, which now conjures up the image of someone whose tall white hat stops *cheveux* falling in the food, but which formerly in French, like *caboche*, meant 'head'. (Kerchief is from *couvre-chef*, 'cover-head'; a handkerchief is literally a 'hand-cover-head'.)

Latin has *caput* (head), *capillus* (hair), and *caper* or *capra* (goat). Etymologists tell us that *caballus* (horse) isn't native Latin, but a word assimilated from languages in countries conquered by the Romans. That repeated root, though, *cap-* in Latin, *chev-* in French, sets one wondering whether the similarity of names for the head, hair, goats, and horses in Latin and the Romance languages might not be a sign that they were all once perceived in terms of one another. The

* *Flavus* and *blavus* survive in the Serbo-Croatian for blue, *plav*.

apparent chain of association is particularly striking in Spanish: *cabeza* (head), *cabra* (goat), *cabellos* (hair), *caballo* (horse).

That is speculation, however. More substantially, whether or not Romance words for head are related to Romance words for hair, horses, and goats, the head of hair – its colour, type, and style, or its complete absence – is after skin colour the primary means by which human beings cursorily identify and mentally classify one another. It tends to be the first thing we notice about a stranger's appearance, and the last thing we forget, almost as though our hair instantly identified us as belonging to this or that suit in the human pack.

This is territory today seen as fraught with sexism and racism. Men classify women by their hair. A woman's crowning glory stands synecdochically, like the Crown for the Queen, for the woman herself, as in the quasi-nouns redhead, blonde, brunette. In Japan women will sometimes classify certain 'older men' with their distinguished silver-grey manes of hair, and well-lined pockets, as *romansu gurei*, or 'romance grey' – that term, however, was coined by the Japanese advertising industry. French has *blond* and *brunet*, but the only men that other men commonly tend to classify in this way are redheads, torch thatches, Titian tops – we shall see, however, that red-headedness is a subject in its own right.

The range of colour difference is matched by differences in hair texture, from blonde hair (the finest, with an average diameter of fifty microns), through brown and black hair, to red (which, at around a hundred microns thick, is the coarsest). Typically, a blonde person will have more hair than a redhead.

Hair types also differ between races. Japanese men rarely go bald – in the words of an expert on hair, it isn't 'in their genetic inheritance' to do so. Certain American Indians cannot grow beards. The hair of the typical Caucasian male will start thinning at around thirty-five years of age, ten years earlier than the Afro-Caribbean average. Afro-Caribbean hair tends to be stronger, curlier, springier, frizzier, and under the microscope, studied in cross-section, it is not round in shape, but elliptical.

Perception of this distinctive Afro-Caribbean hair type has left its mark in the European languages. It is a perception based essentially in the brain-mind's capacity for 'pattern recognition' – in geometry. It has proved an important vehicle for racial stereotyping through metaphor and metonymy – the transferential substitute of a single attribute, hair, for the complex whole: the human being. In this way dominant language-cultures have lumped black people generically together as, in effect, 'fuzzy-wuzzies'.

Grifo and Mota

If 'fuzzy-wuzzy' is a dodo as dead terms go, other slang words for black people based on hair-perception are dinosaurs, still deader. Some are simply abusive, like the American 'kink', with its unpleasant ring of a word coined to be spat out and cause maximum offence. With the Spanish *grifo*, however, we enter what I would argue to be a more complex and interesting area of metaphor-making. I don't doubt that the usage of *grifo* and its spin-offs, like that of 'fuzzy-wuzzy', has an ugly and unfortunate history, but I suggest that the word originated, not in culturally conditioned contempt, but in fresh, even wondering observation.

From the context set out above (see pages 17–20) I hope it may be agreed that 'fuzzy-wuzzy' has the hallmarks of a term arising from an extended family of descriptive 'frizzy' words originally owing nothing to racial fear/hatred, prejudice, or stereotyping. I believe the same is true of the *grifo* words, which exhibit some astonishing parallels of multiple meaning with *friser* and its family.

Grif- is at the root of what, for all its variants, appears to be essentially a single burr-word that attached itself readily from language to language, so travelling and propagating itself. English has, or once had, a number of variants – griffin, griffon, griff(e). Like many words for 'foreigners' (in this instance, black people) they appear to be echoic derivations from an often-heard foreign word. With rough jocularity (and a hint of popular etymology) they relate the 'foreign' black person to a mythological monster, the griffin, and there is perhaps the distant suggestion of the griffin's hooked claws echoing the black person's hooked (or frizzy) hair.

Among the variety of meanings of Spanish *grifo* is 'having tangled hair'. In Latin America it acquired the extra meaning 'Negro or coloured person' (*Collins Spanish Dictionary*). A *grifería* is a collective noun for black people. Santamaría's dictionary of Mexican Spanish (1959), gives *grifo* as 'curly, bristly, hirsute', and adds that it is used 'of kinky hair and even of someone who has such hair'. In Louisiana, in the southern United States, the word entered American, then metropolitan English, according to the *Oxford Dictionary*, as 'griffin', but the *OED* gives griffin's ultimate origin in this sense as 'obscure'. According to Bartlett's *American Dictionary* (1859) the word in various forms was 'constantly used in Louisiana, both in conversation and in print, for a mulatto [a highly offensive word, meaning 'young mule'], particularly the woman'. Corominas, in his dictionary of Castilian Spanish, is sure that it entered both French and English in America, and for him its origin is not at all obscure: it is from Spanish *grifo*.

So far the transferential use of *grifo* from hair to other phenomena (or vice versa) exactly matches that of *friser* and its particles. Like *friser* it was used with great metaphorical freedom, despite which its main range of metaphorical reference does not part company with that of *friser* but faithfully shadows it, even though (and this must be emphasized) there is no etymological relationship between the two words. Such relationship as there is between them, then, appears to be based on their manifestation of shared patterns of perception, independently arrived at within different language-cultures.

From this angle, a known etymology in one language may be cited in support of a supposed etymology in another. Earlier, for example, it was suggested that a correlation of frizziness and freezing may be implicit in *frisson*. In *grifo*, however, that correlation is etymologically explicit. Corominas tells us that 'from the idea of "bristly" [*erizado*] came the expression *grifos* or *grifes* or *grius de fred*' – 'bristly with cold'. Spanish takes the idea a metaphorical step further. Horror too, like cold, may provoke a shiver, a *frisson* (horror is from *horridus*, barley, with its bristling head), and Corominas instances the Catalan *esgarrfar-se*, with its assimilated *grifo* – 'to horrify oneself', 'to feel feverish chills'.

Similarly, a known French etymology for *friser* lends support to the view that an English word, griff, is a metaphor ultimately derived from *grifo*. We know that *friser* was used of weaving, and a griff was 'a frame composed of horizontal bars employed in pattern weaving' (*OED*). A griff, that is, bore a marked resemblance to a *chevaux de frise*. We suppose, then, that 'griff' embodies a perceived similarity of weaving and tangled hair. In the absence of hard etymological evidence that it belongs to the same deep pattern on the loom of language as *grifo*, the coincidence of sound, sense, and metaphorical bias nevertheless draws us to the conclusion that it does belong. As further evidence, it may be relevant that the heraldic griffin was a motif very commonly woven into clothing in the Middle Ages.

In Latin America, *grifo* also means drunk, high on drugs, under the influence of marijuana, which is *grifa*. Is this another metaphorical elaboration, like that of freezing, upon the central, semi-abstract notion of frizziness/fuzziness, or merely a semantic blip, the same *grif*-root arbitrarily pressed into extra service? There is some evidence, however, to suggest that ideas of curliness and intoxication may be linked in the circuitry of the brain–mind – in English, for example, strong drink is sometimes commended with 'This'll make your hair curl'. The mind and habitual behaviour-patterns may also be 'bent out of shape', by drink or psychotropic, 'mind-turning' drugs, and the drunk or drugged person walks weavingly. Is the idea of tangled, fuzzy perception, fuzzy vision implicit in this sense of *grifo*, just as curliness is implicit when we refer to a 'crisp' lettuce? Marijuana is 'grass', which like whitecaps and clouds may also be seen in terms of hair: in Papua New Guinea Pidgin, for example, *gras* is hair.

The linkage of marijuana, weaving, and perceptual difficulty is more explicit in another Spanish word, *mota*, which is related both in its multiple meanings, and etymologically, to similar words in German, Dutch, French, and English ('mote', and in all probability, 'moat' and 'mud' as well). In its Latin American slang sense, *mota* is marijuana, a meaning which, so Corominas suggests, derives from the underlying notion of a 'handful of grass' (*manojo de hierba*). The suggestion is not as obscure as it may seem. *Mota*'s range of reference is wide, as that of 'mote' once was. Both words resume a broad idea of earthiness, encompassing everything from a hill or mound on which a castle or windmill stands, to a speck of dust. There is also an accompanying idea of contamination. Again and again, *mota*/mote is not simply earth but earth that has been disturbed, whether the ploughman's clods or clouds of dust. A clod of turf, a 'handful of grass', falls easily within this range of associative reference.

33

Implicit in 'mote' is the idea 'foreign body, contaminating or obstructive matter, blemish'. In the most famous mention of a mote in English, in Matthew 7: 3, 'And why beholdest thou the mote that is in thy brother's eye, but considerest not the beam that is in thine own eye?', the notion of perceptual difficulty, obstruction, is implicit in the moral homily. *Mota*/mote again resembles *frise* (and possibly *grifo*/griff) in that it is a term in weaving. In a now-obsolete usage, a mote was 'an imperfection in wool or cotton', or a 'burl', matted mud, excrement, or knotted wool that refused to be teased from the fleece. A mote-knife was used 'for removing motes from textile fibres'. *Mota* similarly has the meaning 'burl', and in Latin America it can refer, like *grifo*, to a tangled lock of human hair.

Through consideration of metaphor, we have entered a muddy, mote-tormented world where smoothness, whiteness, purity, fineness, homogeneity, silkiness, were rarely attained ideals. Earth got in everywhere, matter, mud, and there was no Mr Teasy-Weasy to comb out stubborn locks of hair. We shall encounter this pervasive sense of contamination again when we come to look at bran and bread-making – the underlying idea of 'mote' has much in common with 'bran' – and when we glance again at 'burl' and 'mote' in other contexts.

Meanwhile, *mota* sheds light on the shared or overlapping meanings of *friser* and *grifo*, and augments our sense of a consistent pattern of perception underlying these words. Etymology becomes a tool in perceptual archaeology, as for example in the repeated references to weaving: the mote-knife, the burl, the griff, the loom of the moon, *frise*, *Vries*, the *rayon de soleil frisant*. At their simplest, these metaphors are manifestations of the overwhelming importance of weaving in the peasant way of life. Weaving left its mark, like the dyer's hand, deep in language.

At a more complex level, the words in their varieties of meaning are clues to a lost way of seeing aspects of reality simultaneously, as interlocked and all but interchangeable – lost: except that this complex vision of reality remains embedded in the words themselves. Their various meanings arose from long experience and intensely close observation.

The transferential meanings of words seem to owe more to this vision than to etymology, so that people in different cultures, of different language-stock, but sharing roughly the same way of life, may naturally turn the same root word to the same or similar purposes without borrowing from one another's word-store.

There is an instinctive conceptual intelligence at work which finds common ground between otherwise disparate phenomena. In examining and teasing out the matted multiple meanings of words we reassess reality and see it again with new, or old, eyes.

II SPRING DAY

Butter-Birds

'Moth' (for example the character of the page Moth in Shakespeare's *Love's Labour's Lost*) was once pronounced 'mote', and perhaps acquired its modern pronunciation by rhyming sound-association with the *cloth* on which moth-larvae feed. 'In early use', the *OED* informs us, the word was 'applied to the larva' – which was, of course, a special kind of mote, or *mota*, an impurity in the raw fabric, just as 'moth' is apparently a specialized extension of the 'mote' family of words.

A moth was an impure, dowdy destroyer from the world of darkness in direct contrast to the brilliant and colourful butterfly, a creature of light, fancy, spring and summer. The return of the sun and its light, the spring flowers, the birds, the rising sap and the buds, the butterflies, the lambs and kids, all roughly coincide with the moveable feast of Easter, which in Greek (with the lilac – springtime is lilac time) is *Páschaliá*.★

The swallows which in folklore tried to relieve Christ's suffering on the Cross, return in March from Paradise. Throughout Europe, names for the swallow glow with gratitude for its good deed: 'messenger of peace' (Wales), 'bird of God' (Périgord in France), 'bird of the Madonna' (Germany), 'chicken of the Lord' (Piedmont), 'bird of blessing' (Lincolnshire).

It is also gratitude for the spring, the light. Names for the swallow are reminiscent of names for the butterfly, which in the dead language of Cornish was 'God's little gift', and in Sicily is 'little bird of good

★ The lilac is *paschaliá*.

news'. I know of no folkloric connection between butterflies and the Bible, but the 'good news' there is probably that of Christ's resurrection. It has been noted elsewhere that the miraculous Easter-season emergence of the butterfly, like crinkled paper from its chrysalis, matches that of Christ from the tomb, even if, as the natural historian Pliny observed two thousand years ago, butterflies sometimes miscalculate and emerge prematurely, to die in the cold.

The birth or rebirth once complete, the golden sheath of the chrysalis counts for nothing. *Garabina*, a chrysalis in Cuba, means in Bolivia cheap finery, a trifling thing of no account. An empty chrysalis is flocculent and easily wind-blown, like the 'bamboo ashes' which in Jamaica express the same idea. The butterfly is fragile, beautiful, and it flies like the soul on delicate wings. In Greek it is *psyché*, which also has the meanings 'soul, heart, energy, spirit, courage'. In medieval and Renaissance art, angels were sometimes represented with multicoloured wings, like those of butterflies. The modern Dutch *kapel*, meaning both butterfly (or moth) and chapel, seems to imply yet another association with the Christian story. Is it from the resemblance of butterfly-wings to stained-glass windows?

The butterfly symbolizes the soul or human spirit, though, independently of Christianity. In Eskimo, a *tar-* root to a word carries suggestions of evanescence, airiness, change, movement, fluttering. The butterfly, *tarralikitak*, belongs with a family of words following one another in the Eskimo dictionary and including the soul, shadows, looking-glasses, and film-projectors.

The image of fluttering is inherent too in the French *papillon* for butterfly. The Latin *palpebrae*, eyelids, are from *palpitare*, to wink or flutter, to palpitate, and likewise the French *paupière*, eyelid, which in its turn is related to *papillon* and *peuplier*, the poplar tree, 'so named because their leaves are set on long flexible stalks, with an odd twist, so that they move in the slightest breeze'.

An idiomatic meaning of *papillon* is a parking ticket: pinned to the windscreen by the black 'abdomen' of the windscreen-wiper, the ticket flutters like a butterfly (or for that matter the end of a roll of film in a projector's gate). The Spanish *mariposa*, butterfly, is also a bedside candle, whose flame, fluttering in draughts, attracts moths.

In Cuba *mariposa* has the additional sense of a songbird. As with the

Sicilian expression, there seems to be an element of doubt around *mariposa* as to whether the butterfly should be 'placed' as an insect or as a bird. Or, for that matter, as a bat. In the West Indies, a bat meant a butterfly or moth; a bat, to distinguish it from the lepidoptera, was a rat-bat.

Even the English 'butterfly' seems to recognize that it's no ordinary insect. The word's precise origin is unknown, but the German *Butter-vogel*, 'butter bird', probably played a part, doubtless helped along by the echo of 'flutter', as in 'flutter-by'.

The name, it has been suggested, may have originated in Holland, and may be underpinned by the perceived buttery colour and texture of butterfly faeces. If so, it has as much inherent poetry as 'cheese-mite', but the English word now seems, like 'buttercup', to reflect warm melted butter, and to conjure up a fancy of summer and the summer sun.

Eggs in the Mirror

Melted butter reflects, and in French, eggs fried in it are *œufs au miroir*, eggs in the mirror, the German *Spiegeleier*, mirror-eggs.

Let us hold a mirror up to eggs. Imagine them fried in butter, dully reflected in a silver chafing-dish in a great country house at breakfast. It's springtime. What do the eggs remind you of? When was the last time you looked at primroses? True, the common primrose's petals are yellow, but the flowers are very 'pale', 'faint', 'wan', as Shakespeare, Milton, Keats all called the primrose, and the pallid yellow is almost like the buttery white of an egg against the primrose's bright orange eye, or 'yolk'.

In his novel *Coningsby*, Benjamin Disraeli makes passing mention of fried eggs looking 'like tufts of primroses'. In the 1950s, the English gardener Roy Genders visited the Shrine of Our Lady at Knock, County Mayo, and wrote that he had never seen 'such a profusion of blooms before, in appearance exactly like the yolks of countless fried eggs'.

'Primrose' is from the Old French *primerose*, because it was the 'first rose', 'first flower', of the *primus tempus*, the 'first time', the Latin forebear of the French *printemps*, spring.

Since the primrose isn't notably the earliest flower of the spring (although they may sometimes bloom as early as January), 'first' seems to mean 'best', or rather perhaps, *primus inter pares*, the prime minister of the primula family. Another etymology gives French *primerole*, primula, as the aboriginal antecedent of 'primrose'. This is probably true. In most languages with a word for primrose it is simply the 'primula', and German, which has several words for the primrose, has one that equally names the cowslip.

In English, before 'primula' came to name the primula, it named what we now call the cowslip, and was a name too, once, for the daisy, the day's eye (the daisy, like the human eye, shuts at night).

> The 'dayeseye' or elles the 'ye of day',
> The emperice and flour of floures alle.
>
> (Chaucer, *The Legend of Good Women*)

And in Milton's *Song on May Morning* the primula family is equated with the morning star, Venus, the dawn, and spring:

> Now the bright morning star, Days harbinger
> Comes dancing from the East, and leads with her
> The Flowry May, who from her green lap throws
> The yellow Cowslip and the pale Primrose . . .

In modern French, *primerose* is now among names for the hollyhock, while Old French for the spring, *primevère*, names the flower we now in English call the primula. Modern French for the primrose, the banally descriptive *primevère à grandes fleurs* (primula with big flowers) has none of the poetic and suggestive power of the 'primrose' which English purloined from French. It was a fair swap for the Norman Conquest.

What all these spring flowers may be said to have in common is a startling simplicity and freshness. Primroses like daffodils may sometimes 'come before the swallow dares', and they too are 'gallant', like the *galanto*, Spanish for the snowdrop (its Linnaean name is *Galanthus nivalis*). I cannot believe what I once heard an expert on snowdrops suggest, that Linnaeus coined this name.

The English language is brilliant at covering its tracks. The word 'primrose' is a sort of ennobled cowslip whose peasant origins were conveniently forgotten and dropped with the clod-hopping central 'e' of *primerose*. Since the seventeenth century 'primrose' has had the figurative adjectival meaning, 'peerless': it is, among flowers, a member of the House of Peers, as Disraeli himself was after he became Lord Beaconsfield.

Beaconsfield's funeral was in the primrose-time of 1881. Queen Victoria sent a large wreath of his favourite flowers, primroses. It was in the following year that 'primrose' was first used as an adjective of colour. Kid gloves, often, were 'primrose'. The year after that, 1883, aristocratic admirers of Lord Beaconsfield formed the Primrose League to nourish values the primrose-loving prime minister had held dear.

The private primrose – the prime ministerial flower – was now a public emblem, appropriated as a social symbol in exactly the same way, and at exactly the same time, as Oscar Wilde and the aesthetes appropriated the sunflower and the lily. Members of Britain's Conservative Party – lords and ladies, a scattering of knights – still (somewhat wanly now) observe the date of Disraeli's funeral, 19 April, as Primrose Day. From humble beginnings, that skeletal 'e' locked away in the cupboard, the primrose has with Beaconsfield's backing climbed the dizzy heights of the English class system.

But let us forget Lord Beaconsfield for a moment, and return to Disraeli the novelist. And let us, for the moment, forget primroses and look more closely at those fried eggs with which Disraeli compared them.

Fried eggs. They're peasant enough. And so, eventually, is perception of the aristocratic primrose. Look at Disraeli's simile more closely and the apparently private primrose path of his apparently individual fancy opens out into a broad avenue of common perception, at whose end the eggs, the primroses, the spring itself, all seem subtly different. For what we see staring back at us when we hold eggs up to the mirror of language are eyes, startled eyes.

Just as the 'e' is suppressed in 'primrose' so the image of an eye is suppressed in Disraeli's simile. In English we speak of the white of an eye and the white of an egg, but other languages go much further. In the Malay-based language of Javanese, for example, a fried egg is *mata sapi*, a 'cow's eye'. In Greek, more basically, it is *avgò máti*, 'egg eye', and Greek has *krókos*, too, to mean both a crocus and the yolk of an egg – crocuses, like primroses, are early flowers. Even in US hobo slang, fried eggs are 'redeyes'.

It is at least a striking coincidence that the English 'eye' sounds exactly like the German *Ei* (egg) and that the English 'egg' is not at all unlike the German *Auge* (eye).

Yes, I'm aware that 'egg' is a Scandinavian word, having entered English from Old Norse. Caxton in the fifteenth century told a story of a Yorkshireman landing in Kent and asking at a farmhouse for eggs, to be told by the farmer's wife that she didn't speak French. But what was *her* word for eggs? It was 'eyren'. On 'eye' and the German for egg, *Ei*, Professor Max Müller commented last century that 'it would not be unreasonable to take both words as expressive of roundness', but he gives the similarity as a warning to beginners in etymology who would base relationships between words solely on their sound and spelling.

I note, though, the egg–eyes in other languages, and also the similarity of the Old High German *eigir* (eggs) and the Anglo-Saxon *eáge* (eye), and most of all I note the extraordinary similarity of eggs and eyes themselves. I remain impressed by *Ei*–eye, egg–*Auge*, or for that matter the French *œuf–œil*. And I repeat: the English language is superb at covering its tracks.

It is an emphatic roundness, a ring within a ring, the 'O' which in Hebrew is *ain*, eye, that fried eggs, eyes, and primroses have, most obviously, conceptually in common. The roundness is also simplicity, openness, vulnerability. Spring is a time of daring to create and daring to be vulnerable, a time of fragile new life, when the birds are building nests and laying their eggs.

The Italian *primavera*, spring, can be used figuratively in the sense of venturing upon something entirely new, like the pure, path-finding research known in English as 'blue skies', while the Spanish spring, *primavera* again, is also the primrose (and the blue tit). In Spanish too, *ser un primavera* is 'to be a simple soul', a bit of an innocent, a village idiot, an April fool, while *inocentada*, an April Fool joke, is also a naïve remark, and a simple or simple-minded pleasure or person.

The Russian *glaz* is an eye, *glazún* (feminine) *glazúnya* is a 'gazer, gaper, nincompoop', and *glazúnya* (*yaíchnitsa*) are 'eggs dressed in a dish, fried eggs' – a dish in which the yolks are unbroken. Semantically,

Russian fried eggs are equated with the wide eyes of a nincompoop – or, as a Spaniard might say, *un primavera*. In different languages, then, the primrose (or spring) and the fried egg are *both* representative of naïve, trusting, simple-mindedness. They are, essentially, the same phenomenon in different guises. The fresh light shed on Disraeli's apparently simple simile takes us into unsuspected depths in the psychology of perception.

Spring is the time of the creator and holy fool, the Russian *yuródivy*, the German *reine Tor*. We remember that 'silly' once meant 'blessed', and is related to the German *selig*, holy; recall too the line from one of Shakespeare's sonnets, 'And simple truth miscalled simplicity'. It is easy to see creators, courageously in the van or ahead of their time, as silly fools.

The spring is forward: we persist in seeing it as a backward child. 'April', wrote Edna St Vincent Millay, 'comes like an idiot, babbling and strewing flowers.' It is extraordinary, the persistent equation in language of goodness and idiocy, producing, for example, 'ninny' from 'innocent' and 'cretin' from the French *chrétien*, a Christian. Usually, euphemism is given as the reason behind changes of meaning of this kind; but it is a harsh world where 'goodness' comes to mean 'stupidity'.

In the winter of the Cold War, those behind the Iron Curtain who believed in upheaval, reform, and the 'simple truth' appeared to adherents of the Brezhnev Doctrine to be *glazúnya*, political simpletons; and yet the *glásnost*, the 'openness', of Mikhaíl Gorbachóv's Russia was rooted in the ideals of the Czechoslovak reformers and the failed 'Prague Spring' of 1968.

The dissidents of the former Eastern bloc didn't stop believing in the spring. In politics they are (still, at the time of writing) the Primrose League of our time, and when there were votes to be got, they got them, just as Disraeli did. And there, perhaps, a little refreshing cynicism is in order. As Norman Douglas wrote in *South Wind*: 'That sentimental primrose-business. Dizzy as flower-expert! What cared he for primroses? Votes and moneybags was what he was after. But he knew the British Public. And that accounts for the pious domestic button-hole.'

The Halfwit in the Hedgerow

From Dr Johnson's *Dictionary*: '**Gawk** 1. A cuckoo. 2. A foolish fellow.' From the *Oxford Dictionary*: '**Gawk** An awkward person; a fool; a simpleton. (Confounded by Johnson and others with **Gowk**.)' And turning to **Gowk**: '1. The cuckoo. 2. A half-witted person; a fool.'

The *Oxford Dictionary*, then, while agreeing with Dr Johnson that a gawk is a halfwit, does not agree that it also means 'cuckoo'. That meaning belongs to 'gowk', which is distinct from 'gawk' only by the change of a single vowel, and which also, like 'gawk', means halfwit. Dr Johnson (and others) have supposedly 'confounded' the two words, and 'gawk' in the sense of a cuckoo is therefore supposedly the result of an entrenched lexicographical error.

'Gowk' is the English phonetic counterpart of the German *Gauch*, which in Austria is a fool, a simpleton, and in German dialect, a cuckoo. I don't doubt that the English 'gowk' may have meant cuckoo before 'gawk' did, but equally don't doubt that the English dialect use of 'gawk' to mean 'cuckoo' owes nothing to scholarly 'confounding' of the two words.

The showers of April, the cuckoo's month, were known as 'gawk storms', while 'gawk oats' were those sown in April after the bird's return from its migratory 'cuckooland'. I see no reason to believe that the cuckoo in the old Yorkshire saying, 'In the month of Averil / The Gawk comes over the hill / In a shower of rain,' owed anything to Dr Johnson, and no reason to disbelieve Johnson's comment on 'gawk' that, 'In both senses it is retained in Scotland.'

In fact 'gawk' to mean 'cuckoo' has the hallmarks of a popular etymology based on 'gowk'. 'Gowk' is what the English ear hears in *Gauch*: 'gawk' is what the eye sees. But there is more to it than that. The coloration of the cuckoo's plumage, ash-grey with black bars, closely resembles that of certain hawks. (I recall a discussion in Gibraltar Point bird sanctuary, in Lincolnshire, between my cousin and another visitor as to whether a particular bird was a hawk or a cuckoo.)

The cuckoo's reappearance in April roughly coincides with the hawk's disappearance, and a popular belief which flew blithely in the face of its early rejection by Aristotle was that the cuckoo's migratory disappearance at the summer's end was accounted for by cuckoos turning into hawks, just as hawks when they migrated, at about the time the cuckoo arrived, supposedly turned into cuckoos. 'Gawk', which identifies the cuckoo, by rhyme, with the hawk, seems to reflect this old fragment of folklore. A cuckoo, a gawk, is an ungainly joke-hawk. This reasoning tends to confirm what common sense anyway suggests: that it wasn't Dr Johnson and the lexicographers but popular imagination that rang the changes on the central vowel, so that the two words, 'gowk' and 'gawk', once embodied the same central concept in slightly different disguises.

The people as a whole were the 'others' who 'confounded' the words. But 'gawk' seemingly possessed more imaginative potential and metaphorical mileage than 'gowk', and while forms of 'gawk', like 'gawky', have survived into modern English, the dialect 'gowk' has fallen by the wayside. Nor is 'gawky' (of which more later) the only English survival from the apparently Germanic gowk–*Gauch* family. 'Gowk' and 'gawk' also have verbal meanings, whose identity is added evidence to suggest an intimate and essentially interchangeable relationship between the two words. Thus, while the *Oxford Dictionary* strictly distinguishes between the substantive senses of 'gowk' and 'gawk', it gives, for the verb 'gowk', '[Of unknown origin . . .] To stare foolishly', and for 'gawk', the virtually identical 'to stare or gape'. 'Gawk' in this sense also existed as 'gaw', and is the antecedent of the commonly used modern English 'gawp'.

Taking it, then, that old verbs for gawping are related to old disputed nouns for the cuckoo, we are back, once again, to wide eyes and the apparent identification of a simple-minded staring, or gawping, with a springtime phenomenon, this time the cuckoo. In the context already outlined (the fried eggs and the primroses) this identification is entirely to be expected. Approached from another direction, however, it is most unexpected, and even startling. The above analysis of 'gowk' and 'gawk' may seem so far to have been somewhat pedantic, but hidden in it is an unusual problem, to tackle which is to come up with some surprising conclusions. Stated simply, the problem is this: gawping conjures up a visual image, while the cuckoo is *par excellence* the *aurally* perceived bird, just as 'cuckoo' is *par excellence* the aurally derived word. Dr Johnson again, this time on the cuckoo: 'This bird is remarkable for the uniformity of his note, from which his name in most tongues seems to have been formed.'

'Cuckoo', with its close approximations in other languages, is an entirely self-referring word. We name the bird by the sound we take it to make, and languages show a remarkable degree of unanimity in the translation of that sound into syllables. Another such word – and there are very few of them – is the American bird-name 'whippoorwill'. 'Words of this kind', wrote Professor Müller, 'are, like artificial flowers, without a root . . . As the word *cuckoo* predicates nothing but the sound of a particular bird, it could never be applied for expressing any general quality in which other birds might share.'

Like the cuckoo itself, then, the word 'cuckoo' is, according to Müller, orphaned and rootless, apparently parentless, and a poor parent to other words. The cuckoo is an oddity in the bird world; the word 'cuckoo' is an onomatopoeic oddity in the word world.

Certainly the onomatopoeia 'cuckoo' is incapable of transference outside its immediate context, and is strictly applicable only to the bird we know by that name (and to the clock imitative of the cuckoo). But the bird we resume by 'cuckoo' has very marked and unusual habits – habits altogether ignored by Professor Müller in his etymological absorption in 'cuckoo' – by association with which other phenomena may acquire the designation 'cuckoo' to refer, not to the sound, but to one or other of the characteristic behaviour-patterns, real or supposed, of the bird we know by the sound.

Some metaphorical expressions incorporating or involving 'cuckoo' depend on the bird's aspect as aural calendar, or annual cuckoo-clock of the spring – 'the first cuckoo', whose average date in England was calculated in 1936 to be 28 April. The gawk storms and gawk oats of April have already been mentioned; there are also the small and backward 'cuckoo lambs' not born until well on in April, while Greek has 'cuckoo' to refer to young April figs. Perhaps most startlingly, the sound 'cuckoo' in Welsh is not merely onomatopoeic. The Welsh *ku* means 'Where?', and the cuckoo is taken to be asking the whereabouts of people who were alive last spring, whom the winter's cold has carried away: 'Where? Where?' In Welsh the cuckoo is known as 'the sorrowful bird'.

Other 'cuckoo' expressions depend not on a distant overhearing of the bird's disembodied voice but on close if often imperfect *visual* observation of it.

I have already mentioned observation of the similar coloration of the cuckoo and some hawks. Additionally, Greek has an expression incorporating 'cuckoo' meaning 'to be left on one's own', or abandoned, which recognizes the most idiosyncratic aspect of the cuckoo's behaviour – its abandonment of its egg, ultimately its young one, in the nest of the bird it chooses for the surrogate parent, usually some unlucky hedge sparrow, wagtail, or pipit. Against this background in natural history, the cuckoo also typifies hard-hearted filial ingratitude in idiomatic French and German expressions (and in lines in Shakespeare's *King Lear*). But this territory, like the explanations for 'cuckoo-spit' and the cuckoo-derived 'cuckold', although interesting, has been well covered elsewhere. I have, I hope, a more original and far-reaching point to make.

How do *Gauch*, gowk, gawk connect the cuckoo with a gawping halfwittedness, and how did 'cuckoo' come to acquire the idiomatic adjectival sense of 'halfwitted'? Do we turn for an explanation yet again to the sound the bird makes – that uniform and, Dr Johnson might have added, repetitive call? Is that what's so cuckoo about the cuckoo, the cuckoo-sound it makes, the *coucou* which in French rhymes with *fou* (mad)? No, I don't believe so. The squawk-like *Gauch*-words identifying the cuckoo with the halfwit sound nothing like 'cuckoo' and are by no stretch of the imagination mimetic of the bird's call. It is this aural perception of the cuckoo that has largely triumphed in the European languages, while the Germanic and Anglo-Saxon *Gauch*-family of cuckoo-words, if they haven't by now died out altogether in the places where they were once in common use, at most survive in pockets of dialect, or, as I have already suggested, in metaphorical offshoots like 'gawky' and 'gawp'. The exception is Scandinavia, where the 'gawk'-perception of the cuckoo has survived intact in everyday use: in Danish it is *gøg*, in Swedish *gök*, and in Norwegian *gauk*.

The *Gauch*-words, I believe, embody a now almost extinct and forgotten tradition whereby the human mind primarily perceived and conceived of the cuckoo not aurally, but visually; and the picture that stuck in the mind until the cuckoo's insistent sound displaced it was that of huge staring eyes above a huge gawping beak, and a big clumsy body cramped in a small space.

'Gawping' suggests not only round staring eyes, but a dropped jaw, a gaping mouth giving added emphasis to the eyes' roundness. Physiologically, the musculature of the face is such that the opening wide of the mouth stretches the facial muscles so as to open the eyes wide too. It can work in reverse, as when a woman, opening her eyes wide in order to make them up, finds her mouth involuntarily hanging open too. It is also a fact (try it for yourself) that the muscles round the eyes tend to stretch when one pronounces the hard 'g', and especially when it is followed by '-ow'. Try saying 'Gowrie', or 'gowk'. Or try those traditional expressions of eye-opening shock or surprise, 'Gosh', 'Golly', 'God', or 'Good grief!'

A young cuckoo in a hedge sparrow's nest opens its beak – or its 'gape', the part of the beak that opens – very wide indeed, a gaping wideness seemingly all the wider against the smallness of its surroundings and its diminutive, harassed foster-parents. How many people now have ever seen a young cuckoo in another bird's nest? I did, in Sussex, as a child. It's a sight that sticks in the mind:

The young cuckoo grows very fast. Within three days its skin has blackened, and shortly afterwards its feathers begin to sprout. Its appetite is insatiable, and the appearance of the nestling as it rises and falls in the nest, snapping with its gaping crimson mouth, is quite a terrifying one.

(Edgar Chance, *The Cuckoo's Secret*, 1922).

Here, I think, is our *Gauch*, gowk, gawk, whose gawping stare, when the aurally based cuckoo-name triumphed, went to give the onomatopoeic 'cuckoo' its adjectival sense of 'halfwitted', just as the visually based 'gawk' had earlier been used as an adjective for storms and oats coinciding with the cuckoo's call.

Whether gawping, or gawking, is so called because it was reminiscent of the gawk, or the gawk was so called because it gawked, there is no way of knowing. But most language bearing a relationship to the closely observed natural world works from the natural world outwards, and it seems probable that an ancient word 'gawk' or 'gowk' came first, and that 'gawking' and 'gawping' are, therefore, words that we ultimately owe to the cuckoo.

If so, we would also owe to the cuckoo 'gawky', a word once associated with halfwittedness (a 'gawky' was a halfwit) as well as with clumsiness. Gawkiness implies size: one can't be small and gawky. A young cuckoo in the nest, a big bird in a space too small for it, a misfit in a place where by the rules of orthodox biology it doesn't belong, is all wings, the picture of cramped uncomfortable awkwardness and clumsiness.

Gaulish

The English 'gawk' once had the dialect sense 'left', as in left-handed, in which sense the *Oxford Dictionary* gives it as being: 'Of difficult etymology; apparently a contraction of a disyllabic word which appears in many north-English dialects as *gaulick-*, *galloc-*, *gaulish-* (hand, handed).'

Gaulish indeed, and very reminiscent too of Gaul; or of Frankish, the Germanic tribal tongue which Paul Robert's dictionary puts in the far background of *gauche*, the French for 'clumsy' and, as an adjective or noun, for 'left', the left-handedness so often equated with awkwardness.

In its double significance *gauche* exactly parallels the English 'gawk' in its 'left' sense and in its other sense (with which the first is wholly compatible) of 'an awkward [or clumsy] person'. *Gauche* also means, when used of wood, 'warped', and Robert gives it as being from *gauchir*, to flinch or warp, a 'probable alternative', writes Robert, of the Old French *guenchir*, 'to deviate'. Robert proposes some shaping input also from the Old French *gauchier*, 'to press', the modern French *fouler*, whence *foule*, a crowd, a press of people. *Fouler* underlies the English 'fuller', a man who cleans cloth by beating and crushing it.

The young cuckoo is an anti-social misfit who is not at all one of the crowd but who is himself extremely crowded and pressed in his nest. The fool is not one of the *foule*. If a metaphorical impetus underlies *gauchier*, one wonders what it might be. But let that pass. The problem is bigger than *gauchier*.

Robert supplies no central underlying and controlling image from the world outside etymology for *any* of the concepts his etymology covers – neither clumsiness, nor left-handedness, warpedness, flinching, pressing, nor crowding. Somehow – in some immaculate conception of language – all these concepts have supposedly contributed towards the making of one of the most common words in French, *gauche*, which continues to embody several of them.

In going via *guenchir*, 'to deviate', hasn't Robert himself taken a devious or 'warped' etymological route? I am aware that words in their relationships can be as devious as the rhododendron, which almost incredibly is a member of the heather family. But that doesn't mean that their relationships are *invariably* so devious.

The context I have given is an argument for a straighter line, as the crow if not the cuckoo flies, running from nature as well as language – the Frankish-based *gauche* coming from the same eventual source that gave the German *Gauch*, fool or cuckoo, the German guttural *-ch* hardening in the English 'gowk' and 'gawk' and softening in the French.

If this is a linguistic coincidence then it is a most extraordinary one, requiring the agreement of sound, multiple meanings, and even spelling in at least three mainstream European languages. The English words tend to support a reading other than Robert's *guenchir*, and so, more generally and conceptually, does the background, explicit in the English and German, equating clumsiness and halfwittedness with the cuckoo.

Spots and Dots

In the budding branches of the bushes and trees in springtime we come across the source for an important and wide-ranging set of metaphors, and a curious and persistent feature of the pre-scientific world that language has led us into: what might be characterized as a minute attention to spottedness in things, an attention so marked that one sometimes has the impression of an obsessively *pointilliste* word-painter at work behind the scenes.

This is a world required to read alterations in surface appearance for tiny signs of danger, divine displeasure, the malign influence of the stars: the eruption on the face which might mean plague; the tell-tale spottings of blight, blast, or rust on the wheat-grain; the tiny, dark-violet 'cock's spur' of ergot; or the scrap of food spotted with mildew, which the Italians call *lupa*, she-wolf, after the luxuriant, wolflike grey hair of some mildews that can still inspire an atavistic superstitious dread when one finds it on food or in the fridge today.

Over and again in this area of word-making the dominant motif is the bud, the eruption signalling the onset of spring. It isn't invariably associated with spots and spottedness. Spanish has *gema*, gem or bud – the bud, compact, shining with moisture, freshly coloured, resembles a jewel. Tennyson's image in *Maud* – 'A million emeralds break from the ruby-budded lime' – is not as original as it appears. Neither, however, is *gema* itself. It appears at first glance to be a metaphor for a bud, but in reality the idea of a bud is the vehicle for the word 'gem'. It is a metaphor from Latin *gemma*, whose primary meaning was 'bud'. In modern botany, *gemmae* are leaf-buds, the 'emeralds' of Tennyson's image.

The Russian *póchka* or *póchechka*, bud, is also the glistening, compact, bud-like kidney, and other Russian words relate kidneys, or buds, to haemorrhoids. The Spanish *nacerse*, the reflexive form of 'to be born', means to bud and, of a seam in clothing, to split: the bud's green seam splits to give a secret glimpse of the flower or shoot inside.

In Greek a bud can be an eye, *máti*, and in Japanese also, *me*, which is an eye and many other things including, in one form of the word, a bud.★ The idea of the bud as a gem and the bud as an eye combine in the Russian *glazok*, from *glaz*, eye, meaning the bud of a flower or leaf and the bezel – the facets – of a cut gemstone.

Spanish *yema*, as well as a bud, is the heart or the best part of anything and the yolk of an egg (where eyes are, eggs are never far away). Spanish also has, beautifully to my mind, *yema del dedo*, the bud of the finger, for fingertip, in which it is as though the fingers were shoots and their tips were the human body's own tender and

★ Although, admittedly, *me* is one of those instances where, because of the historical entanglement of Japanese with Chinese, it is particularly difficult to be certain that a Japanese word is a metaphor. The context suggests that it is, however.

delicately questing buds. Green fingers indeed. In the same vein, but with a metaphorical precision that is less conceptual, more visual, Spanish has *capillo*, rosebud, for the foreskin. The foreskin is visually implied also in the idiomatic Spanish use of *pito* for the penis: among the primary meanings of *pito* is an empty chrysalis torn open at one end, where the butterfly has departed.

Spots in Spanish can be *barros*, which also means terracotta ware (the red pots, the red spots), while the Latin American *lunarejo*, spotty, compares a spotty face to the surface of the moon. Spots also return us to weaving. The English 'burl', an imperfection in cloth, once had the transferential meaning of a pimple (which causes us to think again about what is meant by a 'burly' man). The Spanish for 'burl', *mota*, is also a polka dot in clothing patterns. *Moteado*, used of fabrics, means dotted; used of skin it means mottled, freckled, spotted with burls.

Foremost among these relatively simple metaphors is the one Flaubert had in mind when he wrote of a character in *Madame Bovary* that 'she was ugly, thin as a lath, with as many pimples as the spring has buds'. The original French is a pun requiring only the one word, *bouton*, meaning both bud and pimple, or *bourgeon* (bud; or pimple, pustule). The nineteenth-century writer on Gypsy life, George Borrow, found evidence of the same correlation in Romany, and placed *bourgeon* with the Wallachian *mourgour* (bud) in the background of the Romany *bugnes* or *bugnior*, meaning smallpox or blisters.

In spring the trees and bushes come out in aperiodic spots, which are sticky, oozing, and vivid against their background, as virulent pustules are on a face. Similarly, someone with spots is in bud; the spotty-faced adolescent is in the bud of adulthood. This body of association underlies a passage in Samuel Beckett's *Waiting for Godot* where the mention of 'pus' follows the observation that, in the spring, 'Everything oozes.' It seems cynical, but Beckett is merely making explicit a metaphor inherent in the language, French, in which he wrote the play.

Similar associations exist vestigially in the English 'dot', a word suggestive of mathematics and Morse code and seemingly unrelated to the natural world, but deriving from the Old English *dott*, the head of a boil. Dottedness is spottedness, or spottiness, under another name.

A spot is a bud that has moved to a face. A dot is a spot that has moved to a piece of paper.

Buds and Buttons

Things get a tiny bit more complicated when we move from *bouton* meaning bud or pimple to *bouton* meaning, as it also does, button.

The first buttons on clothing weren't metal or plastic discs but bulbously knotted cord or fabric, origins remembered in the modern Greek *kómbion*, button, from *kómbos*, knot. Buttons resembled flower-buds with their tightly packed petals, and so, in French, were *boutons*. The same sense of buttons as an organic extension of the natural world into the social is in the Italian *olivetta*, a small olive or a cloth-covered button.

There was also a sense, though, at the beginning of buttons, that they were strange and unnatural – not so much functional as for show, and worn by show-offs. To the Amish and the Mennonites, buttons were sinful signs of vanity and pride – to this day members of these sects won't wear them. The poet Apollinaire wrote in *Annie*: 'She is a Mennonite, who knows / Neither buttons on her clothing / Nor buds on her rose.'

'Button' in its sense of a mechanical or electrical operating device derives by transference from the image of a modern, machine-made button on clothing. Once again, the semi-abstract notion of spotted-ness is paramount. The buttons on the control-panel are coloured eruptions on an otherwise monochromatic and smooth surface. Dashboards are dotted.

While English has 'button' to describe small, bud-like mushrooms, colloquial French for a car's accelerator-pedal, or button, is *le champignon*, the mushroom. In a popular model of French car, the accelerator-pedal was shaped exactly like a mushroom. The resemblance once perceived, the idiomatic metaphor took off and successfully entered French.

The idea of a bore as a 'buttonholer' presents a mystery which my delvings into the history of tailoring, lapels, buttons, and button-holes have so far failed to solve. If 'buttonhole' is a corruption of buttonhold', as it is said to be, why is it that on neither lapel of a man's suit is there a button to hold but that on one of them, the left, there is a buttonhole? And what is the purpose of this buttonhole, this 'eye', with no button to fill it? Why, it is there for special occasions when a *boutonnière* is to be worn. It is there solely to put a flower-bud into.

Is this nature imitating art, reality reflecting its own supposed mirror, language? It may be. For when we say of someone that he's 'unbuttoned' we are saying in effect that he's in bloom, it's springtime in his soul, the buds are opening up along with his shirt-front and his spirit.

This original sense, clouded over in English, is still alive in the Spanish *desabotonar*, which is both to bloom (unbutton) and to undo buttons. A buttonhole is just the place to put a bud; someone whose buttonhole sports one – a primrose on 19 April, a daffodil on St David's Day – is a show-off sporting a visual pun.

III DAY SPRING

Death of the Dawn

Dawn, a literary cliché, comes wonderfully alive when it is looked at through literature's raw material, language. It is perhaps almost impossible now for a writer to describe a dawn without falling into cliché: Homer's 'rosy-fingered' dawn is definitive, and its original freshness is not easily recaptured.

Dawn as literary subject-matter seems to belong to the dawn of literature. Writers have gone to great lengths to try and reinvigorate it, but their dawns are forced and artificial compared to Homer's or the dawn that language itself shows us; and however cynical the writer may try to be in his effort to be original, he always and perhaps inevitably draws upon the dawn we find in language, which is not cynical at all.

Already in the first century BC the anonymous author of a book known only as the *Ad Herennium* was world-wearily writing that 'A sunrise, the sun's course, a sunset are marvellous to no one because they occur daily'. In language, on the contrary, dawn is marvellous precisely for that reason, just as spring – another literary cliché – is marvellous because it occurs annually and without fail. Embodied in language is the perception of a profound association between dawn, the rebirth of the day, and spring, the rebirth of the year. More mysteriously, perhaps, language reveals also the perception of a connectedness (or a confusion) between dawn, the day's birth, and sunset, the day's death and the apparent antithesis of dawn. Much of this apparent confusion, I suspect, can be traced to the strange behaviour of Venus, the 'star' both of the morning and the evening.

Bernard Mandeville (1670–1733) cynically portrayed the Roman

54

goddess of the dawn, Aurora, as a London whore starting the day:

> *Aurora* rous'd by some damn'd Cock,
> From a pure dream, how in her Smock
> She wrestled, with the Man she doats on;
> Jump'd out of Bed, and slipt her Coats on;
> And just then as the blowzy Lass,
> Before the Sea, her looking Glass
> Stood dressing of [her] Carrot Head,
> And dawbing her blue chops with Red;
> Dame Earth pull'd off her Mask to *Sol*,
> As Strumpets do to Sentinel;
> Whose Red Coat, in St James's Park,
> From every Face dispels the dark.

Some of the above, like the pun on 'Cock', is crude and obvious enough. Deeper students of the dawn will be more interested in the references to Aurora's 'Carrot Head', her rouge, and the red-coated sentinel. And the 'blowzy Lass / Before the Sea' – is that a sideswipe at the goddess Venus, and in particular Botticelli's painting of her birth from the sea?

Mandeville, for all the (forced) originality of his treatment, drew on an ancient stock of images and epithets for the dawn, as did Shakespeare in *Hamlet*, again personifying dawn as a redcoat, or rather, as a russet-coated rustic: '. . . look the morn, in russet mantle clad, / Walks o'er the dew of yon high eastern hill.'

Samuel Butler in *Hudibras* had to struggle to come up with a novel (and grotesque) image for the dawn: '. . . like a lobster boil'd, the dawn / From black to red began to turn.' (Like Aurora's blue chops daubed with red – but more on lobsters elsewhere: see the Lexicon, **Lobster**.)

Against this background, I am sceptical of a striking statement in Paul Fussell's marvellous book *The Great War and Modern Memory*. 'Dawn', wrote Fussell, 'has never recovered from what the Great War did to it.' We are to believe that ideas or images too can be killed in action, as surely as any soldier.

In considering ironies arising from the collision of received ideas with personal experience in the Great War Fussell was himself ironic.

Dawn is traditionally the recovery of light from darkness. What never recovered, then, was recovery, or more accurately the idea of dawn as perpetual and inevitable recovery. If in T. S. Eliot's post-Great War image of a sunset, the evening was '. . . spread out against the sky / Like a patient etherized upon a table', then the patient died under the surgeon's knife, or at best was reduced to the 'brown fog of a winter dawn' of *The Waste Land*. But isn't Eliot's image every bit as forced and grotesque in its originality as Butler's or Mandeville's – brown sunglasses in place of Homer's rose-tinted spectacles?

Let's look more closely at this dawn that supposedly died. Fussell takes as his starting point what he calls 'the crucial document in the history of British awareness of the sky', Ruskin's *Modern Painters*. 'Those attentive to the history of taste', writes Fussell, 'know that sky-awareness is a fairly late development. There is little of it, for example, in the eighteenth century, which felt no pressing need for such emblems of infinity as sky or sea.'

I have a quarrel there with 'awareness'. The sky in all its moods was a subject to which the Romantic writers and painters returned (Constable, for example, called the sky 'the chief organ of sentiment' in a painting). But so, to take another example almost at random, was the phosphorescence of the sea. 'It is only in relatively recent times', wrote E. Newton Harvey in *A History of Luminescence*, 'that poets and travelers became ecstatic in their description of the light of the ocean.' But if the sky or phosphorescence suddenly loomed large as literary subject-matter, that isn't to say that there was no previous keen awareness of them, only that there was literary lack of interest. The history of skyscape is intimately bound up with that of the Romantic movement. Language shows us what common sense anyway suggests: that 'sky-awareness', far from being recent, is in all likelihood commensurate with the existence of the race. It is that 'ecstasy' referred to by Harvey that Fussell means, not awareness. It is the sky-rapture of Ruskin, in whose description of an Alpine sunrise 'the whole heaven, one scarlet canopy, is interwoven with a roof of waving flame, and tossing, vault beyond vault, as with the drifted wings of many companies of angels: and then, when you can look no more for gladness, and when you are bowed down with fear and love of the Maker and Doer of this, tell me who has best delivered this His message unto men!'

Ruskin's sky is so top-heavy with God that it must have had a lead roof, like a church. God was the 'Maker and Doer' of this gigantic, fluffy, cherub-infested wedding-cake of a dawn, and it was only this (I think preposterous) God-heavy version of dawn that died in the Great War, not dawn itself. What was killed off, as it were – what died – was the literary overkill of Ruskin's sky-writing. On this Fussell is wonderfully illuminating. Sunrise and sunset in the Great War were the times of 'stand-to', times of high tension and danger when everyone was alert for attack: 'What one stared at twice daily for years on end, thus, was sunrise and sunset.'

It was just when the sun was most spectacularly spilling its light across the sky that human blood was most likely to be spilt too. The irony of this was not lost on the men themselves, as Fussell convincingly illustrates with many apt quotations, commenting after one of them, 'Ruskin has been invited to squat in a jump-off trench on a hill near Albert.' But Fussell draws no distinction between literature and popular taste – or what might be termed the popular preciosity of late nineteenth-century aestheticism. When *Modern Painters* came out, Charlotte Brontë said, 'This book seems to give me eyes'; but towards the end of the century Oscar Wilde on being asked to admire a sunset remarked (in *The Decay of Lying*, 1889): 'It was simply a very second-rate Turner, a Turner of a bad period.'

The skies that Turner's paintings had taught Ruskin to see – and that Ruskin in turn taught the public – were already a cliché; the vision that gave Charlotte Brontë new eyes had become a standardized pair of spectacles which too many people had seen through, a cultural reflex. Ruskin had entered the popular bloodstream. Fussell quotes Evelyn Waugh on himself at fifteen: 'I had not read much Ruskin, but I had in some way imbibed most of his opinions.' In later life, Waugh would be repelled by the sight of a sunset over Mount Etna.

The ironic juxtapositions of the Great War, far from killing dawn off for writers, renewed it as subject-matter and gave it a new lease of literary life. The novelty can be exaggerated. The juxtaposition of blood and morning or evening sunlight wasn't altogether new to literature. Fussell doesn't quote Christopher Marlowe's 'See, see where Christ's blood streams in the firmament!' – a line which Eliot approvingly quotes in his essays, and which perhaps underlies his image of a patient etherized upon an operating table.

If dawn may be said to have died in the Great War it was only Ruskin's, and Fussell's allegedly terminally wounded dawn must be located still more narrowly. If *Modern Painters* was the crucial document in British sky-awareness, as Fussell argues, then sky-cynicism arising from the Great War seems also to have been exclusively British. The Italian poet Giuseppe Ungaretti, a veteran of the Great War, produced out of it his two-line 'Mattina' (Morning) with its odd grammar (an adjective serving as a noun)

> M'illumino
> D'immenso

– the most condensed and joyous image of the dawn known to me.

Goodly Light

Illuminate yourself with immense. Experience the novel thrill of watching a dawn from the first streaks . . .

No, it's even earlier, still dark. 'Before the flies are astir' this last moment of darkness before the dawn is called – *belung terbang lalat* in Malay, and in Japan, *akegure*, which the lexicographer J. C. Hepburn, last century, defined as 'the moment before the Buddhist temple bell sounds for sunrise', a somewhat Zen definition drawing, perhaps, on poetic licence.

Imagine it, though. The Shinto temple bell is just about to sound and the flies about to stir; night trembles at the very edge of day. It is a difficult moment to pinpoint, and already it has passed. A black thread, in the Koran's phrase, may be distinguished from a white one; and according to the Talmud, blue may be distinguished from white. Imperceptibly, light has begun to bathe the eastern sky, home of the morning star, Venus. But Venus is also the *evening* star. It is not, of course, a star at all, but a planet, moving on an orbit closer to the sun than our own and so seen always in proximity to the sun, whether it is rising in the east or sinking in the west.

Because of this proximity, Venus was known to the Indians of the Orinoco as 'the wife of the sun'. The ancient Romans had two names to accommodate its dual identity as the first star of the evening, the last star of the dawn. The star with two stage-names is bright enough at night to cast shadows, and now, as it sheds its evening-name — Hesperus or Hesper — it is still visible under its dawn-name, Phosphorus or Phosphor, the light-bearer Lucifer, the fallen angel.

It is peep of day. The sun's light, but not yet the sun itself, glows over the skyline, and Homer's 'rosy-fingered dawn' brushes the clouds. The temple bell rings. One by one, the stars have been outshone, all but the bright and wandering Venus, now shining alone. The moon has gone too, unless it is one of those mornings the moon-watching Japanese once had a special word for, *ari-ake*, a morning with a moon.

'Dawn [*Aurora*]', wrote the Roman etymologist Varro, 'is said of the phenomenon before sunrise, from the fact that the air "grows golden" [*aurescit*] from the sun's fire, which at that time is golden.' Aurora, related to *aurum*, gold, in the Roman personification of the dawn arose each morning from the saffron-coloured (golden, or yellow) bed of Tithonus. But as we shall see, by this 'gold' aurora we have to understand something subtly different from what we now mean by the word, a colour-adjective for a wider segment of the spectrum than we take 'gold' today to encompass.

To the Romans this time when the air grew golden was *mane* (morning), 'because then', wrote Varro, 'the day "trickles" [*manat*] from the east ...' More contentiously, Varro thought that *mane* might owe something also to *manum*, 'the good', 'from a superstitious belief of the same kind as influences the Greeks, who, when a light is brought, make a practice of saying "Goodly light!"'

It's a seductive idea, and while reserving judgement on that supposed relationship of *mane* and *manum*, we shall find ample evidence in language of a consensus that the dawn light is indeed 'goodly'.

In language, dawn gets an overwhelmingly good press. Languages are far from unanimous, however, in the way they stress dawn's 'goodliness'; different ideas of the dawn tend to dominate in different languages, or, to put that more tentatively, certain dawn-associations are more explicit in some languages than in others. By a roundabout route, for example, two languages owing nothing to one another etymologically, Spanish and Eskimo, have some common conceptual ground in their expression of the idea of dawning light. The Spanish *alumbrar* means to supply someone in the darkness with light. Used figuratively, it also means to give birth. And in Eskimo, we are told (by Arthur Thiebert in his Eskimo dictionary of 1954), 'The main idea expressed by words beginning with the letter U is the opening of the eyes and the feelings of the soul expressed by the opening of the eyes.'

'U' is the exposed negative of night, the exact opposite of shut-eye. By its initial letter, Eskimo for the year's longest day, *ublurtulak*, is related to *ugtuk* or *uttuk*, the vulva. The Eskimo *aggak* is the afterbirth and the caul – the membrane protecting the foetus – and also the retina of the eye. Light dawning upon the retina or caul is birth. The longest day is the eye at its widest open, the sky filled with light.

Orient

The sun rises and warms the earth. Venus vanishes at last, and in Malay it is 'the time when the dew dries ...' At dawn the tiny dewdrops are scattered like seed-pearls; 'orient' – the east, the dawn – is a conventional epithet for both dewdrops and pearls. From the morning dew, the Latin *ros*, the Romans got *rorarii*, skirmishers, those who start the battle, Varro tells us, 'because it "sprinkles" [*rorat*] before it really rains'.

The scattering of the dew bears a discreet resemblance to the sowing of corn – one of many associations, implicit and explicit, linking ideas of dawn with ideas of spring. Milton exploits the linkage in Book Five of *Paradise Lost*: 'Now Morn her rosie steps in th'Eastern clime / Advancing, sowd the earth with Orient Pearl.' The metaphor extends further, from the dew to the sun's light itself. In discussing metaphor, Aristotle looked at the phrase 'sowing around a god-created flame', whereby the act called sowing provides a name for a phenomenon otherwise nameless (the sun shedding its light).

The sun is fully in the sky now – the sun which the Russians once called *práotets*, our forefather; the sun which at a linguists' conference in Turkey in 1934 was proposed as the first object to strike the human fancy sufficiently to demand a name; and that first word, it was claimed, the forefather of all language, was a Turkish one, the word for 'sun', *gunes* ... The idea of the sun as our father may go further. The scholar Desmond Stewart suggested that when Christ on the

Cross called *Eli, eli, lama sabacthani*, 'My God, my God, why hast thou forsaken me?', he may have been calling on the sun – *Elie, elie*, the Greek demotic vocative of *helios*.

It is day, the Latin *dies*, related to *deus*, god, a cognate (or word 'born with') of the Greek *Dia*, Zeus, who rolls the sun on its westward course . . .

His westward course. In Greek myth, dawn is identified with the god Apollo and with Delos, Apollo's island in the Cyclades. Apollo is the sun's charioteer. In the myth, the cock crow wakes him, and his chariot rises over Delos, the sun bathing the barren island in molten gold . . .

The Returning Bird

In Delos we find an explicit linkage of dawn with spring. The golden Delos of the Greeks was called by the Romans Ortygia – from *ortyx*, the quail, the Sanskrit *vartika*, 'the returning bird' . . .

Bird migration is mysterious enough today. In this time before science when much of the world is unexplored, its annual rhythms and wider patterns are seen from one viewpoint only. No one knows where the birds fly to. It might be Paradise, where Russian peasants once believed the swallows went. It might be the moon, where swallows were 'proved' to migrate to in a book by an English 'Person of Learning and Piety', published as late as 1703.

In the Mediterranean every autumn, the grapes harvested, the quails mysteriously congregate in their thousands, and fly away in the night in great flocks – and then, in warmer climes, where they speak of 'the Christmas birds', they arrive as mysteriously. They fly south, to Africa – in his play, *The White Chameleon*, Christopher Hampton has his characters eating quail caught easily in nets on the beaches of Egypt – but the Greeks and Romans think they fly with the light. Then in Europe every springtime, when the light returns, the quails are among the first birds to return with it, to build their scrappy nests among the stones, *les cailles parmi les cailloux* (the quails among the pebbles) as a Frenchman might say – not a proven etymology, but an intriguing whiff of a possible relationship.

The going and coming back of the quails – flocking on Delos *en route* – belongs to a recurrent cosmic pattern of death and rebirth. A daily, yearly pattern. When the night is gone the day will spring from the quail-land – Ortygia. When winter's long night is over the spring will dawn, the quail will return with the sun.

Alektor

There is another bird that returns, not every spring, but every dawn: the cock, which we have coyly learned (from the United States) to call the 'rooster' (the Americans also turned 'arse' into 'ass', while the English are responsible for the 'ass' euphemism, 'donkey'). 'Cock' was felt to be unsuitable for polite society, and there is the story of a young lady who described her brother, a sailor, as a 'rooster-swain'.

The cock, then, is each day's 'returning bird', starting the dawn chorus and the day – and ending it, too – with its raucous cock crow. Like Venus, or the red sky, the cock makes its presence felt at both ends of the day. It is 'both fyrst and last', and seemingly sleepless:

> The cocke dyd say,
> I use alway
> To crow both fyrst and last;
> Like a postle I am
> For I preche to man
> And tell him the nyght is past.

In Greek the rooster is *aléktor*, literally 'the one without a bed', 'who doesn't go to bed', 'the watchful one'. It is the clarion of the work ethic. When it is cock crow it is time to get up and get dressed, and in the West Indies, the cock crow is popularly transcribed as 'Gi' me trousers!'

Day Clean

Also in the West Indies, dawn is 'day clean', a time defined as when there is just enough goodly light by which to see one's way to work (with one's trousers on) without stumbling. 'Day clean' is a term calqued, or copied by translation, into English from African languages, and carried across the Atlantic by slaves. It exists also in French Creole, as *ju netye*, the French *jour nettoyé*, or 'cleaned day'. In this view the dawn may be white, and indeed in Spanish and Italian it is simply *alba*, 'the white', and in French *l'aube*, the Latin *alba* again, in another guise.

'Day clean' appears to fall in with the pattern of one of those complexes of opposed associations, and words similarly perceived as being in opposition, known as 'universal binomials', polarized pairs which describe both aspects of external reality and more intangible, arguably metaphorical qualities. They include straight/crooked, sweet/sour, and white/black. In *After Babel* George Steiner calls the last 'of particular interest, as it appears to convey a positive/negative valuation in all cultures, regardless of skin-colour. It is as if all men, since the beginning of time, had set the light above the dark.' Certainly we shall see, in several contexts, that a white/black binomial does seem to be deeply ingrained in language. Perceived in these terms, if dawn is clean then the dusk, by implication, is dirty. 'Day clean' tends to suggest cosmic spring-cleaning. The clean dawn light's 'rosy fingers' wipe away time's smears, shadowy dust, dirt, and sins, and even last night's hangover, in a new beginning to the world.

Dawn, like the priest, comes dressed in an alb denoting goodliness, godliness. This is not the only perception of the dawn light, however; nor, from the evidence, is it the most widespread one. Running alongside the perception of dawn as 'the white', there is an alternative perception of it as golden, red, yellow, or orange. Both traditional perceptions are ancient – it is profitless to speculate which 'came first' – and both are found in the intriguing word 'auburn'. Based on *albus*, white, it originally meant 'blonde'; only later did it acquire that au-prefix suggestive of the golden dawn, aurora.

In passing, it may be suggested that 'the white' dawn lends itself more readily to moral and didactic interpretation than the dawn at the red and yellow end of the spectrum. Here, no universal binomial is at stake; it is rather a question of perceptual nuance, and we do better if we think, not of binomials, but of a centuries-long aesthetic debate, as it were, conducted through language with the means which language, in any one place and at any one historical moment, had at its disposal.

The Hesperides

In his poem *The Hesperides* Tennyson saw Venus in each of her two aspects – evening and morning star – as implacably opposed to one another. 'Hesper hateth Phosphor,' he wrote, 'evening hateth morn.'

This is the black-and-white, binomial view. In fact, the Greek myth of the Garden of the Hesperides suggests quite different received perceptions, which Tennyson or any classically educated Christian was bound to find profoundly puzzling. The myth is both the chief example, and the chief source, of the confusion surrounding the dawn, and colours and objects associated with the dawn. To the west, it says, in the land of the setting sun, there is an orchard where golden apples grow. The orchard is tended by an old man, Hesper, and his three daughters, whose collective name, the Hesperides, translates from the Greek as meaning 'in the west'. This western garden is guarded by a dragon called Ladon. The eleventh labour of Heracles, in which he succeeded by stealth and cunning, was to steal the golden apples.

The Hesperides is not Tennyson at his best. Its muddled, neo-Blakeian mysticism perhaps explains why Tennyson chose to suppress it. Written in 1833, before Victoria came to the throne, it wasn't published until 1910, after Tennyson's and Victoria's deaths. In 1910, it could still be said of the British Empire that the sun never set upon it, and Tennyson's poem reads now as a kind of sibylline meditation upon that empire, a precursor to Kipling's *Recessional* with its well-known refrain, 'Lest we forget'.

Anachronistically reminiscent of Kipling is Tennyson's idea of east/west as a universal binomial:

> . . . watch the treasure
> Of the wisdom of the West . . .
>
> Guard the apple night and day
> Lest one from the East come and take it away

Look from west to east along:
Father, old Himla weakens, Caucasus is bold and strong.

Tennyson put a Western, Christian gloss on the Greek, pagan myth –
'Western' as in 'Western civilization', 'Western values', the golden
apple as symbolic of 'the wisdom of the West'. In this moralizing
gloss the myth, with its firm location of the orchard 'in the west', of
course encouraged him.

There is a problem here, however, which may help to explain the
muddle of Tennyson's poem. Traditional imagery identifies goodness
or prelapsarian innocence with goldenness (as good as gold), and
firmly locates the source of that golden goodness, that ultimate moral
authority, not in the West, where Tennyson, obedient to the myth,
insisted it was, but, on the contrary, in the East.

The Garden of the Hesperides is a myth of the Golden Age. The
myth of the orchard with a dragon in it parallels the Christian myth
of the Garden of Eden with a serpent in it. Both the golden apple of
the Greeks and the Christian apple of knowledge were stolen. The
close parallels between the two stories were always perfectly clear to
classically educated Christians. So, however, was the major disagree-
ment between them. The Garden of the Hesperides was located
where the day died, 'in the west', while scriptural sources clearly
located Eden where day is born, at the opposite point of the compass,
in the aurora of the east. That is where Milton firmly set it in *Paradise
Lost*, in which, following the Latin Vulgate, he made its westernmost
point 'Auran', the 'Haran' of Scripture. In the Tremellius-Junius Latin
version of the Bible (Milton's favourite version, just as the Garden of
the Hesperides was his favourite Greek myth) it is Auranitis, described
by Joseph E. Duncan (in *Milton's Earthly Paradise*) as 'believed derived
from Eden'.

Whatever the origin of 'Auranitis', both it and 'Auran' are strongly
reminiscent of the dawn's 'aurora'. We shall see that Milton, like
Tennyson later, was apparently puzzled by the reversal of the east–
west axis in the Greek myth, and that he too resorted to assertion in
order to resolve the problem. So did Sir Walter Ralegh, who in his
History of the World (1614) wrote that: 'Paradise itself [was] transported
out of Asia into Africa, and made the Garden of the Hesperides.'

He meant, of course, imaginatively transported, from east to west. Ralegh was writing from the Christian perspective whereby the story of Adam and Eve in Eden was the original and only true account of Paradise and the Fall, of which the Greek myth was a garbled, as it were 'pidgin' version, a 'Fiction', as he calls it.

Gold

'Golden Delos'. But what colour *is* gold? And what colour is the dawn light?

'Orange' is an interesting colour conundrum. Our word for the colour comes from the word for the fruit of that colour. Oranges – and with them the concept of the colour orange –, were introduced into Europe in the fifteenth century. Before their introduction, what was the name for the colour that results when red and yellow paints are mixed together?

It was probably 'gold'. It may be agreed, I think, that gold is not the same colour as orange. Nor is gold the same as yellow. The words 'gold', 'orange', 'yellow' resume subtle differences within the same segment of the spectrum. But the word 'yellow' is semantically related to 'gold'. In fact, in words like 'yolk', the yellowish bile produced by the 'gall'-bladder, and the golden 'gall', or oak-apple, used in dyeing, we can almost see, in linguistic slow motion, the hesitant segmentation of 'yellow' and 'gold', and the consonant shift between 'y' and the guttural 'g'.

So, we shall see, is 'orange' related to gold. And if we were struggling to describe the colour gold we might reach, just as we would in trying to describe 'orange', for the colour-adjectives 'yellow' and 'red'. Earlier (see pages 26–9), we encountered language problems at the blue end of the spectrum. But the segmentation of the red or 'hot' end is not a simple matter either.

In Middle English, and in archaic English thieves' cant, or specialized slang, 'red' was gold; jewellers still speak of red gold. Red, like gold, can be emblematic of excellence and beauty. Japanese has *aka*, red, to mean also 'naked', and, as an adverb, 'completely, perfectly'; and *akai*, red, with the additional metaphorical meaning of 'sincere, loyal'. We find that suggestive dab of red to suggest dawn in the Japanese *akegure* and *ari-ake*, mentioned earlier.

Red – in the shape of the adjective *krásny* – is in widespread figurative use in Russian. It is the root of *krasotá*, beauty in Russian (see the Lexicon, **Beauty**). Moscow's Red or Beautiful Square (*Krásnaya Plóshchad*) was so called from the seventeenth century, long before Marx and Communism. 'Red' acquired the figurative sense 'revolutionary' at the time of the French Revolution. The Bolsheviks drew on both the revolutionary and the Russian associations of redness when they appropriated 'red' as a congratulatory adjective for themselves and their cause, just as their opponents – the White Russians★ – appropriated a colour, or absence of colour, also typifying excellence in Russian (see **White**). The emblematic, political use of 'white' also derives from the French Revolution.

In Latin, the colour of the sun's light could be described as either red or gold. *Rutulus* (from *rutilare*, to be red) to describe sunlight was also used of 'golden' hair. Red – and red hair in particular (the whore Aurora's 'Carrot Head' in Mandeville's poem) – was associated with sunlight, summer, and sun-ripened wheat, a colour now more often conventionally called 'golden'. The hair colour auburn – connected with the dawn – has already been mentioned (see page 63). 'Auburn', like 'wheat' (see pages 97–8), and like the dawn itself, shows us how the same phenomenon may sometimes be called white, sometimes golden.

The more one looks at it the more the drawing of a firm distinction between 'red' and 'gold', where language and perception are concerned, comes to look modern and dubious. In modern Greek, the yellow-golden yolk of an egg is the *kókkino*, which adjectivally, however, means 'red'. *Kókkino* commonly refers to the colour of the wine the French, and the Anglo-Saxons after them, call *rosé*. If the gauchos have horse sense (they have more than two hundred expressions for the colours of horse-hide), the French are wine-wise, and they further distinguish certain types of *rosé* with the subtly observant *peau d'oignon*, 'onion-skin'. French and English agree on calling the darker wines simply *rouge*, red. That seems self-evident, but dark red wine in Greek is *mavros*, 'black'.

★ Byelorussia: White Russia.

In German poetry, a conventional epithet for the light of the morning sun, *trinkbar Gold*, or 'drinkable gold', equates it with wines also known as *trinkbares Gold*. *Flüssiges Gold*, 'liquid gold', a German epithet for wine (*flüssiges Brot*, 'liquid bread', is beer), to the modern mind implicitly equates the delicately scented, yellow-golden German 'white' wine with the sun's aurora – much later, the old *flüssiges Gold* became a German adman's catch-phrase for wine.

In the Graves/Ali-Shah translation of the twelfth-century Persian poet Omar Khayyám we read:

> Dawn, Day's herald straddling the whole sky
> Offers the drowsy world a toast 'To Wine',
> The Sun spills early gold on city roofs
> Day's regal Host, replenishing his jug.

We talk of wine emblematically, as we talk of Bolsheviks and Tsarists, or the antagonists in the English Wars of the Roses, in terms of red and white. It is necessary to make the rather literal point that 'white' wine is more accurately a shade of yellow, or gold, just as 'white' coffee is, in reality, coffee-coloured. What colour of wine did Omar Khayyám have in mind? How much red was there in his 'early gold'? How much white? How much yellow? What colour *is* the dawn aurora?

Language apart, its precise coloration depends on a wide variety of meteorological and other factors. The colour-differences were perceivable long before the reasons for them were scientifically understood, but there didn't therefore necessarily exist terms corresponding to the various nuances of colour, by which they could readily be named. Language lags behind perception.

'Aurora' in English evolved from its literal semantic root to refer to spectacularly coloured and not necessarily golden atmospheric phenomena in general. The word is more used now of the electrical light-shows, unrelated either to dawn or sunset, found at the earth's magnetic poles, the aurora australis and aurora borealis, the latter more commonly called 'the northern lights' or, once upon a time, 'streamers' or 'merry dancers'.

Akkisukpok

The Eskimos, or Inuit, of the extreme northern latitudes lump all these phenomena – the northern lights, the dawn's aurora, the glow of sunset – together in the one word *akkisukpok*. In language, as already noted, there is a tendency to distinguish between the twilight of dawn and the twilight of dusk, and to give them a moral or didactic gloss. In one of the oldest proverbs in English, the red sky at night is a shepherd's delight; in the morning it is a warning.

There is evidence, however, of what appears to be a deeply buried tendency *not* to distinguish between the two red (or golden) skies, but, on the contrary, to identify them, as though sunrise and sunset were once perceived not as opposites but as in some sense interchangeable. And so, visually, they are. The sun rises and sets at opposite points of the compass; sunrise spells coming day, sunset coming night. But both at sunrise and sunset the wandering star, Venus, is present, and both sunrise and sunset, each considered independently of its location and the time of day at which it occurs, are the same more or less multicoloured, more or less subtly shaded, show of red, or yellow – gold or, more in keeping with our modern sense of the spectrum, orange.

Looked at in this light, Eden, or the Garden of the Hesperides, might equally be either in the east or in the west.

In the late eighteenth century, 'aurora' in English came to acquire the meaning of 'a rich orange colour, as of the sky at sunrise' (*Oxford Dictionary*). Or, one might add, as of the sunset sky, which tends to a still richer orange. If dawn is a blood-orange birth, sunset is a blood-orange death. Remove the didactic gloss and the two phenomena are essentially interchangeable.

Hesper and Phosphor – two stage-names for the same star: it is this sameness, this identity, that is conveyed by *akkisukpok*. It tells us, not that 'evening hateth morn', as Tennyson insisted, but on the contrary that it resembleth it.

★

The Sunshine Breakfast

Kellogg's advertises its cornflakes as 'the sunshine breakfast'. Have you a pack of Kellogg's cornflakes in the house? If so, glance at the packaging 'concept'. It is very rise-and-shine. On the front of the pack you will see a stylized *aléktor*, a cock, or 'rooster'. The bedless one, suitable company for someone who's just got up, is entirely to be expected on a packet of sunshine breakfast.

There is also an anecdote explaining its presence. Earlier this century, the founder of Kellogg's was entertaining a Welsh musician at his home in the American mid-West. She told him how much his name, Kellogg (which in fact means 'kill hog'), resembled the Welsh *ceiliog*, a cock. So the *ceiliog* became the Kellogg's cornflakes logo.

From familiarity with traditional imagery of the dawn, however, it is clear that not only cornflakes but all our traditional breakfast foods are rise-and-shine. At break of day we break our overnight fast with things suggestive of the sun – one might even call them representative of the sun. For example, take the eggs which the hens have newly laid overnight. The Greek *kókkino*, the red or golden yolk, has already been referred to. But Greek goes further. The dawn – *avgí* – is close to *avgò*, egg, and it implicitly catches subtleties of the dawn light. The dawn, the day's eye with its yellow yolk, its sunlike centre and white petals, is also the egg the day emerges from.

There may be good dietary reasons for eating toast and cornflakes (which are themselves toasted) at breakfast-time. But from another perspective it is striking that both of them may (like egg-yolk) broadly be described as 'golden' in colour, and so suggestive of the sun's aurora. So, for that matter, is Mr Kill Hog's crispy bacon, whose associations with the sun are looked at elsewhere (see page 102).

Seen from this admittedly rather odd angle, toast and cornflakes are foods only in the sense that the host in Holy Communion is food: vehicles, in edible form, for profound and powerful associations. One is swallowing those associations too. Night is a fast from light as well as food: the fast is broken by eating the sun.

At this point I may seem guilty of preciosity. Cornflakes and communion wafers? Egg and bacon, toast, and the sun? Come off it! But a German proverb corresponding to English 'early to bed and early to rise', *Morgenstunde hat Gold im Munde*, is literally 'The morning hour has gold in its mouth', and in a Spanish proverb oranges are gold in the morning, silver in the afternoon, and death in the evening.

Let's look at the ultimate 'sunshine breakfast' . . .

Orange

On the face of it, the Spanish proverb just quoted means only that the balanced acid-sweetness of orange juice kick-starts the sluggish overnight digestion, and tastes best in the morning. The tastiness erodes as the day progresses.

There is, however, another sense in which oranges are gold in the morning, death in the evening. The original home of oranges and all the citrus family was the east, the gold of the morning. Semantically, just as in Ralegh's view Greek myth transposed the story of Eden into the west, the home of citrus has been transposed westwards. To locate the real home more precisely, it is thought to have been the Malay archipelago. Drop the 'e' from 'orange', and one has one of the commonest words in the Malay lexicon and, in passing, part of the origin of Anthony Burgess's 1962 book title *A Clockwork Orange*.

That is otherwise a Cockney expression for something queer or out of the ordinary, but 'When I worked in Malaysia as a teacher', wrote Burgess, 'my pupils, when asked to write an essay on a day out in the jungle, often referred to their taking a bottle of "orang squash" with them. "Orang" . . . means a human being. The Cockney and the Malay fused in my mind to give an image of human beings, who are juicy and sweet like oranges, being forced into the condition of mechanical objects.'

'Orange', to a Malay, looks like a misprint for a person, and *A Clockwork Orange*, like the orange itself, ultimately originated in the Malay archipelago.

Let us move still further east. The perceived aristocrat among oranges, and the citrus family in general, is, as its name implies, the mandarin, or, as much of the botanical literature refers to it, *Citrus nobilis*. According to an American writer, Harold H. Hume (1915):*

Two explanations have been given for the name Mandarin . . . either because the fruit was regarded as the best of the citrus family, just as the Chinese Mandarin or grandee stood in social rank above his fellowmen, or because this orange was the fruit of the rich and therefore only within the reach of the nobility. The fact that the fruit is extensively cultivated in China and Japan and that it is there held in such high esteem leads to the belief that the first explanation [i.e. 'the best of the citrus family'] is the more correct one.

The mandarin orange is one of those natural phenomena that seems to partake of art, because of its superior taste and, especially, the conveniently easy, somewhat magical detachability of its skin and pith. Good taste, art, and high social status.

In the United States in the last century, mandarins were known as 'kid-glove oranges' (the skin fitted comfortably and came off like a glove; inside the rind, the white pith resembled kid leather). 'The term,' a Mr E. H. Hart told the American Pomological Society in 1889, 'originally a joke of our facetious countryman Colonel Dancy, of Orange Mills, was gravely accepted as a synonym by our first nomenclature committee, and like many another whimsical what-do-you-call-him, it stuck, where one more dignified would have glanced off.'

But where is the indignity? The mandarin's kid gloves are the mark of its aristocratic breeding, acknowledged by Colonel Dancy in his now-archaic name for the fruit.

The mandarin's ultimately Chinese origins underlie the name *china* used in Mexico, Venezuela, and the Spanish Antilles for all oranges. 'China' remains the horticultural name for the mandarin in several of its varieties, such as the China Celestial, or the Willow-Leaved China, the latter so called because its tree is very much like the willow in appearance, almost thornless and with small, deep green leaves, with the fruit borne singly at the tips of slender, willowy branches. What is the true identity of the 'willows' in willow-pattern china?

Geographical names pointing to real or supposed places of origin

* *Citrus Fruits and Their Culture*, New York, Orange Judd Co.

are often used for natural phenomena translated, or transplanted, into cultures where they are, at first, perceived as marvels or extreme oddities. For example, in one of the most pinpoint examples of such naming, the grapefruit in French is *pamplemousse*, from the Mauritian village (Pompelmousses) where the Dutch first found it (English 'grapefruit' is from the West Indies, after the fact that the fruit grows in grape-like clusters).

Now we swing dramatically westwards. The mandarin is also known as the tangerine, in reference to Tangiers, in whose region it was extensively cultivated after its transplantation to the Mediterranean. By a similar logic, modern Greek, Albanian, Italian, Kurdish, and colloquial Arabic all call the sweet, or dessert, orange a 'Portugal', that being the country where it was first extensively propagated in Europe. In English, too, the sweet orange was once distinguished from other varieties as the Portugal, and for similar reasons of geography, the blood-orange was known as the Malta orange. English greengrocers still refer to 'Seville' and 'Jaffa' oranges.

So identified did the name 'Portugal' become with oranges that it is sometimes said that the Portuguese orange-growing area of Cintra was the origin of 'citrus'. Even that word has been seductively transposed westwards. It was first used by Pliny the Elder, from the eastern 'citron' used to make lemonade, candied peel, and sherbet.

Malay for an orange is *limau manis*, sweet lemon or lime, roughly corresponding to the Latin botanical name *Citrus aurantium dulce*, or 'sweet [orangey-]golden citrus'. That *aurantium* is a coined word, derived by Yule and Burnell from the Arabic for an orange, *nāranj*, modified by *aurum* (gold) and the French *or*.

Aurantium is essentially a Latinate translation for 'orange', which derived from *nāranj* under the modifying influence of *or*, gold. Without that influence, the French *orange* (whence the English word) would logically, after the Arabic, have been *arange*.

That faint suggestion of gold is not found in words for 'orange' in other European languages. In Italian *nāranj* has become *arancia*. In Italian, French, and English, the *-n* ending of the indefinite article has eroded the *n-* beginning to *nāranj*, although Spanish has most purely preserved the original, as it so often does, in *naranja*. In Portuguese it is, strangely, *laranja*, a peculiarity attributed to the influence of the

Portuguese *definite* article, which is simply *a*. W. V. Quine, a philosopher who has interested himself in 'orange', writes that 'Portuguese is the one Romance language whose definite article lacks the *l*, and it is the one Romance language whose word for "orange" has undeservedly acquired it'.

More interesting than *laranja*, however, is 'orange', with its hint of gold. 'Maybe', Quine remarks, 'those oranges [i.e. those from which French derived its word] were yellow, or there were thoughts of the golden apples of the Hesperides. The Conca d'Oro or Golden Shell that ensconces Palermo is said likewise to be named for oranges, though lemons are not wanting.'

Quine's whimsical yellow oranges can be discounted, but he might have developed his passing hunch about the golden apples of the Hesperides. When European civilization first encountered the oranges of the east, it did indeed identify them with the golden apples ('in the west') of Greek myth. Furthermore, the evidence is that the classically educated dared to see in oranges an explanation for the myth's origin. In the first half of the nineteenth century, for example, Thomas Bulfinch wrote in his *Age of Fable* that the apples of the Hesperides 'are supposed by some to be the oranges of Spain, of which the Greeks had heard some obscure accounts'.

Imagine never having seen an orange. A journalist friend, in Romania just after the revolution of 1989, saw some children studying oranges in a shop window, and wondering what they were. All Europe once shared their perplexity and wonder. Fernand Braudel tells us, in *Capitalism and Material Life, 1400–1800*, that 'Oranges . . . were still a luxury in England in the Stuart period: they appeared around Christmas and were preciously guarded until April or May'.

Golden Delicious apples exist. Golden apples pure and simple – Yeats's 'golden apples of the sun' – don't. But just as those Romanian children might have called the strange objects in the greengrocer's window 'golden apples' so there was a suspicion, when oranges first arrived in Europe, that these were the golden apples of the mysterious myth.

We shall never know for certain what fruit, if any, inspired the myth of the Garden of the Hesperides, nor whether, when the Venus de Milo had arms, it was an apple or an orange that she held in her hand. But it is the suspicion of the reality that concerns us, or the probable reality, not the reality itself.

Braudel's mention of Christmas is interesting. The modern Anglican Church sometimes celebrates a Christmas carol service called 'Christingle', in which children file through the church carrying lighted candles ensconced in oranges. The service recalls the ceremony whereby, until quite recently, Charles II's mistress, the 'Orange Girl' Nell Gwynne, was commemorated over the Christmas period in London's Savoy Chapel: on one particular Sunday, on a chair near the chapel door, an orange was displayed on a cloth (Nell Gwynne, incidentally, probably sold tangerines: the city of Tangiers was part of the dowry when Charles married Princess Catherine of Braganza in 1662).

At a Christingle service I attended the vicar assured us the orange represented the world: I am sure that like other Christmas manifestations of redness (holly berries, the turkey's wattle, even Santa Claus's outfit which in its modern form, was a Coca-Cola marketing wheeze) it represents the sun in its winter absence. In D. H. Lawrence's story, 'Sun', the mother undresses her small son and rolls him 'an orange across the red tiles':

'Bring me the orange,' she said, amazed at her own deep indifference to his trepidation. 'Bring Mummy the orange.'

'He shall not grow up like his father,' she said to herself. 'Like a worm that the sun has never seen.'

Christingle, the Savoy Chapel ceremony, the jealous guarding of oranges until the spring, all testify to the sense of wonder this 'sunshine breakfast' once inspired. There are also Northern Ireland's emblematically named 'Orangemen', after the Dutch House of Orange. Originally, and serendipitously, they were known (after the dawn) as the 'Peep of Day boys'.

In Dutch, German, and Russian, the orange is known as the 'China [or Chinese] apple'. 'Apple' is one of only two native European names for fruit (the other is 'berry') and is there used generically. It might equally be 'fruit'. A berry is a small apple. An apple is a big berry. The Greenland Eskimos, who knew berries but not apples, told the early Scandinavian missionaries that Adam and Eve 'must have been very fond of fruit since they would rather die and suffer pain than forgo a few big berries'.

And so, while in most European languages we have 'earth-berry' for the English strawberry, we have the French *pomme de terre* ('earth apple') for the potato; also pomegranate ('apple with seeds'), and 'pineapple' (which was originally a pine-cone: the fruit is named from the resemblance to the cone). German also has *Pomeranze* (*pomme* + *nāranj*) for the orange. The Romans used 'apple' (*malum*) to refer to all sorts of fruits (such as the quince and the peach) and so did the Greeks: a melon, for example, is only a Greek apple (*mîlon*). It surprises me, therefore, that Robert Graves in *The Greek Myths* should have taken the apples of the Hesperides literally. At sunset, he wrote,

... the sky is green, yellow, and red, as if it were an apple-tree in full bearing; and the Sun, cut by the horizon like a crimson half-apple, meets his death dramatically in the western waves. When the Sun has gone, Hesperus appears. This star was sacred to the Love-goddess Aphrodite [Venus], and the apple was the gift by which her priestess decoyed the king, the Sun's representative, to his death with love-songs.

Death in the evening, in fact. And Graves gives us another, somewhat arcane resemblance: 'If an apple is cut in two transversely, her five-pointed star appears in the centre of each half.'

Personally, I have never seen a sky with green in it,* and the sunset has never reminded me either of apples or apple-trees. It has made me think of oranges, though, and if you cut an orange in two (as I've just done) the resemblance to a star, and to a setting sun, is even more marked.

But then, I have seen oranges. They were, we believe, unknown to the ancient Greeks. It is all very puzzling, and the puzzle is essentially the same one which confronted Sir Walter Ralegh, Tennyson, and Milton in Book IV of *Paradise Lost* (ll. 249–51):

> ... fruit burnisht with Golden Rinde
> Hung amiable, *Hesperian* Fables true
> If true, here only, and of delicious taste ...

* Nor have I seen the momentary 'green flash' with which, scientists say, the sunset ends.

Milton, like Ralegh some fifty years earlier, was asserting that the myth of the Hesperides, if there was truth in it at all, was set not 'in the west' but only in Eden, in the east.

It has been remarked that Milton in his description of Eden borrowed the style of the travel writers of his day, and here there is the suggestion that the golden apples of the Hesperides were themselves once a traveller's tale, impossibly distant in time. In his description of the fruit 'with Golden Rinde . . . and of delicious taste' he gently turned those mythic 'apples' into oranges. We might note, also, that the Puritan Milton was here touching upon a dreadful absurdity. If the (stolen) apples of the Hesperides were oranges, so, by implication and extension, was the biblical Apple of Knowledge stolen in the Garden of Eden.

Certainly oranges (or tangerines) were what Milton's contemporary, the Earl of Rochester, had in mind in the 'Hesperian Fruit' of his *Panegyric on Nelly* (Nell Gwynne):

> But first the Basket her fair arm did suit
> Laden with pippins and Hesperian Fruit.
> The first step rais'd, to the wond'ring Pit she sold,
> The lovely fruit, smiling with streaks of gold.

The *Oxford Dictionary* dates 'Hesperian' in this sense from 1622, and it seems to be over the seventeenth century (when orangeries were becoming well established in Europe) that the apples of the Hesperides turned, semantically, into citrus fruit. The myth is invoked in several botanical texts about oranges in this (pre-Linnaean) period, for example the Jesuit monk Baptiste Ferrari's *Hesperides sive de Malorum aureorum* (1646), which even has those 'golden apples' in its title. Today, the whole citrus family in modern Greek is the *esperididí*, and in English, following the classification of Linnaeus (who himself followed the earlier texts), the 'Hesperides' are the 'name for a class of plants, containing the orange family'.

Not only was the Golden Age 'transported out of Asia' then; so was the supposed original home of the golden oranges so closely associated with that age. The evidence is abundant that the 'Portugal', the fruit from the Malay archipelago, is seen in terms of an ancient Greek myth. In looking at the gold of the orange we see *akkisukpok* in action, east and west identified or transposed. In the orange and in words for it – even that tiny touch of gold in 'or-' – we find an extraordinary instance of the confusion sown by the planet Venus, the 'wandering star' with, confusingly, two names, Phosphor and Hesper.

IV PLOUGHING THE SEA

Words like Wheat

Let us imagine the field by the sea now not as green grazing for animals but as ploughed land with spears of new wheat poking out of the soil. These are the most precious of the spring's buds, and the work that has gone into them (and that has yet to go into them) opens up a new territory of metaphor.

The spears of wheat look like soldiers – in Devon one February, someone described such a field to me as 'the field where the soldiers are', an image recalling the myth of Cadmus and Jason, and the armed men, or Sparti, that sprang from the soil where the dragon's teeth were sown.

These spears of wheat are only too vulnerable; however. Much back-breaking work has gone into planting them, and much – even life itself – depends on their successful fruition and harvest. It is a precarious exercise. All of it may be destroyed so easily – in a flood, in a storm, by birds, by pigs rooting up the shoots or, later, trampling the standing corn.

The story of the wheat goes back to the late autumn/early winter of the previous year, when the field was put to the plough. Let us put ourselves at that period of the year, and put our seaside observer to work (the one who saw the resemblances between the animals, the waves, and the clouds). Let us turn him into a ploughman, bare-headed and open-breasted, 'but also all naked and full of dust' as Pliny described the Roman ploughman–dictator Cincinnatus (after whom the US city of Cincinnati is named). His plough is pulled perhaps by oxen muzzled with rush baskets, and hanging from its beam is the hatchet which Pliny recommended, for chopping roots in the plough's path.

This is the archetype who has been so long a figure on the landscape, so immemorially an image in the human mind, that few people actively notice him. The ploughman is simply there, as the trees and the earth are. His weather-beaten skin, like a baked potato's, blends into the earth he bends over, and he seems to blend also into time, merging indistinguishably with Cincinnatus, with Piers, the ploughman of William Langland's twelfth-century poem, or Triptolemus, who in Greek myth was the first ploughman; and further back still, until his image is lost in a time before records began and before the myths that have come down to us. The ploughman has always been there. He always will be.

Ploughing is so ancient an activity of the race, so fundamental to our existence on this earth, that it would really be more noteworthy if there *weren't* a ploughman there this morning, at this season of the year. Even in this remote spot a chance passer-by walks on without looking too closely at him. No more would he think to examine the earth beneath his feet or the grain of the floorboards he walks on in his house.

He is an object of contempt, a clodhopper, a clodpoll, churlish (from 'churl', peasant, the Anglo-Saxon *ceorl*), boorish (from German – *bauer* – or Dutch – *boer* – words for peasant). He is the archetypical *paysan* – the pejorativeness of the word 'peasant' has been a growth industry in English ever since the Norman invasion. In 1912, in his *Change in the Village*, George Bourne wrote that it had become synonymous with 'stupid, ignorant, objectionable', and today it is nothing more than a term of outright abuse ('You're all fucking peasants as far as I can see' – John Lennon).

Our ploughman is probably even a villain (from the Norman *villein*, the lowest of the feudal low). Call him what you like. He is only a clod, mud in human form, on the move; and yet, 'the common ploughman,' wrote Adam Smith in 1776, 'though generally regarded as the pattern of stupidity and ignorance, is seldom defective in his judgment and discretion'.

To which we might add that if nobody much notices the common ploughman, he himself is quite a noticer. In his dreaming at the plough, his intense noticing, associations sow words in his mind and he sows words upon time like the wheat he will sow in this earth . . .

If words are the 'daughters of earth' that Dr Johnson believed them to be, then the ploughman, a son of the soil, is one of their fathers. The metaphors arising in his mind as he works resemble tiny compact poems embodied in words which in time will be smooth and polished, as the wheat-grains he grows will be when they've been harvested and milled. These 'name-poems' are buried at or near the very heart of language, so deeply that surgery is required to see them. Stripped of their husks, ground down, milled, pulverized, transubstantiated into modern English, Russian, Spanish, French, the words will bear no more apparent relationship to their roots in the world and human knowledge and perception of the world than a fairy cake resembles a sack of wheat, or wheat a sack of flour, or a bag of flour a loaf of bread.

But just as the informed eye may discern the ploughman's shaping hand in a landscape cultivated over centuries, so we may find in the wordscape the evidence of his patient and quiet noticing. As an individual he may be one of the 'mute inglorious Miltons' of Gray's *Elegy*. But as an archetype his 'poems' are to be found in our dictionaries, in familiar 'everyday' words we tend to take for granted, as we tend to take him. *There* he isn't mute, but eloquent indeed.

Both Milton and Gray and their well-stocked minds were indebted to the ploughman's linguistic seed-corn; and so are our minds, so are we.

Ploughing the Sea

Metaphor, the verbal traffic 'carrying over' the borderlines, isn't all one-way. The imagination is a free-trade area without customs restrictions, and if the sea can be a blue moor, it can also be cultivated land, and so can the land be sea.

Again, as at the beginning of this book, a crisp, if anything crisper breeze is blowing, and whipping up waves on the sea. Having earlier seen animals in those waves, our observant peasant turned ploughman now sees other resemblances.

Ploughing is repetitive work, furrow after furrow, furlong (a furrow's length) after furlong. But now it's time to stop work for a while, 'elevenses' as the English say, the time, eleven a.m., called in Malay *tulih tenggala*, 'when the plough is idle'.

'Blessed word', H. Atwood Clark calls elevenses in his *Country Mixture*. Today the word suggests a cup of tea and a biscuit, but in the rural England where it originated, it meant a solid ploughman's (or reaper's) lunch of bread, cheese, pickled onions, and home-brewed beer brought to the field by the womenfolk.

In Spanish this is *las once*, the sacred 'elevenses' again. But in Latin America eleven o'clock has been transposed from morning to afternoon, perhaps through confused observation of the English habit of drinking tea both in the morning and afternoon. The Latin American Spanish *las once* is tea or an afternoon snack, and there is even a verb, *oncear*, 'to have an afternoon snack'. *Oncear* might translate as 'to elevense'.

Our ploughman knocks off for his elevenses, and eats it looking out to sea. Between bites, he half-consciously notices that the land he's already ploughed is choppy, as the sea is today. Out at sea is a ship, the one human 'civilizing' presence on the sea's wide impartial surface, as his plough is on this lonely stretch of land. He notices how the ship's bow-wave resembles the earth churned up to either side of his plough's blade, and how its wake resembles one of his furrows.

Clods of water, waves of earth. It pleases him to perceive these veined similarities between earth and sea, plough and ship. Perhaps he imagines himself to be the first man on earth who ever made the connection. And perhaps he is. More probably, however, he is only one in the long succession of millions of men who for millennia have ploughed fields like this all over the world, to whom the same idea has occurred.

Ships have long been said to plough the sea, and ploughs to sail the earth. In a variant of the same ancient metaphor the modern French *faucher le grand pré* for sailing is literally to reap, or to mow, the big field; the reapers too leave a wake behind them. The German lexicographer Max Müller, last century, related 'oar' to a root by which it means 'as it were the plough-share of the water'; he added that 'the English word *plough*, the Slavonic *ploug*, has been identified with the Sanskrit *plava* . . . and with the Greek *ploion*, ship'.

Whether or not these etymologies are sound, language certainly embodies the *perception* of a ship as a plough. It does so in the word 'dock', formerly 'dok'. That word now names the place where ships are tethered to the land, but it originally meant a ploughed furrow (thus the dock-leaves which, as a child, I used as a cure for nettle-stings). When a ship beaches itself, its keel ploughs a furrow – or 'dok' – in the wet shore. The idea is exactly expressed in Gavin Douglas's translation of the *Aeneid* (c. 1513), in which

> Inimicam findite rostris
> Hanc terram sulcumque sibi premat ipsa carina
>
> (Cleave this hostile land with your prows
> and let the keel press for itself a furrow)

is translated as 'Lat every barge do prent hyr self a dok', with 'dok' substituting for *sulcus*, furrow.

'He who serves a revolution ploughs the sea . . .' The reputed dying words of Simon Bolívar, South America's 'Liberator', strike a note of existential despair, Sisyphean futility, which we might think of as distinctively 'modern', as though Bolívar in the nineteenth century had anticipated Camus and Sartre in the twentieth.

There is nothing modern or original in Bolívar's image. The ploughman leaving his furrow behind him, the sailor leaving his wake, had been there long before him. The same idea of a lonely 'ploughing' presence in a large landscape underlies 'ship of the desert' for the camel, and 'prairie schooner' for the covered wagon of the American pioneers.

Pioneer and Clown

The English 'pioneer' is related to the French *pion*, a pawn in chess. In a chess game, the pawns are the first pieces to fan out over the new territory ahead, and they may even be considered (by a bad player) to be expendable foot-soldiers.

Pion, or pawn, in its turn is related to the Spanish *peón*, a pawn in chess, but also, and originally, an unskilled workman. 'Pawn' is the primary meaning of *peón* in metropolitan Spanish, but in the Spanish-speaking countries of Latin America it means 'labourer, farmhand', first, and 'pawn' only secondly. These *peones* were the pioneers of the Spanish colonies established following the discovery of the New World by Christopher Columbus, or Cristóbal Colón.

Extraordinarily, the surname of Columbus, the greatest pioneering colonial of them all, happens to be related to 'colony'. *Colon* in French is 'husbandman, farmer, colonist, settler'. It had an equivalent once in the English 'clown', originally 'countryman, or peasant', the sense in which Keats used the word in *Ode to a Nightingale*, in the phrase 'emperor and clown'. It is related, originally, to words in German and Dutch meaning 'clod', and is therefore another abusive word for the peasant. Pioneers, or clowns, were the first turners of clods in the new colonies, and even in the colonizing countries the first clods must once have been turned by pioneering clodhoppers.

Pigs . . .

Now let us turn to the woodland backing on to our coastal field. It is part of the great forests of early medieval Europe which according to Chateaubriand, in *La Génie du Christianisme*, were the inspiration for the architecture of the Gothic cathedrals. Huysmans makes a similar point in *La Cathédrale*, and Baudelaire in *Correspondances*:

> Grands bois, vous m'effrayez comme des cathédrales
> Vous hurlez comme l'orgue . . .
>
> (Great woods, you frighten me like cathedrals
> You roar like the organ . . .)

The woods covered much of the country. Deep in them were wild boar – which the moralizers of the day identified with the Devil – and perhaps, too, 'wodwos', the wild, hairy men of the woods. Also, woodpeckers, important birds of omen to the growers of wheat.

More to our immediate purpose, however, it is in the woodland that we find the pigs. They will reappear under many other guises, and it's convenient to try and introduce them properly here. I do so with some reluctance. Once pigs get their snouts into the picture they aren't easily dislodged. At the same time they can't be shut out. Their ubiquitousness in language and as a unit of perception is the index of their importance.

Ridiculous though it may sound, nothing in this book – not even the wayward planet Venus – has caused me as much trouble as the pigs. The reason, I am sure, is that nothing in the natural world caused our ancestors more trouble and anxiety, and these difficulties, which are, I think, partly psychological, are fully reflected in language, with its amazing range of pig-metaphors. Some attempt must be made to sketch out this tricky territory, and the background to it.

Historians aren't too sure where the pigs were for most of the year, and conjecture that there must have been fields specially set aside for them. If so, they must have covered a large area. Pigs were plentiful; the Domesday Book abounds in them. Their lives, and deaths, are better documented towards the end of the calendar year. In early autumn, after harvest, they were let on to the stubble fields, to grub up what fallen corn they could find. Then, when the fields were put to the plough, ready for sowing, the pigs were driven into the woods. There, in the care of swineherds, they were fattened up for slaughter – a fee-paying system known in post-Norman England as 'pannage'. The time of pig-fattening was known as *Porculatio*.

> No more the fields with scattered grain supply
> The restless wandering tenants of the STY;
> From oak to oak they run with eager haste,
> And wrangling share the first delicious taste
> Of fallen ACORNS: yet but thinly found
> Till the strong gale has shook them to the ground . . .
> Whole days and nights they tarry midst their store
> Nor quit the wood, till oaks can yield no more.
>
> (Robert Bloomfield, *The Farmer's Boy*, 1800)

The swineherd in Bloomfield's poem is called Giles, which was generic to swineherds just as Piers was to ploughmen. Both names have since moved heavily up-market, but from his association with the filthy pigs one imagines that 'Giles' must have started off as the lowest of the medieval low.

Just to complicate the picture, however (and it always is complicated when pigs are about), pigs were associated with prediction, especially of the weather, and according to Robert Graves (in *The Greek Myths*) '"swineherd", in early European myth, means soothsayer or magician. Thus Eumaeus ("searching well"), Odysseus's swineherd, was addressed as *dios* ("god-like").'

Some typical medieval Gileses are shown in illustrations from the fifteenth-century *Les Très Riches Heures du Duc du Berry*, in which, much as children today collect conkers, a man in a pink smock is helping things along by throwing a stick into the trees to make acorns fall, and in the Luttrell Psalter, where a swineherd high in an oak is shaking the tree.

These illustrations, and anthropomorphic medieval carvings of pigs playing musical instruments, pulling on pairs of trousers, dancing, and so on (these 'lovable' pigs are particularly numerous in England) testify to closeness, and even to a fondness for pigs. And why not? Peasant life was lived in close physical proximity to the pigs. 'Hog' (now figuratively 'a coarse, self-indulgent, gluttonous, or filthy person') was originally an affectionate pet-name for the pig. It is related to the Irish Gaelic *og*, which is 'young' or 'little'. In the early fifties, 'hog' in its affectionate sense could still be heard used of lambs and calves.

And yet, at the same time and at the other extreme, there is a sinister side to the relationship. It wouldn't be sinister, of course, without the (real or apparent) affectionate side. A book called *The Symbolic Pig*, published in 1961, is an anthology of this 'lovable' pig as we 'long pigs' (humans) have represented it in art and literature.

For the whole of the pig–long pig relationship (there is something inherently comic in the very word 'pig') there seems to be no single source. For the sinister side one has to look elsewhere.

True, the authors of *The Symbolic Pig* quote from William Mason's *A Handful of Essaies* (1621) the judgement of the usurer that 'like a swine he never doth good till his death; as an apprentice's box of earth [i.e. 'piggy bank'], apt he is to take all but restoreth none till he be broken'. This is an argument for killing usurers, as pigs are killed, and from there it is but a short step to the hideous *Judensau* – the 'Jew-pig' of medieval German church architecture, which shows a sow suckling Jews.

The image is entirely confined to Germany, and with the abusive label *Saujuden* (pig-Jews) which entered the German language in the sixteenth century, it inculcated the idea that the Jew 'never doth good till his death' and helped to pave the way for the Holocaust.

'The unclean animal', wrote Isiah Schachar (in his essay *The Judensau*, Warburg Institute, 1974), 'symbolizes unclean persons and sinners, and swine stand for Jews.' Schachar took this identification back through the medieval moralists to the encyclopedist Magnentius Hrabanus Maurus (780–856). In his *De rerum naturis** Hrabanus wrote that 'Pig [*porcus*] is as if "dirty" [*spurcus*]; indeed it gorges itself with filth, plunges into mire, smears itself with dirt. Horace: *And the sow is friend to mire* . . . Hence we also name "dirt" [*spurcitia*].' To the same root, English owes the word 'spurious'.

This pejorative use of pig and related words continues to thrive, but it coexists with another tradition, equally long and equally widespread, approvingly equating the pig with succulence and sustenance.

There is yet another perception of the pig, which, like the curl-shape seen in the sea, is purely geometric, as though the shape were somehow stamped in the human 'brain-mind'. I am sure, for example, that 'pigs' of citrus fruit (for example lime in the necks of bottles of Mexican beer) are so called from their hog's-back shape, as are the wild fungi which the Italians call *porcini* (not, as is sometimes claimed, because pigs like to root them up and eat them).

Perhaps I am jumping the gun: there will be more about this pig-shape. For the moment, it is enough to say that, in language, pigs are Protean, versatile, omnipresent. Attitudes towards them are so violently contradictory, they have so many names, and so many things have been named for them, that they deserve to be considered as one of the prime sources for metaphor in language.

Pigs get in everywhere. Of the Romany *baulo* – pig, swine – for example, Borrow writes, 'The proper meaning of this word is anything swollen, anything big or bulky. It is connected with the English bowle or bole, the trunk of a tree; also with bowl, boll, and belly; also with whale [French, *baleine*], the largest of fish, and wale, a

* Usually known as *De Universo*.

tumour; also with the Welsh *bol*, a belly, and *bala*, a place of springs and eruptions.'

I would tend to doubt whether *bala* belongs there, but still borrowing from Borrow: 'It is worthy of remark that the English word pig, besides denoting the same animal as *baulo*, is of the same original import, being clearly derived from the same root as big, that which is bulky, and the Turkish *buyuk*, great, huge, vast.' Other apparent members of Borrow's bulky word-family (to which we might also add 'bell', 'bull', 'ball', and 'bulky' itself) are the Spanish *bellota*, acorn, which additionally means the (acorn-like) bud of a carnation, *bellote*, a nail with a large, round head, and the Aquitaine French for chestnuts, *ballote*.

In the imaginary woodland we have entered pigs are snuffling in the grass for acorns. Among them perhaps is the earlier, large acorn called in Spanish a *breva*, which is also the early fruit of a fig-tree and, by extension from these, a type of cigar. (I once mistook the soggy stub of a *breva* cigar on a pavement for a squashed fig.)

The French *gland*, acorn, is also a tassel, which at its knotted end resembles an acorn or, for that matter, the tip of the penis, which in German is *Eichel*, or acorn. *Glans*, acorn in Latin, is a Latinate and clinical-sounding word in English for penis, (although words don't come much more clinical than 'penis' itself). Internationalize 'acorn', however, and the penis, or anyway its tip, comes by transference to seem to resemble a carnation-bud, the head of a nail, a fig, a cigar, a tassel ... a purse. Why a purse? Well, the root of modern Greek *valántion*, purse, is *válanos*, acorn. Think of one of those small leather pouch-purses with a draw-string. Pull the draw-string tight and it peels back on itself, the leather flap lapping over its main body like an acorn's cupule, a pulled-back foreskin ...

Beta has the value 'v' in modern Greek, 'b' in classical. Make the switch and we have *bálanos* to mean acorn, whose *bal* root takes us back to Borrow's family of 'bulky' words. *Bálanos* is the parent of *bellota* and its metaphorical offshoots and meanings in Spanish, and is also perhaps morphically related to the acorn of the Romans, *glans*.

In Old English, acorns, with other varieties of mast, were *picbrēd*, literally 'pig-bread' or 'swine-food'. Real bread requires real corn, not 'oak-corn', or 'acorn', eventually, via obsolete forms like *æcern*, and *æcirn*, from the Old English *æcer*, or the produce of uncultivated land' (whence 'acre'). The woodland we are in is *not bread* country. It is acornland.

Uncultivated land is without corn, but may be rich in oaks, or, for that matter, ash-trees: 'ash' is the name for the Anglo-Saxon rune represented by the digraph, *æ*. Is the *æ* of *æcer* indicative of the ash, which in Old English is *æsc*, and which like the oak has mast, or meat, fit only for pigs? And the *cer* – could it owe something to that body of words where Latin blends so naturally with Anglo-Saxon, 'cereal', 'corn', 'kern', 'kernel'?

It's tempting to try and jerry-build, first, a bridge between 'acre' and 'ash' and then (perhaps via the German *Eiche*, oak) between *æcer*, ash, and 'oak'. The oak, in Latin, is *quercus* (whence, it is thought, both *Eiche* and 'oak'). But Virgil has *aesculus* for 'the winter or Italian oak', Horace has *aesculetum*, an oak-forest, and Varro has *aesculi*, oaks. Was the oak, then, once semantically related to the ash? Are they both, as it were, seen through the same linguistic lens? That 'ache' sound of *æcer* – even allowing for *quercus*, is it eventually the small acorn that produced the mighty 'oak'? Then 'oak' (*aesculus*) might 'translate' as something like '[tree] where no cultivated land [or corn] is'.

But this is a reverie. The *Oxford Dictionary* absolutely forbids it: 'ultimate connections unknown', 'there is no common Indo-European word for this tree'.

Professor Max Müller seemed to think there was, though. 'English *tree* is Gothic *triu*; in Sanskrit *dru*, wood and tree (*dâru*, a log). In Greek *drŷs* is tree but especially *the* tree, namely the oak. In Irish *darach* and in Welsh *derw* the meaning of oak is said to preponderate, though originally they meant tree in general.'

Robert Graves thought so too. In *The White Goddess* he interrelated words for tree and oak and put them, especially the Welsh or Celtic *derw*, behind 'Druid' and the word 'door' (in English 'sporting the oak' is a phrase for 'keeping the door shut').

Graves has been ridiculed for his oak–door etymology. Perhaps Varro in the first century BC (who was himself ridiculed by Quintilian in the first century AD) may be allowed to come to his defence. 'The man who has made many apt pronouncements on the origins of words', he wrote, 'one should regard with favour. If I have no knowledge of the roots of a tree, still I am not prevented from saying that a pear is from a branch, the branch is from a tree, and the tree from roots which I do not see.'

Neither is Graves prevented from suggesting that 'door' is from old words for 'oak'. We still cannot see clear to the roots of 'oak', or 'ash'. We cannot see to the deepest roots of words in general.

. . . and Ploughs

We are at the point where etymology merges into myth, where words set one dreaming and tease with plausible impossibilities or hypotheses that are perhaps unprovable. Here etymologies are lost, and recognizable words dissolve and turn into mere imagined sounds, puffs of breath upon a mirror as likely to reflect one's own face as the truth.

Where exactness is no longer possible, the search must either be given up, or continued, if at all, with imaginative guesswork and restrained speculation. We cannot say, positively and precisely, that words for 'ship' distantly derive from words for 'plough', only that on the available evidence it seems both etymologically and imaginatively likely.

Nor can we positively state that 'plough' is derived distantly but directly from 'pig', but we can point to strong evidence of an ancient family relationship between sets of 'plough'-words and sets of 'pig'-words. Pig is related to plough, as farrow is to furrow, and thus to furlong, an eighth of an English mile. The Old German *furicha*, furrow, is connected with *farah*, boar. Plutarch derived ancient Greek words for plough from the word for boar. In Latin, *porca*, a ridge between two furrows, was from *porcus*, pig, and *Imporcitor* was a god who presided over the making of furrows.

These examples tempt the thought that 'pig'-words may underlie the idea of a ploughed field lying 'fallow'. Perhaps they do, but the etymological evidence, strong in the above examples, is here lacking, and where pigs are already so plentiful it would be folly to look for them where there may be none.

'A plough', according to Müller, 'is said to be called a pig's nose.' Why? The mind boggles a bit at this. Did pigs once pull ploughs? That, after all, seems to be why ridges between furrows can be called in Spanish 'horses' or 'camels'. But after a little reflection the connection makes sense. Boars have tusks at their noses; the plough's blade, the coulter, is a kind of tusk — in Latin it was called the *dens*, the tooth. A plough turns up the earth and obliterates traces of greenery as a pig does, and digs like a pig's nose among the acorns, hunting for buried truffles. A similar idea exists in Spanish, where *hoz* is a sickle, and *hozar*, used specifically of pigs, is 'to root in, to root among'.

The ninth-century encyclopedist Hrabanus gave an etymology for 'sow' relying on the *Etymologiae* of Isidore of Seville: 'The sow [*sus*] is so named because it turns up [*subigat*] pastures, that is, it searches for food by turning up the soil.' While the plough is sow-like, then, the sow's behaviour is plough-like. This behaviour has a strong bearing on the way pigs are viewed. When the field has been ploughed, and ploughed across, it is harrowed using a toothed length of wood drawn by oxen and called in Latin *irpices*, from *hirpus*, wolf, after the harrow's 'teeth'. Then it is sowing-time, and if ploughing and pigs have something in common, sowing and sows don't mix at all.

The time of pig-sticking varied a little from place to place (but the calendar altered, too, from time to time). In Parma, for example, famous for its cured ham, it was September. But in general in Europe it is in November that the man–pig relationship reaches its climax. This is the time of year when Mr Kellogg comes into his own ('kill-hog' now has the appearance of meaning something like 'kill-pet', even 'kill-darling').

Is it an accident that the time of pig-sticking should coincide so neatly with the time of sowing? In Germany, November is *Slaghtmonat*, 'slaughter-month', and in Spain pig-sticking is in the halcyon November days of Martinmas, *San Martín*, which in the Spanish farmer's mind was once equivalent to *matanza*, the season for slaughtering pigs.

A cada puerco le llega su San Martín, they say in Spain, 'for every pig there's a Martinmas', 'everything comes to an end'. We might translate it 'pride comes before a fall': over *Porculatio*, after all, the pigs have been in clover, they've never had it so good. And in English

November was 'Gore-moone', which is to do with mud but with blood as well, the blood of the pigs.

The field has become taboo territory; property. The husbandman fears that pigs will wander from the woodland and destroy all his labour by digging up the seeds he's planted. However he has felt about the pigs for the rest of the year, he fears and hates them now, and is pleased that in this same month many of them will be killed. That is all they have been fattened for – the kill. This is how the close, even intimate man–pig relationship must end – in blood, one might even say in the murder of the pig. No wonder that language so abundantly reflects neurosis over the pig. In the lives and deaths of the pigs human beings may see their own lives and deaths, parodically, bloodily mirrored. The cookery writer Jane Grigson once wrote that all the world's cuisines could be traced back to the pig. 'Kill the pig!', the cry of the children in Golding's *Lord of the Flies*, may be the cry at the very heart of civilization.

If this seems excessive, sentimental, anthropomorphic, consider the words of the vegetarian Pythagoras, as Ovid quotes him in the *Metamorphoses*. Pythagoras perceived a direct link between sowing and *Slaghtmonat*. 'The swine', he said, or is supposed to have said, 'is believed to have deserved death as the first victim, because it grubbed up the seeds with its turned-up snout, and cut short the hopes of the year.'

Pythagoras saw the slaughter of pigs, then, not primarily as a utilitarian matter of food for the winter, but as a sacrificial rite. Sooner than risk the parable of the Gadarene swine being enacted in one's own wheat-field, it was better to kill the pigs when the seed was sown, before they could nip 'the hopes of the year' in the bud. It was then, in November, that they most 'deserved death'.

And yet, just as pigs were associated in a positive way with ploughing, as we have seen, so they were with sowing. Graves writes of 'the goddess Merpessa, Phorcis, Choere, or Cerdo, who made the corn sprout'. Even so, however, the sow goddess's power of fertility resided in the pig's identity as sacrificial victim. Graves adds that 'though, by Classical times, swineherds had long ceased to exercise their prophetic art, swine were still sacrified to Demeter and Persephone by being thrown down natural chasms'. And 'If I am right,' wrote Frazer in *The Golden Bough*, 'the very freedom with which the boar ranged at will through the corn led people to identify him with the corn-spirit, to whom he was afterwards opposed as an enemy.'

It is all very obscure, but this mythological background is useful in considering the wealth of pig-metaphors in language.

Slugs and Snails

To know when it is time to sow look up to the heavens or down to the earth at your feet. Pliny didn't believe the common ploughman capable of telling when the rain-stars, the Pleiades, have sunk over the horizon. 'This husbandman of ours, who cannot skill at all to look up and to learn the order and position of the heavens, must spy this sign of winter amongst his briers and brambles: he must find (I say) the time of seednes as he looketh downe upon the ground, namely, when he sees the leaves fallen and lying under his feet' (Pliny the Elder, translated by Philemon Holland).

Xenophon considered that a sign from God was needed before sowing, and Cicero, expanding on Xenophon, 'taketh the raines in November to be that signe'. This is, usually, early November, 'Goremoone', mud month, when rain has softened the earth sufficiently for sowing sticks. The field is now a mire called in Latin *limus*, 'slimy mud', a word cognate with the Greek *limón* or *livádi*, pasture. It is in this 'slimy mud', says Varro, that slugs live. A slug, *limax*, is slime, *limus*, on the move. The slug has something in common with our cloddish common ploughman, and his snail's-pace progress over the land. Classical Greek, too, has *limax* for slug, and in French it has become *limaçon* – which is, however, a snail.

A snail is a slug in a helical shell, and in French the helix is responsible for *escalier en limaçon*, 'snail stairs', for a spiral staircase (Russian has the same metaphor). A slug, meanwhile, is a 'naked snail' – the modern Greek *gimnosáliangas*, where the *sali-* root of *salingári*, a snail, relates it to saliva, *sálio*.

This Greek conception of the snail is based on very close observation. The Spanish verb *azogar* means to coat with quicksilver, as in making a mirror, and, in its reflexive form, it means to salivate. Spanish mirror-making has something distantly in common with French window-shopping, which is *lécher les vitrines*, 'to lick the windows'. Window-shopping is lecherous: a lecher salivates and licks his lips. But a licked window, in Spanish, would become a mirror.

Saliva doesn't reflect light, as the snail's shiny trail does once it has dried out. But before it dries, when it is still fresh, it is bubbly, like spit. It is this fresh trail that the Greek word so observantly catches, while another Greek word for saliva, *siagos*, is juice from the jaw, *siagon*.

In English once, 'snail' also meant slug, and both creatures are taken to typify laziness, slowness, sluggishness. One expects aspects of the natural world to form the basis for metaphors for human qualities, not vice versa, but unusually, it is 'slug' that is derived, probably from Scandinavian verbs, from the idea of 'sluggishness', not 'sluggishness' from 'slug'.

As with the shark (see the Lexicon, **Great White Shark**) it is rare in the naming of animals for metaphors to be based in the human world.

Woodpecker

The story of the woodpecker in words is bound up both with the story of the wheat after it has been sown and with the great oaks of the forest, in terms of which, as we have already seen (pages 89–90) there appears to be a tendency to see all trees.

'Woodpecker' has the ring of a utilitarian bird-word, like the Greek *ziophagus*, wood-eater. And indeed, the woodpecker is the utilitarian, the magical tool-user among birds. Its name is more interesting and mysterious than it originally appears. Another name for it, one of several in Greek, *dryokoláptis*, whose root is from *drýs*, oak, takes us deeper into the dark and mysterious world of the forest, and into the forest of names for the woodpecker.

It is time to look at a myth in more detail. In Book 14 of Ovid's *Metamorphoses* the sorceress Circe transforms Picus into a woodpecker:

He fled; wondering that he sped more swiftly than usual he beheld wings on his body; and indignant that he was added suddenly as a strange bird to the Latian woods, he struck the wild oaks with his hard beak, and, in his anger, inflicted wounds on the long branches. His wings took the purple colour of his robe. The piece of gold that had formed a buckle, and had fastened his garment, became feathers, and his neck was encompassed with the colour of yellow gold; and nothing now remained to Picus of his former self, beyond the name.

That name, Picus, has been fertile in language. In English it gives us 'pick' (pickaxe), and its cognate 'peck', and in French, *pic*, whose primary meaning is pickaxe but which also names the woodpecker.

At its simplest, then, the woodpecker is conceived of as a sort of navvy descended from a mythical king, Picus. But the woodpecker is also a craftsman. In Spanish it is *carpintero pájaro*, the carpenter bird, while the ivory-billed woodpecker is *carpintero real* (royal carpenter). Another Greek word for the woodpecker is *pelekâs*, the joiner, or carpenter, bird, which is cognate with Greek words for 'axe' and the verb 'to hew' and related also to *pelekoúdi*, a wood-chip, or wood-shaving. St Jerome referred to the probability of a perceived similarity between the bird's bill and an axe, and suggested *pelekâs*, woodpecker, in the background of 'pelican' – another bird with a long, prominent beak.

A similar idea of the woodpecker as a carpenter exists among the Ainu people of Japan. In *The Ainu and Their Folklore* the Reverend J. Batchelor wrote that: 'The woodpecker appears to be in a peculiar way the boatmakers' bird. The name *Chipta Chiri* [an excellent name for a 'chippie', or carpenter], by which he is known, means "the bird which digs out boats" ... Some Ainu say he was sent by God to teach them how to make boats.'

Beyond its status as a skilled worker, names for the woodpecker reflect its status as a pagan god. The bird was identified, like the gods Zeus and Thor, with thunder, lightning, and rain.

The great black, or European, woodpecker, *Picus martius*, has been said to resemble a dark storm cloud, with the vivid red flash of its crest (which all the woodpeckers have) like a flash of lightning. We are to imagine the flash of this bird's flight through the forest gloom, the hole driven to the tree's heart (a power also possessed by lightning), and, as well as the usual tapping of trees in search of insects, or to build a nest, the distinctive 'drumming' sound, like a roll of thunder, by which the bird attracts a mate in spring.

Thor, with his red hair and beard, and his rock-shattering hammer, was the tool-user of the gods. The woodpecker, likewise, is the tool-user among birds.

Roman literature abounds in references to the woodpecker as a bird of augury, and as a rain-god. Woodpeckers were called *pluviae aves*, or rainbirds. In France one of its nicknames is *Plieu Plieu* (*pluie*, or rain) and in Shropshire 'Weet Weet' (or wet), imitating its cry and naming the hoped-for result. It was believed that the woodpecker always called loudest before rain, and from there it was but a short step to believing that the rain falls *because* of the woodpecker's intervention.

In Germany it is called *Giessvogel*, and in Austria *Gissvogel*, both of which mean 'Torrential Rain Bird'; in the Tyrol it is *Regenvogel*, or Rain Fowl; in Sweden *Regnkrake*, or Rain Crow; and in England 'Rainpic' (also 'Rainbird' for the green woodpecker). And another name for the bird in France was *avocat de meunier*, or miller's adviser, because it supposedly told the miller when there would be rain and so water to drive his water-wheel.

Through the association with water, the woodpecker came to be associated with fertility. As late as the seventeenth century, a god called 'Pikker', a variant of Thor apparently related to 'Picus', was worshipped in Estonia. There was a prayer to him: 'Beloved Pikker ... we would pray thee for our ploughing and our sowing, that our straw be copper red and our grain be golden yellow ... unto us ploughers and sowers give a fruitful season and a sweet rain. Holy Pikker, guard our seed field, that it bear good straw below, good ears above, and good grain within.'

A still more obscure tradition appears to associate the woodpecker with the god Mars, to whom, in classical times, the woodpecker was sacred. In France it has been known variously as *grande Marte* and, like that other long-beaked bird, the kingfisher, as 'St Martin's bird'. There may be some confusion here arising from Mars, martial, *marteau* (hammer). The Latin *Mars, Martis* may have been confused with, and corrupted into, the names of the Christian saints, Martin and Martha.

Then there is the woodpecker's call, which is often compared to mocking, manic laughter. This gives us the imitative dialect words for the woodpecker, 'yaffle' and 'yike' and probably 'yokel' as well: 'yokel' to mean country bumpkin is thought to derive from this 'yokel' which names the yellowhammer as well as the woodpecker.

Another local name for the woodpecker, 'galley bird', also derives from its 'laugh': it is from the Saxon *gall*, which means merry. Inevitably, we wonder whether there was not also some association with 'gall' in the sense of 'oak-apple'.

Another Greek myth, from Crete, has the goddess Rhea placing her son Zeus in a mountain cave, to protect him from his father, Chronos, who had an unfortunate habit of devouring his children. The bees brought the small boy-god honey to eat. To the cave came a man called Keleos, in an attempt to steal the honey. Zeus turned him into a woodpecker. The association is with the black European woodpecker and its fondness for bees' and wasps' nests, which it digs out of hollow trees in order to eat their grubs. The bird appears to disregard the stings of the bees, and from this arose the not very environmentally friendly superstition that those who carry a woodpecker's beak about with them will not get stung.

Keleos is among the classical Greek names for the woodpecker, and in modern Greek *kellion* is cell, or honeycomb. The story of Keleos and Zeus is behind the reference in *The Birds* by Aristophanes: 'Zeus will not lightly restore the sceptre to the oak-tapping woodpecker.' A similar tradition underlies the German woodpecker-name, *Bienenwolf*, or bee-eater, related to the Saxon *Beowolf* or *Beewolf*, a human incarnation of the woodpecker-god.

The White

The yokel has called, and in the field by the sea our yokelish peasant has heard him call. The rains have fallen. The wheat-seed has sprouted, and the sun has shone. Now it is summer, and the wheat is starting to grow tall. In the field the quail is calling 'Wet my lips! Wet my lips!' or *Paie tes dettes*, as the French hear it – pay your debts.

Wheat. But what is it, this *wheat*? Müller has an eloquent answer:

Many names might have been given to *wheat*. It might have been called eared, nutritious, graceful, waving, golden, the child of the earth &c. But it was called simply the *white*, the white colour of its grain seeming to distinguish it best from those plants with which it otherwise had the greatest similarity.* For this is one of the secrets of . . . name-poetry, that each name should express, not the most important or specific quality, but that which strikes our fancy . . .

I have a hypothesis – it is no more – that English words like 'pale', 'pallor', 'pallid', and the Spanish family of words with a *palo-* root, mentioned earlier (see page 11) may be connected with the Latin *palea*, chaff, later the French *paille*, straw. Müller's white wheat also strikes me as a hypothesis. Is whiteness really wheat's most striking quality? Isn't wheat rather, as in the prayer to Pikker, 'copper red' and 'golden yellow'?

Wheat may certainly, however, be said to be white in the figurative sense of 'good', or, as we still say of some foods, 'good for you', and it may be, not that wheat is so named because it is white, but rather that 'white' arose from 'wheat', or alternatively, and more probably, that 'wheat' and 'white' both belong among words denoting goodness, both in the sense of 'good for you' and, metaphorically, in the sense of 'morally good'.†

As we shall see, there is certainly reason to believe that bread, and so perhaps wheat, or 'white', the ultimate source of the bread, has long been perceived in terms of the universal black/white binomial.

---

* German *weiss*, white, *Weizen*, wheat. A wheaten pale ale is a *Weisse*, and in Berlin once I drank a wheat-beer called *Weissherbst*, 'white [or wheat] autumn'. It was red in colour.

† In support of this idea, Greek has *kálos* to mean 'corn'. The adjective *kalós* is 'good, wholesome'.

Little Nails

There is another way of perceiving wheat, and a good way of reaching and appreciating that perception is to take a detour via words for a very different plant – the spice known as the clove.

The English 'clove' comes from the Old French *clou de girofle* meaning 'nail of the clove-tree', alluding to the resemblance of the dried flower-bud of the tree *Caryophyllus aromaticus* to a nail. *Caryophylla* or *garofala*, names by which the clove-tree was known to the ancients, gave *girofle*. The Old English name was 'clove gillofloure' (from *girofle*). The comparison of a clove to a nail exists in many languages. In Persian cloves are *mekhak*, or 'little nails'. In Chinese a clove is *ting-hiang*, or 'nail-spice', and in Spanish it is *clavo de especia* (nail of spice), while in German it is *Gewürtz-nagel*, or 'spice-nail'; German also has *Nelken* or *Nägelchen*, or 'little nails'. In Russian a clove is *gvozdíka*, 'little nails'.

Swahili, in whose catchment area the clove grows, has five words for it, ranging from *karafuu* (close to *caryophylla*, *garofala*, etc.), which are cloves in general, through *misumari*, which means 'nails' (Swahili was originally a pidgin, and the idea behind *misumari* was perhaps a foreign import) to fully grown cloves, *mavi ya panya*, 'rat's dung' (which cloves can also be said to resemble).

English refers indiscriminately both to 'clove' (the spice) and to a 'clove of garlic'. The English word incidentally, and happily, suggests the 'cloven' nature of a head of garlic, but the Spanish and French, with greater descriptive precision, refer to garlic in terms of 'teeth' (*diente de ajo*, *dent d'ail*).

A 'clove' of garlic in both shape and colour does indeed resemble a tooth rather than a nail. Teeth are sharp, however, as nails are; and so, often, are spices, both to taste and, as growing plants, to the touch.

Spike

The spikily named spice, spikenard, has rhizomes 'covered in hair or spikes resembling the ears of corn', while the aloe has 'tall serrated leaves that resemble "the sheaths of knives"' (Patricia Crone, *Meccan Trade and the Rise of Islam*).

The *Oxford Dictionary* comments that 'the ultimate source of the word "sabre" is probably to be sought in some Oriental language'. Could it have been the classical Arabic *sabir* (a now-redundant spelling of 'sabre'), *sabr*, or *sábara* for the aloe, with its curved knifelike leaves?

The 'spike' of 'spikenard' derives from the Latin *spica*, an ear of corn. From the same source come the Spanish *espiga*, the French *épi*, and the English 'spike' in its specialized sense of an ear of corn or, by extension, the sharp part of any plant.

The Greeks, though, have *karphi* to mean both the sharp part of a plant *and* a nail. The Spanish *espiga* can likewise mean 'spigot, tenon, dowel, peg'. Spanish and Greek clearly have no problem in extrapolating, ultimately from the notion of an ear of corn (*spica*), the notion of a nail, and equating them in the one word. Neither does German, in which *Spiek* or *Spieke* are either spikenard or lavender (which is also spiky), and *Spieker* is a large nail, or spike. The suggestion of sharpness seems to go further still, in *espion*, the sharp-eyed spy, and if 'sabre' is from *sabir* might not the French sword, *épée*, be related to *épi*, the French for *spica*?

The *Oxford Dictionary*, in defining the English 'spike' in its sense of nail (Middle English *spyk*), refers to the Swedish and Norwegian *spīk* and a number of its variants as meaning only 'nail', while adding, 'It is possible that these may in some way be derived from L. *spica*.'

Aren't there grounds for being a little less tentative and suggesting that 'spike' (nail) arose from 'spike' (ear of corn, sharp part of plant), whether via Scandinavia or by another, unknown route? The Greek *karphi* (see above) would appear to be closely related to *karuophíllis*, clove. If so, then *karuophíllis* perhaps translates conceptually as something like 'sharp-growing-things-foliage'. The modern Greek *karuophíllis* can mean both a clove and a flintlock. Greek seems to have made the same metaphorical connection as Japanese, in which *chōji* are cloves, and *chōji-gashira* means 'the charred soot, resembling a clove, which forms on the wick of a lamp' (Hepburn). Flintlocks, too, involve soot and charred, clove-like wicks with black, flattened tops.

The richness of metaphor surrounding 'clove' leaves me a little puzzled by the *Oxford Dictionary*'s confident attribution of 'spice' via the French *épice* and *espèce* to the Latin *species*. The dictionary gives an intermediate English term to back up this etymology: *spece*, from species, with usages to mean 'spice' dating from 1300.

Littré (1895) gives *species* as the origin of *épice*, spice, but another strong candidate must surely be *épi* (*espis* in Old French), the cluster of grains of wheat, corn, etc., at the top of the stalk. *Épi/espis* is at least as close to *épice*, and as respectable a forebear of it, as *espèce/species*. Given the close connections between the two words, isn't it likely that 'species' once, or originally, referred to different varieties of 'spices'?

There is, as I hope I have shown, a body of linguistic evidence to back up this interpretation. If it is correct, then 'spice' and 'spike' derive ultimately from the same root, and both belong to a close family of words denoting sharpness. In saying 'spice' (spike), then, one would essentially be saying the same thing as 'clove' (nail).

Cicada

The wheat ripens in the sun of high summer, when 'the cicada sings', *canta la chicharra* as they say for baking heat in Spanish.

If spring, as we have seen, is associated with the dawn, then summer is associated with noon, when the sun, in the Malay word for noon, is *rambang*, bang in the middle of the sky. The Italian *mezzogiorno*, midday, with a capital 'M' means Sicily and the south, Provence in the south of France is *le Midi*, and the Greek *mesibría*, noon, is also the south. Even in Estonia, not notable for its sunshine, *lõuna* is both noon and the south. This is the tourist season, when the sun has moved house in the sky, and we no longer look for it in the east or in the west but in the south, Goethe's 'land where the lemon-tree blooms'. The supposed site of the Golden Age has shifted across the compass from east to south, and while it lasts we want to be golden too, somewhere where the sun is hot enough for near nakedness and a suntan.

> J'aime le souvenir de ces époques nues
> Dont le soleil se plaît à dorer les statues
>
> (I love the memory of those naked epochs
> When the sun amused itself with gilding statues.)

Baudelaire's Golden Age idealism (in his poem 'J'aime le souvenir de ces époques nues') lives on in idiomatic French for acquiring a suntan, *bronzer*, whose original meaning was only to bronze, or to gild, a statue.

If the French language tells us that French people sunbathing on a beach secretly see themselves as godlike Greek statues bathing in liquid gold, the English metaphor 'suntan' is equally telling. The literal image from 'tan' is of someone steeping his skin (his hide) in a tanner's vat, or even staining himself with the tannin of used tea-bags. We might also reasonably picture a cabinet-maker using walnut stain on a piece of wood – nut, the Latin *nux*, 'is so called', Varro tells us, 'because its juice makes a person's skin black, just as "night" [*nox*] makes the air black'.

But back to that Spanish cicada. Its chirping is the very sound of summer, and it has produced some ingenious metaphors for phenomena associated with heat and the summer sun. We aren't surprised that its insistent chirping has given *chicharra* the senses of chatterbox and electric bell, but the perceived affinity between its chirping and the spitting of fat in a roasting hot oven is a subtler and more daring metaphorical leap.

Figuratively, a *chicharrero* (which loosely translates as somewhere jam-packed with cicadas) is an oven or any place of stifling heat, while *chicharrón* (big cicada) is pork crackling, crispy bacon or any burnt meat, someone who's red-faced (a 'red mullet', or *barboúni* in Greek) and someone who's overdosed on the summer sun, and is sunburnt.

By a similar analogy, a tree in Mexico whose bark peels off to reveal the bright red wood beneath is known as 'the tourist tree', while I have heard the Caribbean Creole for a white man, *bakra* (see the Lexicon, **White man**), anecdotally glossed by *compositio* as 'back raw' (i.e. from sunburn).

Spray

One summer day in the field by the sea there's a storm. Waves pound against the shore to make a fine spray of water-droplets floating in the air and lightly falling. If the coast is rocky and the sea really rough the effect of the spray may be of high columns of smoke – the metaphorical impetus behind the Norwegian *brenning*, 'the burning', for surf.

When I spray-paint my car, or use a nasal spray, or spray eau-de-cologne from an atomizer, I am producing a miniature version of this majestic spray of the sea. But the spray of flowers I give to my dinner-party hostess? The cut-price 'sprays' of carnations I saw advertised this morning in the supermarket? What have these flowery sprays to do with the watery one? Or is there no connection at all?

The *Oxford Dictionary*, a lot of help elsewhere, here isn't. It has nothing to say on the subject. Nor can it supply the ultimate origin and the metaphorical basis, if any, of 'spray' in either sense. The etymologies are simply too sketchy. For 'spray' in its sense of an informal bouquet, for example, the dictionary tells us 'the ultimate origin of Old English *spræg* and synonym *spræc* is unknown'. And for 'spray' in its commoner sense of fine water-droplets it has 'immediate source unknown; formally corresponding to Middle Dutch verb *spra[e]yen*'.

'Spray' is one of those highly successful words that have shed their origins and been rolled and milled by usage into functional cylinders. Where are the expressive if unwieldy missing arms of the representational statue we take it once to have been? Etymological practice allows for supposed missing cognates and antecedents of words whose fully documented histories we lack, and if we turn to German we find *Spreuregen*, drizzle.

That's easy enough – 'spray rain', a simple and literal description of drizzle. Except that it isn't literal, because the meaning of *Spreu* on its own isn't 'spray' as we commonly understand it but chaff, the husks which float in the air and lightly fall, like drizzle, or sea-spray, when wheat is threshed. The Japanese language possesses the same idea. *Konuka-ame*, 'rice-bran-rain', exactly repeats the same peasant observation. In similar vein, the small rocky island of Eldey, off the coast of Iceland, was known to fishermen as *Meelsaecken*, or 'the flour bag', after the high columns of fine spray, the *brenning*, produced when the sea pounded upon it.

Spreuregen, then, is a figurative, not literal term for drizzle, in which the modern sense 'spray' seems to be indebted to the sense 'chaff'. And it is possible that other words we connect today only with water and liquids, the English 'sprinkle', or the German *sprengen*, originated out of this metaphor. But what are we to understand by chaff, or rather by *Spreu*? My limited definition of 'chaff' in the sense in which it's commonly understood doesn't encompass 'spray' in its sense of a bunch of flowers. The cloud of fine wheat-husks resembles drizzle, but not a bunch of flowers.

Now let us turn from the sea to face the field where wheat is growing. What do you see, in your mind's eye? This isn't a modern wheat-field tidily ranked with grain, soaked in fertilizers and pre- and post-emergent herbicides, where, in harvest-time, combine-harvesters like assembly lines on the hoof will turn out standardized bales. This field isn't measured in acres. As we have seen, the word 'acreage' when used of cultivated land is an etymological absurdity. This isn't *æcer*-country like the dark woodland. It is a white wheat-field.

Not *only* wheat is growing here, however. Look more closely. Among the wheat are weeds and other plants, such as poppies. They are as inedible as the weeds, but certainly prettier to look at. If you were tending this field you might pull up all these excess plants – especially the poisonous ones, like henbane – but keep the flowers to take home or to give to your lover.

This too is a 'spray', a fountain of flowers whose shape resembles the spray of water from the 'rose' of a watering-can or garden-sprinkler. But the resemblance is fortuitous. This second English 'spray' in the sense of an impromptu bouquet of wild flowers is much older than watering-cans, and it suggests a possible expansion of the German *Spreu* to mean something subtly different from what we ordinarily understand by 'chaff' – not just the drizzle of wheat-husks in threshing, not just the straw, but *all* that part of the crop, both before and after reaping, considered unfit and possibly dangerous to eat, and certainly not wanted for bread.

The weeds and mixed flowers among the wheat would then be the *Spreu* of the periods of growing and reaping just as the husks and straw are the *Spreu* of the threshing. Taking *Spreu* to bear some etymological relationship to the Old English antecedents of both 'spray' synonyms, 'spray' would then amount to a concept roughly definable as 'all the inedible part of the corn crop, both before and after harvest, including weeds and flowers as well as straw and husks'. It may go further still, and denote all that grows, whether or not on cultivated land, that is inedible by man.

This is not a perception of reality we are used to. By this reasoning, someone tending the wheat might once have pointed to a single cornflower growing among it and called it by a generic name we can now only render by 'spray'. Much later, the word and the full body of its significance split into two synonyms both apparently unrelated to wheat and to farming, a watery spray and a flowery one. In support of this interpretation there is the old Devon place-name, Spreyton – Espreitone or Spreitone in the Domesday Book – 'farm in brushwood country', where 'sprey' or 'spray' has connotations of 'uncultivated, wild'. More evidence for it is perhaps to be found in the digraph *æ* in the Old English antecedents for 'spray' given above, a formation which, as we have seen, there is some reason to connect with the idea of uncultivated land; but there, perhaps, I am clutching at straws.*

Garbo

In Spanish *garbo* is 'grace, elegance ... [woman's] glamour, allure, attractiveness'. *¡Qué garbo!* means 'Isn't she lovely?' 'What a good-looking woman!' etc. And in Italian: *garbo*, 'courtesy, good manners; elegance; tact; good cut (of clothes); habit, custom'. Even in English the original primary meaning of *garb*, now commonly only clothing, was 'grace, elegance'.

What a marketing-man's dream of a name for a screen goddess! Was this the thinking behind the process whereby the Swedish shopgirl Greta Gustaffson became Greta Garbo? Well, no, not exactly; or at least, not consciously. The admiring Spanish, Italian, etc. senses

* After writing this I discovered that the idea that the two 'sprays' are ultimately identical was put forward by Ernest Weekley in his *Etymological Dictionary* (1921). But I am not convinced by Weekley's suggestion of a 'ground-idea of what is scattered or sprinkled'.

of *garbo* were, superficially at least, an accidental bonus in Garbo's career. Her name was bestowed by her Polish lover Mauritz Stiller:

'When I saw you the first time', he said, 'you were beautiful, but your beauty was not refined. You were fresh and simple. I said to myself, I must *wygarbować* this girl.'

'What does that word mean?'

'It's the Polish word for the process of making leather. Very often when I was mischievous my parents would say, "We have to *wygarbować* his skin." That was the signal for a good thrashing or at least a tongue-lashing.'

I said: 'I do not deserve such an ugly word.'

'The verb *wygarbować* is beautiful, strong, and important,' he answered. 'It suits you very well. And how beautiful it sounds in English. The great Garbo!'

(Antoni Gronowicz, *Garbo: Her Story*)

Odd, but otherwise apparently straightforward enough. There is, however, an interesting and even somewhat sinister subtext to this offbeat compliment to the beautiful but still 'unrefined' Miss Gustaffson. Stiller's apparently original correlation of leather-making with a (sexually) attractive woman has a precedent in ancient Rome, where the process of turning *pelles*, hides, into soft leather was associated with visiting a prostitute. The Old Latin verb *scortari* was 'to go with a prostitute'. It is from *scortum*, another word for *pelles*, skin. In polite society, *pelles* or *pellicula* was preferred to the equally valid *scortum*, with its extra meaning 'prostitute'.

In modern Spanish *cuero* is 'leather' and *encuerada* is a ribald term for a naked woman. Semantically, to see a woman in terms of her skin and her skin in terms of leather is to see her entirely as a sex-object. Her skin, her body, is to be used, like an animal's hide. There is even the suggestion that the more roughly it (she) is used, the softer it (she) will finally be. Spanish further associates the notion of being 'in leather' with vice – an *encuerista* is a striptease artiste, and in Venezuela *encuerar* is 'to live in sin'.

A Braniff Airlines advertisement in Spanish had to be withdrawn because, intending to inform passengers that they could fly in leather seats (*en cuero*), what it inadvertently told them was that they could fly *encuero* – stark naked.

There is a subconscious undertow of violence. Let's remember what Stiller is said to have said. 'Very often when I was mischievous my parents would say, "We have to *wygarbować* his skin."'

In other words, very often they would say, 'We have to give him a good hiding.' To hide, in this sense in English, is both 'to remove the hide from' and, by extension, 'to beat the hide of', doubtless with a leather (or hide) strap or whip. Another step in the production of leather gives us the figurative 'tanning', for a beating perhaps less severe than a 'hiding'. 'Tanning' naturally associates with 'hiding': the process of obtaining the dye by crushing oak-apples, oak-bark, walnut hulls, etc. also involved physical force.

Why are these reflections upon Garbo, *garbo*, and leather here in the midst of a narrative about wheat-growing? Well, it is possible to go deeper towards the metaphorical base of *wygarbować*. There is also in English the phrase 'to give someone a [good] thrashing' (the word Stiller used), where thrashing is identical with threshing.

The process of separating the grains of wheat or other cereals from the straw and husks also involves violence. Skins are flayed, and grain is flailed. Wheat is threshed, and people are thrashed. 'Flay' and 'flail' have every appearance of being related both to one another and to the Latin *flagellum*, a whip. The making both of leather and of flour are processes of refinement in which physical force (beating, pounding, flaying, etc.) are involved. The metaphorically derived spin-offs in language may refer to the violence, the refined end-product, or to the waste products.

The German verb *gerben* is to 'tan, dress, curry (*hides*)' and used of steel it means 'to refine'. *Ihm das Fell gerben* is 'to give him a good hiding'. Now the various associations converge, as we look at the Spanish and Italian *garbo*, grace, elegance, refinement, etc. from a slightly different angle. *Gerben* is related to the German *Garbe*, Spanish *garba*, a wheat-sheaf; in English too 'garb', in a now obsolete meaning, was once a wheat-sheaf. *Garbe*, *garba*, and 'garb' are all related to those central two syllables of *wygarbować* from which the screen goddess Greta Garbo got her name ('when I saw you the first time . . . you were beautiful, but your beauty was not refined').

Figuratively, Greta Gustaffson's untreated beauty was the raw hide or alloy, or the unthreshed wheat-sheaf; tanned, refined, and milled in the star-making process initiated by Stiller, this raw beauty was treated and transformed as it were into luxurious soft leather, refined steel, pure white flour. The 'garbo-izing' of Garbo by Stiller now strikes us in a rather different light.

And there are other associations. 'Garbage' was once 'wheat straw and the ears, chopped small as food for horses'. The equivalent word in the process of refining spices was 'garble' or 'garbling' – the unwanted rubbish sieved out from the half-processed spices. In London, the official called the 'garbler' was empowered to enter shops selling spices 'and to garble the same and make them clean'. Someone who 'garbles', in the modern sense, talks or writes un-spicy 'garble', or rubbish.

In language, then, the making of leather is metaphorically related to the process of threshing wheat, and via *Garbe*, *garba*, *garbo*, etc. 'garble' like *spica* provides more evidence of a perceived linkage between spices and wheat, and more specifically between the refinement of spices and the refinement of wheat into flour.

Judas's Bran

Dictionaries are compiled to be consulted, not read as continuous prose. Reading one for research can be a bit like crossing a desert. There are the occasional mirages, for example the words called by etymologists 'false friends' (*faux amis*), words in different languages identically spelt but having different significances and etymologies.

More devious still are the false family relations. It is amusing, for example, that *Autriche* (Austria) is at once followed in the French dictionary by *autruche* (ostrich). In the matter of their Nazi past, and notably in the Kurt Waldheim affair a few years ago, Austrians have indeed been ostriches, hiding their heads in the sand. Additionally, it so happens that Austrian for 'ostrich' is *Strauss*, the name of Austria's national popular composer. But of course 'Austria' and 'ostrich' owe nothing to one another. The apparent family relationship is a serendipitous pun, etymological fool's-gold, a mirage.

Sometimes, though, the dictionary's desert terrain, as it can seem, will blaze into life, to give real and original insights, as improbable but once-powerful associations now largely forgotten or altogether ignored are suddenly revealed. The association of disparate phenomena, an association submerged in one language, is visible in another, preserved or partly so. And then one finds oneself engaged in the partial re-creation of a world to which words are the clues, a world lost to us except that some of its words survive.

What have bread, freckles, scurf in common? Etymologically, as words, nothing. As phenomena, then? Again, apparently little or nothing. From language, however, it is clear that there are deep metaphorical associations between them, and that this is no mirage but a real oasis of understanding where words and associations have clustered; an oasis, moreover, where flowers, flour, and butterflies are all to be found.

On the same page of a dictionary of modern Greek we run into *pitsiliá*, a splash of mud, *pitsiláda*, a freckle, and *pitirída*, scurf. Also *pítera*, bran, and *pitta*, bread, all with the same *pit-* root.

The resemblance of a splash of mud to a freckle is straightforward enough. Scurf is 'a morbid condition of the skin', and freckles might equally be thought of as a skin condition. We are back to that obsessive sense of spottedness which we saw earlier in buds, buttons, spots, and dots. In the present context of wheat-growing we might think rather of stubble or stipple (the Latin *stipula*, straw), speckles, and freckles.

Just as freckles and splashes of mud are spots on white skin or white cloth, so bran, the husk of the grain, can be considered an imperfection in white flour, white bread. All-bran or roughage has not always had the good press it currently enjoys. On the contrary, white and brown bread belong on opposing sides of that aforementioned ancient polarity of light and dark, white and black.

This is where the carriages in this curious train of association begin to link up. A secondary, now-defunct meaning of the English 'bran' is scurf in the hair. The *Oxford Dictionary* tells us that scurf is 'characterized by the separation of branny scales'. Dandruff resembles chaff. The bran–scurf connection is vestigially there in English too, but etymologically absent and otherwise forgotten, as it is not in the

Greek. Nor does the English 'freckle', which is related to 'freak' in its sense of flecked, streaked, give us the direct and unbroken connection with bran and bread which *pitsiláda* does.

Freckles marked their possessor as being on the sinister side of the polar opposition of light and dark. Now-antiquated if still-used French for freckles, *bran de Judas*, identifies the freckled person, the freak, with none other than the betrayer of Christ. The mind half-supplies *brandon*, or brand of Judas, but it means Judas's bran, with bran in the extended sense of excrement, muck, filth. French freckles, then, translate figuratively as something like 'Judas's shit', and *bran* retains in modern French the familiar meaning of a baby's excrement.

There is more here than a ghostly comparison of freckled skin to poor-quality flour. The perceived resemblance of freckles and bran has moved beyond metaphor to morality, and acquired a bias that justifies us in connecting the Spanish *peca*, freckle, with *pecado*, sin.

On the 'light side' of the polar opposition, the equation of white bread with white skin is explicit in the modern Greek *aphrātos* – used of bread it means light, soft, crisp; used of flesh, it means plump and white. The freckled person lacks immaculacy, which is freedom not only from sin but also, and originally, from spots. I would hazard that just as it wasn't safe to be a black cat in medieval Europe, so it wasn't safe to have freckles, even if they were only *Sommersprossen* or *Sommerflecken*, as a German variant of the bud–spot motif has it, summer buds or summer spots brought on by the sun.

There was in the Middle Ages a belief that Judas had red hair. But if red hair was thought loathsome, so apparently were freckles, to which redheads, for genetic reasons, are of course peculiarly prone. Here, for example, is John Dryden on his publisher, Jacob Tonson: 'With leering Looks, Bull-fac'd, and freckl'd fair / With two left legs, and *Judas*-coloured hair.'

Recognition of the connection between red-headedness* and freckles seems to be implicit in the French *taches de rousseur* for freckles. 'Stains of redness' seems purely descriptive until one reflects that freckles aren't red. Paul Robert in his dictionary takes the phrase as being descriptive. But the explanation 'stains *consequent upon* redness', i.e.

---

* See the Lexicon, **Fox**.

upon having red hair, makes better sense. There is something sinister about this 'redness', and its attendant stains. Freckles may also explain the name of the 'Judas tree', in which the leaves bud directly from the branches, unnatural buds like *Sommersprossen* (*Sprossen*, incidentally, are also the rungs of a German ladder).

In the Ukraine it was the custom to greet the first swallow of the spring with the cry, 'Swallow, swallow, take my freckles and give me rosy cheeks.' In England, and perhaps elsewhere, the first spring or summer butterflies were omens of the quality of bread, the quality of life, to be expected in the year ahead. If the butterfly seen first was a cabbage white, you would eat pure white bread; but an ill-omened, moth-like meadow brown foretold a dismal year when the fare would be cheap bread badly freaked with bran.

The identification of butterflies with bread goes beyond coloration. There is another feature they share. There is an old rhyme from Dorset, chanted by children when catching and killing white, night-flying moths (perhaps the species called 'whitefoot' by collectors):

> Millery! Millery! Dousty-poll!
> How many sacks hast thou stole?
> Four and twenty and a peck,
> Hang the miller up by's neck.

The moth larvae, the motes, have been eating the flour, which in Romany is *pauno*, literally 'what is white', as a miller is *pauno-mengro*, white fellow. But the moth identified in the rhyme with a dishonest miller, and perhaps incidentally with a leper, is not only a leprous 'white fellow' – he is 'dousty', too, dusty, as flour is, and as all the lepidoptera are. The dust, subtextually the 'flour', is made up of the wing-scales after which the lepidoptera are named, displaced from the wings. Explicitly, Jamaican English has 'flour bat' for a species of large moth with white, dusty wings.

This scaliness of butterflies and moths is also known, in a secondary meaning of the word, as 'scurf'. But I am in effect tautologously drawing an analogy already implicit in 'scale', which goes back to a root meaning 'husk'. Scurf is scaly and scales are chaff, bran. The scaly, speckled sea-trout is called a 'scurf', and Irish Gaelic for a speckled trout, *breac*, connects it with *barm brack*, a kind of sweet loaf speckled with raisins.

It may seem contradictory that scurf should be associated both with bran, the bad, and, in the rhyme from Dorset, with white flour, bran's antithesis, the good; but we are dealing with metaphor and imagination, not mathematical logic, and, to complete the picture, 'scurf' can also be simply *farine*, modern French for 'flour'.

For scurf German has the neutral *Grind*, suggestive of a millstone impartially grinding. It bears no relation to modern German verbs for 'to grind', however, and may be a false friend or relative, although probably not if the evidence above is admissible. The *Oxford Dictionary* roots the English 'to grind' in Old English *grindan*, of which, it says, 'there are no Germanic cognates'. In the context set out here, however, German *Grind* is a clue to suggest that there was once a cognate, now lost.

Flour and Flower

'Pollen', which flowers have, and 'polenta', a kind of flour, have (like 'pollard', another name for bran) a common ancestor, the Latin *pulvis*, dust.* Does this shared dustiness go any way towards explaining the connection between 'flower' and 'flour'? The Latin *farina*, flour, was also 'dust or powder of any kind', and in ancient chemistry the 'flower' was 'the pulverulent [i.e dusty] form of any substance'.

The dustiness of flour is plain enough. The dustiness of flowers is less so. It seems a slender basis for a common name differentiated only by spelling. And it is only comparatively recently that they have been so differentiated. The Old French for 'flower' was *flour*, and 'flower' in England signified 'flour' as well. The two words were first clearly allocated their modern spellings and significances in English by Dr Johnson in his dictionary of 1721, but the *Oxford Dictionary* tells us that 'flower' continued to be used for 'flour' until the early nineteenth century. And the similarity of sound can still, apparently, confuse. In a court case in 1990, a witness was asked about a certain flower-girl in Romford, and replied,' What kind of flower? Flour as in HomePride or flower as in *My Fair Lady*?'

* Even 'dust' appears to be a metaphor from bread-making. It is related to Dutch *duist*, meal-dust or bran.

The confusion was still more deep-seated in French Canada, where it was doubtless helped along by false friends among words spoken by the English settlers. There in the 1880s a flour merchant was still *un marchand de fleur*, or a flower merchant, and further still, the best of the flour was *la fleur de la farine* (the flower of the flour).

But in *fleur de farine*, 'pure wheaten flour', we have the source of the flour–flower identification and confusion. For *farine* we are evidently to understand a meaning originally other than what we now think of as 'flour'. Fine white flour was the 'flower', or emblematically the softest, the whitest, the least freckled and most refined, 'the best', of the *farine*. English took over the emblematic French *flour*, while French settled for the Latinate *farine* to mean also the 'flower' of the *farine*.

Likewise, bread made from completely unsieved flour is sometimes still called in French *safleur*, which it seems fair to guess means '*sans fleur*', that is, 'without flower'. In fourteenth-century France, bread was sold in carefully classified grades. In Poitiers in 1320, for example, there were four grades, ranging from whitest of the white 'canon's bread' at the top of the scale down to *safleur* at the bottom. Braudel comments: 'Nothing is more typical of the extent to which social inequality was the general rule ... Bread was sometimes bread in name alone. Often there was none at all.'

Malaka

The idea of 'chaffing' someone is thought to derive from 'chafing' them, warming them up, getting them heated. It may bear no relation to the chaff of the wheat. But it is also the case that when one person 'chaffs' another he is symbolically stripping off the bran – or, thinking of 'bran' in its excremental sense, refusing to take what Americans figuratively call his 'bullshit'.

A word besprinkling the conversation when Greeks chaff one another is *malaká*. Look at the packaging of a bag of Greek flour and you'll find the word *malakós*, meaning, says Professor Müller, 'soft and smooth, originally rubbed down or polished; and it comes to mean at last weak, or sick, or effeminate'. *Malakós* is related to the

French *moulin* or Spanish *molino* (mill), and the English 'molar', once known as the mill tooth. Indeed it is related also to Professor Müller's (or 'miller's') own name.

Hidden in *malaká* is the sense 'softy', or 'like soft white flour'. It roughly corresponds to the figurative American use of 'milk toast', Milquetoast, or the English 'milksop', bread soaked in milk, 'graveyard stew', the quintessence, or 'flower', of whiteness, wetness, softness, effeminate lack of fibre.

So *malaká*, paradoxically, chaffs with the suggestion that the person has already been well and truly chaffed. Lack of bran, elsewhere perceived as a virtue, is here considered a weakness. That is less a perversity of language, however, than a psychological contrariness reflected in language.

V BIRDS OF A FEATHER

Wine in a Cup

We are where we began, in a field by the sea on a spring day, a crisp breeze blowing. We look out over the sea, and compare the whitecapped waves with the sheep, the spring lambs, the goats and kids and horses grazing around us.

All fancies, figures of speech, metaphors ... Our observer knows the sea isn't *literally* a 'blue moor', and the flecks of foam aren't *real* animals. At the same time these images are something more than a mere prettification of what he sees. The sea scares him. It is the deep unknown, and here his shaky science falters still further. The further out to sea he goes — in imagination or reality — the more outlandish his ideas about it are likely to be.

The field where he stands is a narrow patch of the familiar between two great and mysterious almost-altogether unknowns, the sea before him and the deep woodland behind, all overarched by the sky. There is a sense in which he is reassuring himself when he pictures these coastal waters as a field not unlike this land, grazed by animals. There may even be ancestrally known beds of mussels or oysters out there, farms of a kind, and even pigs, or anyway pork-fish, porpoises (from the French, *porc-poisson*). But there is something else that he sees, or imagines he sees, in the white sea-foam ...

To understand the tremendous power over his mind of this metaphor that is more than fancy we must make what may seem at first to be a wide detour from our main line of enquiry; later, we shall see that we had to go this way, down a rocky path leading from the field's edge to the surf line, close to the foam ...

★

Try to put yourself in the mind of this pre-scientific peasant-observer picking his way among the rocks ... You see things in almost hallucinatory detail, but in the scientific abstract know next to nothing that we would think valid today. Little escapes the finely meshed net cast by your sense-impressions, but you yourself are caught in that net.

Your intense physical seeing is sometimes inimical to your abstract knowing. You believe, for example – you *know* – that the sun goes round the earth. You can see it do so every day, sinking at evening, rising at dawn. You probably believe too, or know, '*by experience* ... that whatever bodies are consumed by length of time, or by dissolving heat, are changed into small animals', as Ovid has Pythagoras say in the final book of the *Metamorphoses*. You believe that bees emanate from the putrefied entrails of bullocks, hornets from horses, and scorpions from crabs. Maggots are spontaneously generated by putrid meat and (a belief held in the sixteenth century even by the sceptical Sir Thomas Browne) mice by wheat.

You are none too certain how *you* came about. You know that sexual intercourse and semen are involved, but you know nothing either of spermatozoa or, even if you are a woman, of the ovum. You are that much more inclined, then, to believe in God, or in gods, and in creation myths.

The prevailing orthodoxy, if one exists yet, is Aristotle's, perhaps reinforced by Aquinas. The stress is on individual fatherhood, the mother being, after all, only a glorified incubator of the foetus, an interchangeable blood-transfusion unit, so that children are regarded as 'engendered' rather than 'conceived'. Your imagery for the sea, if you have any, is not that it is the Great Mother but that it is 'all-fathering'. Facial resemblances between children and their mothers probably puzzle you.

Pliny, of whom you've probably never heard, put physical resemblance down to momentary fancies passing through the mind during sexual intercourse: 'A thought even, momentarily passing through the mind of either of the parents, may be supposed to produce a resemblance to one of them separately, or else to the two combined.'

Six centuries later, in the Dark Ages, the etymologist Isidore,

Bishop of Seville, who drew upon the ancients, thought that the female as well as the male must have semen, or 'seed', and he passed on the belief that 'children resemble their fathers if the paternal seed be stronger; the mother if the maternal seed be stronger ... Those resembling their grandparents and great-grandparents do so since, just as there are many seeds hidden in the soil, seeds also lie hidden in us which will give back the figures of our ancestors.' This is the liquid 'semen' taken literally to mean dry 'seed'.

The microscope, which will defy those sharp senses of yours by 'seeing' things you can't, has yet to be invented, or, if it has been invented, it is not yet the practical working instrument that it will become by the mid sixteenth century. Even then, it will still be more than a century before Leeuwenhoek's 'discovery', in 1677, of spermatozoa, later still before the discovery of the ovum and other secrets of the *loci muliebres*, the 'women's places' of the Romans, and not until the twentieth century that genes, chromosomes, and DNA are discovered.

There are no newspapers yet, or, if there are, you are illiterate. Even after most of these discoveries, it will still take a long while for news of them to reach you, and longer still before you stop believing the stories you made up before the discoveries were made – stories you have been told and have been telling all your life, stories the human race has been telling itself for thousands of years before you, in order to account for reality.

It will be the early eighteenth century before Linnaeus produces, in Latin, his massive tome *De Systema Naturae* classifying nature into exclusive, self-contained kingdoms. There is little or no obstacle in your mind to the idea of promiscuous commerce and metamorphosis between entirely separate biological classes.

You wouldn't, for example, necessarily shut your mind to the belief, once held in China, that hummingbirds are born out of flowers. You don't draw our modern lines between nature's different kingdoms, our lines between belief and knowledge, faith and fact.

Your scientific ignorance is a kind of gift, giving you a metaphysical realm much wider (and more susceptible to priestly interpretation and influence) than ours today, comprising as yours does not only inexplicable phenomena close to hand, but phenomena further afield which today constitute much of our acknowledged physical world – faraway countries, unseen and unvoyaged seas, distant peoples and animals that you will never see for yourself or on television, and that you hear of only in progressively garbled accounts like those of the children's game called 'Chinese whispers', a game made all the more complicated by its being played between different languages and over many centuries.

Causality is your biggest scientific weakness. In a sense you're *too* close to nature. You know and understand so much of it so well that you're all the more acutely aware of what you don't know, don't understand, and all the more likely to explain it away to yourself in terms of the knowledge you do have.

You are eager for explanations, over-eager. Correctly associating the phenomena – like maggots–meat, mice–wheat, hummingbird–flower – you are quite wrong about the causal chains connecting them. But your mind nevertheless insists on making the connections, just as it insists upon metaphors, which are, indeed, sometimes the sole bases for the supposed connections of cause and effect.

Metaphors can break free from beginnings in fancy to be taken literally and join the circulating stream of quasi-metaphysical Chinese whispers, and those whispers can produce very different results. In time, a metaphorical name may settle down until it is apparently only a notional tag, as it were, attached to the thing named. In these cases, repetition and familiarity progressively erode the metaphor. 'Porpoise', for example, doesn't now, if it ever did, conjure up a mental picture of floating pork or a swimming pig, and although the original metaphor is intact in the original French, or better still the German *Meerschwein*, 'sea-pig', the porpoise is verifiably not a pig, and verification was always comparatively easy. *Porc-poisson* would remain a figure of speech.

But what if 'porpoise' had been one of those many instances in our (formerly) scientifically impoverished, largely unexplored, metaphysically rich world where verification was harder or completely out of the question? Then with repetition the metaphor might have swollen into the rumour, the Chinese whisper, of a swimming sea-pig – a metaphor taken literally. This colourful legend, like that of the mermaid (thought to derive from sightings of the manatee, or 'sea-cow'), might if taken literally have been metaphysically embroidered into a full-blown myth. Taken literally again, the myth might have hardened into metaphysical dogma.

Returning to you by the sea, what else do you see in the foam? It isn't only horses, or goats, or sheep. You don't even really see what we now mean by 'sea-foam', but something distinct from the sea, or rather, the sea in its more familiar form metamorphosed into something else. What, though, *is* this 'something else'?

Let us take another example – that of the semi-translucent jellyfish. 'Jellyfish' is a metaphor of fairly recent origin: the word resumes a creature resembling watery gelatine, turned from a Victorian jelly-mould (if the mould isn't so shaped after the jellyfish). If you live round the mouth of the River Plate in South America you call a jellyfish *aguaviva*, 'livewater': thus perceived, it is semi-see-through sea water in semi-solid, living form. And indeed, the jellyfish is the nearest that biology comes to actually *being* water. Or if you are a speaker of the once-dead (but now apparently reviving) tongue of Cornish, you call it *morgowl*, 'sea-curd'.

'Jellyfish' is fanciful, but both in Cornish and in River Plate Spanish the words suggest a vision of the jellyfish as being *of* the sea, formed *out of the sea*. The jellyfish is living water or the living sea in milky, coagulated form, just as the ancients believed that milk itself was whiteness directly curdled from blood.

This is not so much a metaphorical vision of the natural world as a metamorphic one based upon metaphor. How does the slate-blue sea become floating white foam? How does red blood become white milk? According to Isidore in the Dark Ages, the nature of the 'white fluid', milk (the Latin *lac* or *lact*, or Greek *leukós*, white) 'is changed out of that of blood . . . it flows in its natural channel to the breasts, and by their force becoming white, receives the qualities of milk'.

The foam, then, resembles milk, or semen, a resemblance incidentally recognized in the Spanish *leche*, milk, but also semen, and in the milk-like Papua New Guinea Pidgin word for semen, *melek*.

It's more than a fancifully perceived resemblance, however. Isidore again: 'The male's semen is the froth of blood shaken up like water on the rocks at the seashore, which makes the spume white, or as dark wine shaken in the cup turns white.' That is to say, semen, milk, and sea-foam are *all* produced in the same way. Notice that Isidore is using simile only to reinforce the notion of identity, that the other, unfamiliar phenomenon is only the more familiar one in a less familiar form.

The semen or the milk isn't *like* the froth of blood, it *is* the froth of blood, and the sea-foam's whiteness is shaken up from Homer's 'wine-dark sea', or like wine in a cup, exactly as white semen is 'shaken up' from the body's red blood. After a similar fashion, later in history, the resemblance to semen of the soft white fat of the whale would cause it to be called 'spermaceti'. Metaphor becomes the basis for a supposed metamorphosis.

Causality and metaphysical physiology (metaphysiology?) are implicit in this vision of sea-foam – as they are not in the fancies comparing the whitecaps to farm animals. Semen impregnates. Here, potentially, is a missing piece in the causal jigsaw, and the impregnation of a myth.

But supposed perception of a hitherto missing cause presupposes the prior perception of a hitherto inexplicable effect. A myth may originate in a circular argument based on a scientifically fake Eureka, in which not one but several pieces of the jigsaw of cause and effect all fall into place at once.

Our observer finds another piece of that jigsaw among the shells and the shellfish on the beach . . .

Blackamoor's Teeth

There are many shells on the beach and shellfish on the rocks, whose Linnaean scientific names, today compacted in the dead language of Latin, are the fossils of the wonder we felt on first seeing them.

The wonder we felt and the metaphors we made. These shells, for example, look like fingernails, these like razors, these like the combs in a lady's hair, and these (whelks) like trumpets. These have the colouring of a sunset, while these round ones look like 'acorn shells', as the English called them last century and as old fishermen perhaps still call them today. Wonder at shells is found throughout the world, and is the greater when travel brings people into contact with shells they've never seen before. Shells are well travelled, and always were. There is even a book called *Shells as Evidence of the Migrations of Early Culture*. Who hasn't brought home from holiday a sea shell, a free and ready-made memento, picked up on the beach? You are an English sailor in the Pacific last century, and on a beach you see

... the *Nut Crab*, or *Calappa*, whose queer little legs are so closely tucked away under his odd little shell, that rambling '*Jack Tars*' in search of '*Curios*' not unfrequently gather a few ... under the idea that when cut and polished they will serve to form elegant brooches and splendid shirt-pins, for the gay promenades of Portsmouth and Plymouth.

(From an account of 1867)

And here is another shell you would never find on a European beach, although it has been admiringly appraised by European eyes and was once imported into Europe in vast quantities. It is small and glossy, white or creamy-white. It comes from the Indian Ocean, and its common name is the cowrie (from the Urdu or Hindi *kaurī*, shell). Its scientific name is *Cypraea moneta*, and for many centuries in ancient times, in China and the Far East, it was used as money.

The smallness and portability of *moneta* was a plus in its use as currency, for which purpose, according to one account, the shells 'should be small, clean, and white, with a beautiful gloss'. In more recent history it was the money of the African slave trade, by association with which in England the white shells were known as 'blackamoor's teeth'.

A repulsive name for a beautiful shell. For the purpose of slaving, warehouses in Amsterdam were stocked with cowries. A Dutch account of the mid eighteenth century laments that 'the Negroes now set such a value on their countrymen that there is no such thing as having a cargo under 12 or 14 tuns of cowries'. Cowries are still prized, but I understand that a present-day collector on holiday on a beach in the Seychelles or Maldives would be lucky to find one. Cowries – 'blackamoor's teeth' – have been translated into the black populations of the West Indies, the United States, the Americas.

Porcelain

'Each time I see a piece of pork on my fork, I must remind myself that "pork" and "porcelain" are the same word.'

So, over dinner, says the collector of porcelain from whom Bruce

Chatwin's *Utz* (1988) takes its name. The point Utz has to make is in two parts. To illustrate Part One he reaches for a sea shell, a specimen of *Cypraea moneta* conveniently to hand.

The *Cypraea* family of shells is remarkable for the precision with which it imitates animals. Not just one animal – a whole menagerie of them. Among some on display at the Museum of Natural History, Boulogne, the *zebra*, *pantherina*, *tigris*, and *caputserpentis* (snake's head) all strikingly resemble the animals with which they are compared. With the *mus* and the *talpa*, particularly, it is as if the shell kingdom were a toy factory turning out, respectively, mice and moles.

The name of another shell, *Cypraea vitellus*, compares it to a baby calf, although in this observer's opinion it resembles rather a mottled pig – a Gloucester Old Spot, perhaps – all the way from the suggestively curly-wurly 'tail', like pinched pastry dough, over its gibbous 'hog's back', to the pronounced and astonishingly exact 'snout' at the other tip. Turn the shell over, and the tiny, teat-like pleats along its lips recall John Ruskin's disgusted comparison of the multi-towered, or -teated, chapel of King's College, Cambridge, to 'an inverted sow'.

The shell that Utz produces in pursuit of his point, *moneta*, is a smaller and in my opinion less exact piglet than *vitellus*. But this, the money-shell *moneta*, is the one that the Portuguese, the first European traders with the Far East, nicknamed *porcelana*, or 'little sow', a usage apparently already established when the Venetian Marco Polo – who calls the shell *pourcelaine* – travelled the Far East in the thirteenth century.

The creamy white of one of the *moneta* shells in Boulogne seems to owe more to art than to nature, and 'porcelain' is said to owe its name to the perceived similarity between its glaze and the 'beautiful gloss' of the cowrie. Porcelain was exclusive to China (whence its more common name) and to Europeans it was a mysterious, even somewhat miraculous substance. Valuable, too – a German name for it was *weisses Gold*, 'white gold', formerly an alchemical name for quicksilver. But that wasn't the name that stuck. When the Portuguese returned with the first samples, their shell-like appearance suggested a name derived from the porcelain-like cowries which, probably, they had shelled out in exchange for the porcelain.

The long association between pigs and currency lives on, at least lexically, in the (porcelain) 'piggy banks' in which children still collect their weekly pocket money. The authors of *The Symbolic Pig* write that 'despite exhaustive research . . . [they] have been unable to trace the original, authentic money-pig, or when it was first made'.

The earliest money-pigs weren't porcelain but earthenware. And it isn't surprising that so few, and none, perhaps, of the very earliest, have survived. They were made after all to be broken open when full.

But why *piggy* bank? A number of factors must have played a part – the analogy between the progressive and thrifty fattening of the pig on random scraps of food and the thrifty fattening of the piggy bank on small change, the more sinister identification of pigs with usury, and also perhaps, I suggest, the early equation of money with the pig-like cowrie shells. It is in the eighteenth century, when the slave trade was thriving, that we find the first porcelain piggy banks.

But back to Utz, who has almost established the link between the pork on his fork and his priceless collection of porcelain. Now he proceeds to Part Two of his point, producing 'a bottle of translucent white porcelain which dated from the epoch of Kublai Khan' and pointing out the resemblance of its glaze to that of a cowrie.

Quite. And yet, not quite . . .

It was thought too that porcelain was actually made from cowrie shells, or cowries and eggshells pounded together, which seems to justify taking the origin of 'porcelain' beyond simile to a supposed identity of substance with the shell. And perhaps, in support of this, the Portuguese had come across an extraordinarily delicate porcelain, now known as *porcelaine laquée burgautée*, which actually does incorporate mother-of-pearl from a sea shell, not the cowrie, however, but the burgau.

It was for centuries popularly supposed in Europe that the transformation into porcelain was effected by burying the pounded sea shell and eggshell mixture in the earth for a hundred years. In his dictionary of 1755, Dr Johnson gives a French etymology for porcelain from *pour cent années*, 'for a hundred years', and quotes in support of it Francis Bacon and Browne's *Vulgar Errors*, but not the old couplet: 'True fame, like porc'lain earth, for years must lay / Buried and mixed with elemental clay.'

I think I can explain this curious belief. Porcelain, or 'China clay', once it is dug up is left to stand in heaps, but underground burial plays no part in the porcelain production process. It does, however, in the processing of cowries. The shells are harvested rather as lobsters are, by exploitation of their natural habits. A branch of coconut-palm is left in the sea for the gastropod inhabitants of the shells to adhere to in clusters. They are then picked from the branch, and buried. Several years later the clean white shells are dug up, with all trace of the gastropods gone.

A garbling of *porcelana* to mean shells and *porcelana* to mean porcelain probably underlies the myth behind Dr Johnson's false etymology. China and the Indian Ocean were far from Europe. Cowrie shells were buried; porcelain was not. But 'Chinese whispers' confused the two.

I leave it to others to establish whether the equally mythical story of China's buried 'hundred-year-old eggs' owes anything to this apparent confusion over eggshells, sea shells, centuries, and porcelain.

A final caveat. As well as a supposed Chinese propensity for burying things for a century, we have to bear in mind in the story of 'porcelain' that peculiar but marked European tendency to name things, including shellfish and sea shells, after pigs or parts of pigs.

Perna

You don't have to take my word for it. Here is an experiment you can try for yourself – the next time you eat *moules marinières*. Single out a mussel, preferably one of the larger, juicier, and paler ones. Look at it closely. Turn it over with your fork. You will see that this once-living inhabitant of a sea shell, the mussel, itself looks like a sea shell. In fact, its shape resembles a cowrie. Refer, if you like, to my description above. In the mussel you will see the same pinched 'tail', the same gibbous 'hog's back', the same hint of a 'snout', the same pleats or 'teats' along the lips. If you have never seen a cowrie, you will almost certainly have seen sea shells on some seashore that look very like it, and very like the mussel too.

I am aware that that has about it the ring of Polonius humouring

Hamlet ('Very like a whale'). But 'though this be madness, yet there is method in't', and here is a third curious thing. If the cowrie resembles, as it was thought to do, a little pig, a *porcelana*, then the mussel's resemblance to a pig is still more striking, because the mussel, like no cowrie shell but like most pigs, is (often) pink, and the mussel, like no cowrie but like all pigs, is edible meat, flesh.

Extraordinary, but true. Inside a sea shell, in the shape of a mussel's pink cooked flesh, nature gives us a very fair representation of a pig.

Europe has long known the mussel, but has known the tropical cowrie only since the early days of empire. Both are perceivable as 'pork-fish', and so is the shellfish, of a species no one has confidently been able to identify, described by Pliny two thousand years ago in Book XXXII of his *Natural History*:

There are also shells [*pinnas*] of a kind for which the name 'perna' is given; they are abundant round the Pontiae islands. They stand like pigs' hams fixed bolt upright in the sand; and, gaping not less than a foot wide where there is broad enough space, they lie in wait for food. They have, all round the edges of the shells, teeth set thick like those of a comb; inside is a large fleshy muscle.

It sounds like a species of giant clam. But what is significant is Pliny's comparison of its appearance to that of a pig's ham, *perna*, a ham or leg of pork in Latin.

There is something of a puzzle surrounding this *perna*, in which a word for the meatiest part of a pig is also a word for a shellfish. And not only one kind of shellfish. In a somewhat confusing passage (confusing because he gives so many possible etymologies for 'barnacle'), Professor Max Müller suggested a possible derivation of 'barnacle' from the diminutive of *perna*, *pernacula*. A barnacle certainly looks something like a miniature leg of pork, and certainly *pernacula* is a highly respectable antecedent for 'barnacle'. As certainly, however, a barnacle is not the creature that Pliny describes.

Pernacula, wrote Müller, became *bernacula*, the medieval *bernekke*, barnacle. But he also gave *bernacula* to mean 'muscle', the Latin *musculus*, the diminutive of *mus*, mouse, whence 'mussel'. We find ourselves stirring a loathsome lexical stew of muscles, mice, mussels, and pork, an indigestible mixture into which we may as well also toss a cat (the Latin *mus*, mouse, could also mean cat) and a whale (Pliny, elsewhere, gives *musculus*, little mouse, as a species of whale).

We do better if we think in terms, not of specific phenomena, but general ideas of meatiness, muscularity, edibility. Pliny's *perna* had 'a large fleshy muscle', and a mussel has a small one. A muscle may be thought to twitch like a mouse, or a mouse like a muscle, and mice, cats, and whales may all be thought to have a certain muscularity in common (although that *is* pushing it).

'Hams' in English are the meaty and muscular backs of the thighs, or the thighs and buttocks together, while *perna* in modern Portuguese is a human leg. *Perna* moves us into a new territory of pig-metaphor, where we see that 'pig' seems to have been used as a rough-and-ready coefficient both of filth and, much as 'apple' or 'berry' was used of fruit, of meaty edibility. English gets 'succulent' from *sucula*, a little sow, whence also suckling pig. It is related to *succidia*, which is a leg of pork, or *perna* under another guise; and *succidia*, in one of Varro's correct etymologies, is from *sues caedendae* – 'the cutting up of the swine; for this was the first domestic animal that the owners began to slaughter and to salt in order to keep the meat unspoiled'.

This 'succulent' range of reference underlies the remark of an English traveller in the Pacific in the 1840s that so-called 'spiny lobsters' are 'in their spiked armour like Egyptian *porke pigs*'. Spiny lobsters look nothing like pigs, but are good to eat, at least our traveller found them so: 'To our taste, a well-conditioned "*porke pig*", in the shape of a Crayfish, is by no means to be despised.'

Nor is this the most incongruous juxtaposition, in the same breath as it were, of pigs and crayfish. Thomas Huxley recorded (in *An Introduction to the Study of Zoology*, 1880) a story from the Mark of Brandenburg in Germany that dealers in crayfish were obliged to transport them to market by night, 'lest a pig should run under the cart. For if such a misfortune should happen, every crayfish would be found dead in the morning.' And he quotes another author saying that 'the steam of a pig-stye, or of a herd of swine, is instantly fatal to crayfish'.

Perhaps fear of food-poisoning explains this conjunction of pigs and crayfish, but it is, as Huxley himself notes, very odd, and he cites the Latin tag: *tam exitiatis est porcus cancro* (so fatal is the pig to the crab). More generally, it was thought bad luck to mention pigs, or even porpoises, when at sea, and taboos – a sure sign of veneration, loathing, fear, or all combined – surrounded the naming of the pig even when on land. It was referred to variously as 'the short-legged one', 'the grunting animal', 'the thing', even 'the beautiful one', and in China, where Darwin argued that the pig was first domesticated *circa* 5000 BC, it is 'the long-nosed general'.

This reluctance to call a pig a pig is odd given the almost excessive readiness elsewhere to call things after pigs. And oddest of all is the violent veering between the pig as the type of succulent excellence and the pig as the type of disgusting filth. That veering – which in an individual psyche would be reasonable evidence of insanity – is central to cultural perception of the pig.

We seem to be touching upon some very ancient connections in language and deep connections in psychology – and in particular the psychology of perception. I am under no illusions as to the likelihood of reaching the psychological bottom of it, and will be content if the reader is convinced with me that 'it' exists: a dreamlike clustering and unconscious crystallization of associations so apparently remote that the rational mind may find them absurd, and rebel, associations which both shape and are shaped by language, in which they are evident.

Pigs and shellfish: if the next piece of evidence for a perceived connection between them doesn't convince the reader, nothing will.

Pearls before Swine

We find ourselves skirting absurdity, or rather, perhaps, seeing under the skirt a glimpse of white thigh – naked nature usually hidden beneath the artifice of language. For words can be wonderful hiders, and with some it is almost as though they had been designer-made to cover a sense of shame and absurdity with a civilized illusion of grace and style. The instinct towards civilization is also a turning away from nature, and words are a way of making this deep denial.

It may seem faintly indecent, stripping away the clothes so shyly hiding words' (and our) nakedness. The elegant 'porcelain', for example. And yet, isn't it true? Undress the Dresden shepherdess and one finds a pig. A bit of a shock, really. Likewise when one picks up 'pearl' and peels away her layers.

'Neither cast ye your pearls before swine . . .' (Matthew 7: 6) has entered English as a proverb, while in Flemish (*rosen voor de verkens*) roses take the place of pearls in a proverb having the same broad meaning. In a church carving at Kempen in the Netherlands, men are shown throwing roses to pigs, a wood-carver's joke thought to originate, or so *The Symbolic Pig* informs us, in a carving on a misericord in Rouen of an old woman with a basketful of blossoms, throwing them to her two pigs.

Those blossoms aren't roses, however, but the white flowers, ox-eye daisies, also called marguerites, and this time the joke is better because marguerite *means* pearl. It is from the Latin *margarita*, which Pliny calls originally a barbarian, and therefore probably an eastern word (it is thought to be Babylonian). To the same root we owe the woman's name Margaret and the name of the nacreous, mother-of-pearl-like 'margarine'.

The real joke, however, is still to come: semantically, pearls *are* swine . . .

Modern Italian for the oyster is *pernocchio*, 'leg-of-pork-eye', the 'eye', the tenderest part of the *perna*, with perhaps too the suggestion of a resemblance between the watery membranes of the oyster and those of the eye. So here is *perna* again, and this time we are at a loss to suggest a visual basis for the metaphor in geometric similarity. The shape of an oyster is not like that of the barnacle, or the cowrie, or the pig, or the part of the pig called a ham.

Oysters, however, are eminently edible, succulent, as I'm sure Utz's pork was. They are also eminently 'raw', like freshly butchered meat. It may be that *perna* has this connotation of fresh, raw meat, and that from the killing of the pig this sense was transferred to other similarly 'raw' phenomena.

As for the Italian for 'pearl', it is simply *perna* again, in yet another of its marine manifestations. From the same source we get the English 'pearl'. *Perna*, the 'a' dropped, the tip of the tongue no longer flattened against the frontal palate, but just tiptoe-touching it, the 'n' gradually ground down and milled by use into an 'l' – and hey presto, from *perna* to 'pearl'.

Birds of a Feather

In the aftermath of a storm, the trunk of a tree washes up on the shore. It has been in the sea for weeks or months, long enough to have become home to the crustacea we have known for many centuries as 'barnacles'. The storm may be of relevance in what is to follow. The late nineteenth-century French biologist, Frédéric Houssay, wrote that the discovery on shore of barnacles, taking place as it always does 'at a period of fatigue and of nerve-strain caused by several days of barometric depression . . . must cause at least a moment of surprise to the ignorant fishermen . . . The finding of barnacles is therefore always associated with an idea of surprise, astonishment, or mystery.'

To enter this atmosphere of mystery we must shed associations which the word 'barnacle' conjures up, associations which are, largely, humorous. 'She'll never leave him,' punned James Joyce's father on hearing his son was to marry a woman called Nora Barnacle, a pun depending on the barnacle's reputation as the epitome, the type, of tenacity and adhesiveness.

It is only comparatively recently, however, that the metaphorically derived 'barnacle' has itself been barnacled with the accretion of this metaphorical bias all its own. Superfluous though it may seem to say so, its reputation depends on perception of the barnacle and the thing it adheres to as separate entities or organisms, as we *know* this tree-trunk and these barnacles to be.

We may know (if not, we can look it up) something of the barnacle's life-cycle. How it begins as a sightless and itself barely visible larva enclosed in a minute case like a canary seed, how it develops, in its second stage, eyes, and, in its third, hard calcareous plates and six pairs of forked legs with which it actively paddles about, before turning into the barnacle known to beachcombers. We may even know the wonderful description (originally by Thomas Huxley, later refined by others) of this final transformation as comparable 'to that experienced by a man who should begin life as an active boy, running about as others do, but be compelled suddenly, by some strange spell or Arabian Djinn, to become glued by the top of his head to the pavement, and to spend the rest of his life in kicking his food into his mouth with his legs'.

It is thanks to marine biology and the microscope that we know all this. But forget marine biology – it doesn't exist yet. Forget what you know. Stick like a barnacle to what you see.

In this piece of driftwood on the beach the sea seems to have sent our essentially land-bound 'ignorant fisherman' (none other than our ignorant all-noticing eye, formerly in the field) a message in language he can understand. He knows what is happening here. These shells are budding from the wood. Not metaphorically but *really* budding, the buds putting forth, like those on land, out of the wood's sap. In French a name for these barnacles is the conceptual *sapinettes*, from *sapin*, the pine-tree.

Look more closely, though. They are shells, a fact which together with their suggestive shapes prompts visual comparison rather with nuts than with buds. We've already looked at some acorn-like shells, but these, by contrast, look more like almonds, as learned commentators in centuries to come will not fail to notice; or rather, attached as they are to long peduncles, or foot-stalks, they resemble mushrooms, the metaphor which will be preferred by the Sieur du Bartas, a French poet of the sixteenth century.

They won't get called after almonds, though, or mushrooms, for there is something still more remarkably mimetic about them, a set of detailed resemblances that will spawn one of the most tenacious myths ever to glue itself upon mankind's imagination and stand physiological reality on its head.

Look again at the stalk the almond-shaped shell is mounted on, and see how closely it mimics the long sinuous neck of a goose, even to the 'head' at its tip, the shell partly open like a bird's beak. And the shell's browny-black colour, its markings. It looks variously like a bird's beak, like a bird's egg, a bird's wings, and like the dark plumage of that goose, the branclake, which we see every summer and often find here at the sea's edge, but whose nests and eggs we never see, whose origins and life-cycle we've always wondered about.

Could this be the explanation? For these creatures not only resemble the grown birds in so many detailed particulars, their partly open shells reveal what look like the partly formed bodies of baby birds.

And what's this? No, it can't be. *There are feathers peeping out of them!*

But why the surprise? One more wrinkle in this story of the birth of a myth is that at any point in the history of Europe in the last three thousand years at least our observer would find it already born and pre-existing him, his observations confirmed by received wisdom. For we aren't now looking at barnacles in the modern sense either of the word or of the creatures resumed by the word. These barnacles generated out of the driftwood partake, in the medieval formula, of its nature, or essence. This isn't, moreover, the final stage of a marine life-form in its own right, but a transitional stage towards another, airborne life-form.

These are goose-barnacles, or duck mussels, whose Linnaean name to this day incorporates *anatifera*, 'duck-bearing'. We must think now of 'barnacle' as having a sense inseparable from the modern sense of 'goose' or 'duck' (the least of the confusions in this tale) – as a term essentially interchangeable between the bird and the crustacean.

The tree-trunk too has undergone a transformation. No longer are we looking simply at a piece of pine or other driftwood. No. This is a trunk of the wondrous goose- or duck-bearing tree.

The clinching detail is that of the plumose or feathery appendages sticking out of the barnacle's shell. They are its feet, more precisely the *cirripedes*, or 'curl-feet', with which it feeds itself. There remains a genus of barnacles known as the *pinna*, Latin for 'feather' (and including Pliny's '*perna*', above).

But our imaginary observer doesn't know that these are feet not feathers. Nor does he know that the barnacle goose is migratory, making its nests and rearing its young in the Arctic Circle, away from his and other human eyes. (As late as 1936, their breeding grounds were described as having been discovered 'only recently'.)

His first-hand observation and supposed knowledge of nature is usually impeccable. It must be, if he's this perplexed by his inability fully to account for the life-cycle of the barnacle or that of the barnacle bird. And how brilliantly accurate his observation and metaphor-making are. Seeing so clearly, however, knowing so much, blinds him to the possibility that there may be things he cannot see and does not know at all. Scientifically, his precise noticing has led him astray.

It has, however, provided the rich bonus of a myth, for if necessity is the mother of invention then scientific ignorance is sometimes the mother of myth and imagination. Our keen-eyed observer has married in his mind two phenomena having, visually, much in common, but nothing otherwise except that he finds them both inexplicable – the hermaphroditic barnacle magically reproducing itself and seemingly growing out of the driftwood, and the migratory bird that is apparently immaculately conceived and that is known in French, in a reference to its seeming chastity, as *l'oie nonnette*, 'the young nun goose'.

He has added two minuses to make one dubious plus, and so supplied at a stroke, in one complex causal chain, two explanations which before were both disturbingly absent – two birds with one stone, as it were. *Qui se ressemblent s'assemblent*, they say in French: those who look alike keep one another's company. Not a bad definition of metaphor. The English equivalent is: birds of a feather flock together.

Or, on this occasion, a bird and a barnacle.

'Of Ireland . . .'

Which came first, the chicken or the egg? Which name came first, the name of the barnacle goose or that of its 'egg', the goose-barnacle?

The *Oxford Dictionary* is sure the geese were first: 'The name [barnacle] was orig. applied to the bird, not to the shell.' But if 'barnacle' evolved from *perna*, or is related to it, it must surely have named the shellfish first. And how can we hope for etymological exactness when the goose and the barnacle have kept such immemorial metaphorical company? By the time of the most ancient records that have come down to us their perceived physical association (the basis for the metaphor) was already ancient, lost in time.

Those first records are not written, but pictorial: pottery from Mycenae and an ossuary from Crete bearing a motif which Frédéric Houssay called *lepas anserisé* (or 'goosified limpet') and the English naturalist Sir Ray Lankester called 'barnaculized goose'. If the bird and the barnacle were identified pictorially, doubtless they were identified etymologically too. 'A legend', Houssay called it, 'which has reached us from a nebulous antiquity adown the ages.'

Nowhere in Western Europe did the legend take more vigorous root than Ireland, one of the bird's first landfalls on its return from the Arctic. In the 1860s Max Müller offered the most attractive of his etymologies for 'barnacle' – that it derived from the Latin of the early Irish monks, from *Hiberniae*, 'of Ireland', or from a garbling of its diminutive, *Hiberniculae*.

Müller, with his perplexing variety of etymologies for 'barnacle' on offer, and stumped as to the real one, wriggled out of his difficulty with the idea of a fantastic coincidence: that the birds were independently called *berniculae* (from Hibernia) and the barnacles *bernaculae* (from *perna*) 'and as their names seemed one, so the creatures were supposed to be one. Everything afterwards seemed to conspire to confirm the first mistake.'

This is to be, in Dr Johnson's phrase, 'lost in lexicography', and blind to the metaphor-based relationship between language and the physical world. The pictorial 'barnaculized goose' motif on its own proves there was an ancient identification of bird and barnacle rooted, not in sound similarities between words, but in visual similarities. The names are identical because they were thought to be stages of the same life-form. We may agree with Müller, however, when he writes: 'If the story was once started, there are many things that would keep it alive; and its vitality has certainly been extraordinary.'

Over the centuries, the scientifically inclined awkward squad would ask tricky questions. Do the geese impregnate the tree, like weevils or gall wasps? Do they fly from the barnacles like winged insects? Why does no one ever seem to have witnessed this? Why are there no really reliable eyewitness reports of a goose-bearing tree? If there is such a tree, why are barnacles found also on ships' hulls? And so on. Yet the metamorphic metaphor – the myth – would stand time's test as received truth very well, finding no shortage of takers and no shortage either, over the centuries, of 'reliable' eyewitnesses vouching for its accuracy.

Some of the factors that 'kept it alive' have already been noted: physical similarities between the bird and the barnacle, and ignorance of their respective life-cycles. There is another, rather surprising reason. In the end it would be exploded by science, but in the meantime pseudo- or para-science helped to sustain it. This myth was not simply and demonstrably a fancy, like, for example, the myth of Picus changing into a woodpecker (pages 94–7ff). It was *explanatory*. That is, it accounted for things that were genuinely puzzling.

Another important factor was religion. Over the centuries, religious wishful-thinking, and religious dogma, would help to fill the evidential gap. The legend, very much older than Christianity, nevertheless found fertile ground in Christian doctrine. The barnacle myth demonstrated a metaphysical dimension to the natural world. Here was evidence both of miraculous metamorphosis and of parthenogenesis, or virgin birth (*l'oie nonnette*).

No other explanation seemed to fit the facts. In the early eighteenth century, the Norwegian bishop and missionary Hans Egede wrote of the bird he called *Stok-ænder*, or tree-goose, that they 'do not breed by the pairing of male and female like other birds'. And back in 1603, a chronicler called Gerald of Wales had horribly harangued, 'Be wise at length wretched Jew. She [the barnacle goose] is an argument for the faith, and for our conviction procreates and produces every day families without either male or female.'

No, Gerald, no. But how do you reason with a man who had 'frequently, with [his] own eyes, seen more than a thousand of these small bodies of birds, hanging down on the sea-shore from one piece of timber, enclosed in shells and already formed'?

Gerald, anyway, was only endorsing the chronicler, William Camden, who wrote (in his *Britannia* of 1586): 'That there be little birds engendred of old and rotten Keeles of ships, they can bear witnesse, who saw that ship [the *Golden Hind*] wherein Francis Drake sailed about the world, standing in a dock near the *Tamis* [Thames]: To the outside of the Keele whereof a number of such little birds without life and fethers stucke close.'

No, William. But the *Golden Hind*'s sailors weren't to know, were they? Some took the barnacles home with them in the hope they would hatch into birds. Doubtless they intended to eat them, for, more mundanely, the metaphysical significance of the barnacle myth made it a loophole in the strict religious rules governing diet.

Evolving as it supposedly did from marine life, the barnacle bird in its essence was a sort of feathered flying fish. For some, it was therefore suitable fare for Fridays and times of fast, 'a testaceous [i.e. shelled] fish', in the words of another chronicler (J. C. Rieger, 1742): 'Therefore in fast-times those who eat the bird eat fish.' For others, by the same reasoning, the bird was neither fish, flesh, fowl, nor good red herring. While Gerald of Wales lectured the Jews, taking the goose as his text, the Jews argued among themselves over its status in their dietary code, with rabbinical edicts on the subject spanning centuries.

The Irish were more relaxed. Gerald of Wales had a bad-tempered go at them, too: 'Bishops and religious men in some parts of Ireland do not scruple to dine of these birds at the time of fasting, because they are not flesh, nor born of flesh. But these are thus drawn into sin; for if a man during Lent had dined of a leg of Adam, our first parent, who was not born of flesh, surely we would not consider him innocent of having eaten what is flesh.'

Gerald had a point there, but he thundered to no avail. In Ireland, the people of a parish in County Derry shortly before the Great War were, according to their priest, 'in the habit of eating the Barnacle-Goose during Lent, under the impression that it was more fish than fowl'. The myth was especially prevalent in the west of Ireland, where Nora Barnacle came from. And of course James Joyce was aware of the playful possibilities of his wife's maiden surname. Among his notes for *Finnegans Wake* he scribbled 'glorious name of Irish goose', and it was noted by Nora's biographer, Brenda Maddox, that references to waterbirds and geese are found in Joyce's work 'tucked into the text, much as mediaeval monks wove their favourite flowers and animals into their illuminated capitals'.

Maddox says of Nora's name, 'It was derived from "barnacle goose".' It survives as a surname in the west of Ireland, usually in the form 'Barnicle', but also in Gaelic versions (for example, Kane).

If Müller was right, though, Nora and the goose both independently derived their names from the name of Ireland. By this explanation (unknown to Maddox and, as far as I am aware, to Joyce as well) Nora Barnacle would translate literally as 'Nora of Ireland', hardly an etymology that Joyce was likely to have ignored.

★

Canard

There are intriguing resemblances between elements of the barnacle myth and Samuel Beckett's play *Waiting for Godot*. Beckett was an Irishman who knew Joyce and Nora. Through his friendship with the painter Jack Yeats, he also knew the west of Ireland, where the barnacle myth was then still a living reality. He could very well have come into contact with the myth there, but if not he had certainly encountered it in Shakespeare's *The Tempest*, a play he knew very well. In Act 4, Scene 1, Caliban remarks: '. . . We shall lose our time / And all be turned to barnacles.'

It might easily be a desolate Jack Yeats landscape that Beckett's characters, Vladimir and Estragon, find themselves stuck in, as so many of Beckett's characters are stuck, like barnacles 'stucke close', paralysed or glued to the spot 'by some strange spell', truly mobile only in their memories of their 'active' earlier lives. Huxley's description (pages 129–30 above) of the barnacle's life-cycle could double for a description of the life-cycles of Beckett's people – Hamm in *Endgame*, Winnie and Willie in *Happy Days*, Krapp in *Krapp's Last Tape*, and Malone in *Malone Dies*, to name but a few. Often physically paralysed, and always infirm of purpose, Beckett's typical characters have lost their time, and been turned to barnacles.

Vladimir and Estragon are stuck because they are waiting for Godot. In French, the language in which Beckett wrote, the hope that he will come is a *canard*, a duck, figuratively a preposterous piece of exaggerated hearsay, or a newspaper, like the ironically entitled *Le Canard Enchaîné*, dealing in gossip and hearsay. French gets that figurative expression directly from the barnacle myth – *l'histoire d'un canard* the French called it when it was exploded by science (exploded, in historical terms, almost overnight), 'the story of a duck'.

And that story begun in peasant noticing was, as Müller noted, specifically 'a good Irish *canard*' – a tale almost if not quite as tall as that of God.

In teasing Gerald of Wales and William Camden just now, I did not stray from my purpose. The barnacle myth *is* comic, but it – or rather, its explosion – is also tragic. We are in a position now to see that the word 'barnacle' resumes what is one of the more amazing, not exactly achievements, but manifestations of the human imagination – and yet, it was all a *canard*. How very disappointing. How disappointed those sailors from Drake's ship must have been, when their barnacles didn't hatch into birds.

The barnacle myth is the outstanding instance of the belated survival into modern times, and then the death, of a perceived metaphysical dimension to the world. Its death – the last gasp of the metamorphic idea – is the story also of the loss of faith, and that, whatever else it is, is not primarily funny. But it is tragi-comic, a sorry absurdity.

The set of *Waiting for Godot*, 'a tragi-comedy in two acts', is featureless but for one bare tree, which, at the start of the second act, has sprouted a few leaves. The great interest that Vladimir and Estragon take in this tree is reminiscent of a story of 1435, when Aeneas Sylvius Piccolomini, the future Pope Pius II, visited Scotland. With Ireland and the Orkney Islands, Scotland in the Middle Ages was one of the places where speculation over the whereabouts of the miraculous goose-bearing tree tended to concentrate.

Piccolomini enquired of the King of Scotland, but received no satisfactory answer. Whereupon he said, 'Miracles flee further and further.' Having come all that way, the future Pope's 'appointment' was not kept. How disappointing for him.

His very 'Beckettian' observation on his disappointment is the perfect epigraph to Beckett's play. It is just what Estragon or Vladimir might have said, in effect just what they *do* say, and just the predicament they are in – their perpetually flagging but never-quite-extinguished faith is pinned on the Chinese whisper, the *canard*, of a Godot who will never come. Miracles flee further – over the horizon of time as well as space. Somewhere over that horizon grows the goose-bearing tree, but always, where one actually *is*, it is conspicuous only by its absence.

I ransacked *Waiting for Godot*, looking for clues to the presence of that 'good Irish *canard*' at the back of it. The tree interested me most. In Act I Vladimir and Estragon puzzle over its identity. Is it a tree, or a shrub? If a tree, is it, perhaps, a willow? If so, where are its leaves? 'What are you insinuating?' Vladimir asks Estragon, 'That we've come to the wrong place?' (That was the future Pope's ironic insinu-ation, too.)

Pozzo arrives, leading Lucky 'to the fair'. Lucky might be a goose on a string, and later, when he dances, Pozzo says his dance is called 'The Net. He thinks he's entangled in a net' (nets are used to catch geese and other wild birds). Lucky's big speech is punctuated by 'qua qua qua', the sound of quacking.

They all look at the sky, 'pale and luminous like any sky at this hour of the day. [*Pause*] In these latitudes.' Are those 'latitudes' the north? They are waiting for a *canard*, but are they also waiting for geese? (The north wind, and the return of the geese from the north, were popularly associated with fertility.)

Act I ends with the non-news of Godot's non-arrival, and Act II begins with a sign of springtime fertility: the bare tree has sprouted a few leaves. But it isn't leaves they are waiting for. Soon afterwards Vladimir remarks, 'Decidedly this tree will not have been the slightest use to us.'

Vladimir and Estragon discuss some bones: are they fish or chicken? (Fish, flesh, or fowl?) Most intriguingly, perhaps, Vladimir remarks: 'Let us represent worthily for once the foul brood to which a cruel fate consigned us.' 'Foul brood' is Beckett's own pun from his original French into English. The French text has *engeance*, 'breed', a word particularly associated with poultry. Exactly the same pun, foul/fowl, occurs in *The Tempest*, Act 2, Scene 1. In the same play it is questioned whether Caliban is 'a man or a fish', and whether a particular plant is a shrub or a bush. Stefano says to Trinculo, 'Though thou canst swim like a duck, thou art made like a goose.'

Qua qua qua. Preposterous, isn't it? What should one expect from the theatre of the absurd, however, if not absurdity? And of course, if *Waiting for Godot* is indebted to the barnacle myth, or to *The Tempest*, it is less at the level of detail than of deep structure. The Godot that is being waited for can't be defined in detail, can't be furnished with a clear-cut identity.

I was in hot pursuit of an Irish *canard*. I was on a wild-goose chase.

Certainly, however, the rumour of Godot is a *canard*, and certainly 'duck' (like 'pig', or 'barnacle') is a word dangerously freighted with absurdity. In a play by the American playwright David Mamet, a lakeside dialogue between two old men, 'ducks', according to one commentator, 'prove a trampoline for observations about such things as the poisoning of the environment, the endurance of generational cycles and the inevitability of death'.

Mamet modelled his play on *Waiting for Godot* – he called it *The Duck Variations*.

Foam-Born

There are various accounts of the birth of the goddess Aphrodite, whom classical Rome assimilated with its own goddess, Venus. The best-known is a myth which scholars are agreed came to Greece from the east. It was told by the poet Hesiod in his *Theogony*, three thousand years ago.

Setting aside the wider ramifications of the myth, the story of the birth is as follows. When Kronos castrated his father, Uranos, he threw the dismembered genitals into the sea, whereupon, according to Hesiod, 'a white foam spread around them from the immortal flesh, and in it there grew a maiden'.

That coy 'maiden' is typical of the 1914 translation of the *Theogony* from which I am quoting. A note to the same translation glosses the robust epithet 'member-loving', used of Aphrodite, as 'perhaps a perversion' of another 'regular' Greek phrase meaning 'laughter-loving'. A slightly earlier edition, of 1909, omits the offending phrase altogether, calling it 'probably spurious'. But this is raunchy territory – Aphrodite is member-loving all right, as we shall see.

There is a modest, maidenly quality to the woman depicted in Botticelli's painting, *The Birth of Venus*. Butter probably wouldn't melt in her mouth. The maidenliness owes something to the Christian ideal of womanhood and ultimately, I am sure, it derives from a discreet identification of the pagan goddess with the Maid or Queen of Heaven, the blessed Virgin Mary. She is Venus in her nakedness, but her face is the Virgin's. Botticelli shows his naked Venus chastely wrapping her long hair about her, and he follows Pliny's account in placing her on a sea shell, afloat on a foamy sea. That sea shell is important, and so is the identity which Botticelli ascribes to it. We shall return to it, and to the Virgin Mary.

There are intriguing similarities between the Venus myth and the folkloric, para-scientific story of the barnacle-bird. In his learned and witty *Barnacles in Nature and in Myth* (1928), Edward Heron-Allen wrote that 'Neither in the legends of Greece nor of Rome do we find any trace of the Barnacle-Goose Myth'; this, even though 'it seems to have had its origin, as it were, at their gates'. Certainly the Venus and barnacle-bird myths cannot be said to be one and the same. They do markedly resemble one another, however, both in deep structure and in several significant details. They seem to belong to branches of the same mythic family, and it may even be that they bear traces of one another.

Both are myths of marine birth without 'the pairing of male and female' (although male and female elements are heavily sublimated in the Venus myth). The bird's 'womb' was a sea shell – its 'foetus' was a shellfish. The sea shell on which Venus stands is in Pliny but not in Hesiod, which is not necessarily to say that it was a later accretion to the myth: the identification of sea shells with goddesses was characteristic of the pre-Hellenic civilizations in which the myth originated. Hesiod may simply have omitted it; or ideas about sea shells as the sources of other life-forms, as evinced by the story of the barnacle-bird, may have put it there. We do not know, but if the sea shell in the Birth of Venus myth is not actually a 'trace of the Barnacle-Goose Myth' it certainly has every appearance of being a family heirloom passed down within the same set of myths to which we take the barnacle-goose myth to belong.

What matters most, though, is the hold on the mind of the *idea* of miraculous 'virgin' birth and suspension of the usual natural order as a physical as well as philosophical reality. Let us remind ourselves that the barnacle is hermaphroditic, and that in the reproductive cycle of the barnacle goose sexual intercourse was believed to play no part: Venus, a personification if not exactly a person, was also supposed to have been conceived without the agency of human sexual intercourse. The barnacle arose from the sea as an airborne life-form, a bird, and in the shape of the supposed 'star' named after her, so did Venus. The 'nun-goose' was an argument for virgin birth, and therefore also 'an argument for the faith'; that is to say, an argument in support of that central plank of Christian faith which holds that Christ was born of a virgin.

The literal-minded barnacle myth, with all its self-justificatory pseudo-scientific trappings, was highly vulnerable when real science came along. In a sense science was the test which it had to pass in order to qualify as a full-blown myth. By that criterion it failed. It was demonstrably false. But the myth of the Birth of Venus existed and indeed still exists on another plane of discourse. If it is explanatory, it is opaquely so. If it was open to disbelieving scorn, it was also impervious to logic. It survived among the canon of myths, those stories from which we expect 'poetic' but not literal truth, and more tenuously it survived into Christianity.

However strong our sense of Christianity's complex debt to the myth of the Birth of Venus, it would be a mistake to attempt to pin it down too closely. We cannot hope finally to *know* 'the origin of the gods' (which is the meaning of *theogony*), and we risk being risible if we were simply and bluntly to state for example that *The Gods Had Wings* (the title of a book of the 1930s arguing that birds were the original models for certain divinities) and that the barnacle goose was the original 'model' for Venus. That way leads only to Erich von Daniken-land.

An exploration of metaphor nevertheless reveals rich parallels between the Birth of Venus and the birth of Christianity. We can put that in another way. If the barnacle myth, exploded, is a powerful and absurd after-image of the death of Christian faith, the myth of Venus is an intriguing advance image of its birth.

'Mary' is thought like 'Miriam' to be from Latin *mare*, the sea. St Jerome in his *On the Interpretation of Hebrew Names* gave 'Miriam' as *stilla maris*, 'drop of the sea'. This relates 'Mary' – relates her not etymologically but metaphorically – to 'Aphrodite'. The Greek *aphrós* means 'foam'. 'Aphrodite' is 'foam-born'. The 'drop of the sea' and the 'foam-born' appear to keep the same metaphorical company.

The consensus among classical scholars is that Aphrodite's name was concocted by the Greeks, purpose-built as it were to supply a need. Roland G. Kent of the University of Pennsylvania wrote in 1951, for example, that the story was a 'Greek legend invented to connect the name of Aphrodite with *aphrós*, foam'. According to Professor Kent, the name 'Aphrodite' is 'probably of Semitic origin'. Likewise, the editor of the Oxford edition of Hesiod's *Theogony*,

M. L. West, wrote in 1966: 'Aphrodite is formed in foam to explain her name.'

We are asked to believe that the name or something resembling it came first, and that the association with foam followed by sound association in its wake. By this reasoning, the myth of the Birth of Venus is an elaborate, punning, and altogether spurious etymology.

That is to concede too much power to words, however, and too little to metaphor, which (this book argues) although it may manifest itself most notably in language yet remains finally independent of it. Language needs metaphor, we might say, more than metaphor needs language. Essentially, the notion of a concocted myth follows the same erroneous 'lost in lexicography' line of argument that Max Müller pursued in his etymology for 'barnacle'.

The obvious objection to it may be found in *The Origin of the Gods*, Richard Caldwell's 1989 study of the *Theogony*. 'Why the connection with foam?' Caldwell asked, 'Hesiod may put Aphrodite in foam because he found foam in her name. but how is foam connected with Aphrodite in the first place?'

Everything in this book supports the answer Caldwell gives: 'The association must result, I would think, from a prior connection with the phallus [i.e. the castration of Uranos] and consequently from a visual similarity between semen and the foam excreted by the sea.'

This is not some obscure quibble, but an argument over how the human mind actually works. The view taken here is that the Birth of Venus myth is not some clever and conscious 'invention', but that it is based upon *metaphor*, and the myth that has come down to us is inconceivable without the metaphors of which it is composed and of which it is expressive. The myth is metaphor, in dynamic, metamorphic action.

Earlier we saw that Isidore of Seville identified semen with sea-foam. The same metaphor is equally valid in reverse, however. Aphrodite, or Venus, arose from the 'all-fathering' sea precisely *because* sea-foam was identified with semen. Thus the 'foam' in her name. To suggest that 'foam' was added after the event is to suggest that it is essentially accidental, an afterthought. But it is not. On the contrary, it is the proposition – one of the propositions – upon which the myth is founded and with which it begins.

Remembering our earlier glance at the linked perception of semen, sea-foam, and milk, let's spread the metaphorical net a little wider . . .

There are doubtless many metaphors arising from the churning of milk. It was always one of the most startling yet most everyday and accessible instances of metamorphosis. The separation of milk into curds and whey, and the solidifying of liquid milk into cream, butter, or cheese, was a fundamental transformation which, unlike the alleged 'shaking up' of blood into breast-milk or semen, it was possible to witness taking place under one's own eyes.

In the Hindu myth cycle, the *Mahabharata*, we find the story of how amrita, or *sōma*, the 'water of life', was obtained by churning the sea. 'For a churning-staff the Gods used Mount Mandara, which they tore from its base with the help of the mighty serpent Ananta. They then went to the shore of Ocean and said: "O Ocean, we have come to churn your waters in order to obtain amrita".'

The Sanskrit verb used there in the sense of churning as if churning milk, *manth*, has the primary meaning of 'vigorous backwards and forwards motion of any sort'. It is used also for the act of sexual intercourse and the act of making fire using tinder and wooden sticks.* *Manth* is semantically related to the name of the 'churning-staff', the mountain, Mandara.

One needs no special knowledge or bias to see the sublimated phallic significance of that mountainous 'churning-staff'. The Hindu myth of churning the sea is a dynamic metaphor for sexual intercourse, the production of semen, and subsequent conception. The things that emerge from the Ocean as a result of the churning are markedly milky and white, 'the mild moon', 'Lakshmi, all in white', and 'the divine Dhanwantari with a white vessel in his hand'.†

Among those apparitions, 'the White Horse Uchchaisravas' takes us all the way back to that first, and then apparently quite straightforward, metaphor with which this book began, 'white horses' on the sea . . .

* The two acts are anciently identified: 'punk', which had come to mean 'prostitute' by the eighteenth century, in one etymology originally meant 'tinder'.

† Containing the drink *sōma*, the mythic version of semen. The Sanskrit homonym, *soma*, is the moon. Greek *sôma*, as in 'psychosomatic', is the body. 'Soma' in English is 'the body of an organism in contrast to the germ-cells'.

In the Birth of Venus myth the dismembered phallus of Uranos fills the role played in Hindu myth by an uprooted mountain. That is its 'churning-staff'. But let us not forget the churn, the 'female' dimension to this myth of birth. For if semen and sea-foam are interchangeable on the metaphorical plane, so are shellfish and the female reproductive organs. Evidence for the perceived identification, or assimilation, of the two goes back to neolithic times. Nor is it contained by geography or culture: we find it among the Aztecs in Mexico and in ancient China and Japan as well as in India, the Near East, and Europe.

This ancient metaphor still obtains widely today. Evidence for it is legion in language: to take only two examples, the Spanish *concha*, mollusc, or in figurative slang, vulva, and the alarmingly direct Danish *kudefisk*, oyster, but literally 'cuntfish'. More generally, we have the widespread vague popular belief in the aphrodisiac properties of oysters and other shellfish: 'Eat Beef or Pye-crust if you'd serious be: / Your shell-fish raises *Venus* from the Sea.'

The strength of that now-archaic, transferential use of 'Venus' was its absence of specificity and its accompanying wide range of application. 'Venus' was a generic name for things having certain qualities conceptually in common. It evoked the sense of a yielding softness and juiciness, whether found in the body of a woman, the succulent pleasures of the flesh, the raw nakedness of shellfish, the juicy tropical guava, or even, in the Roman writer Gnaeus Naevius, boiled vegetables. The French phrase for tomatoes, *pommes d'amour*, 'apples of love', falls in with this pattern (I remember a line from a Caribbean calypso of the 1950s: 'My baby got squashed tomato').

As used of a woman and sexual desire 'Venus' was at once euphemism and innuendo. It resembled the modern American slang use of soft and tasty 'cheesecake', or, as I argue in the Lexicon, the slang cant term 'box' (see **Box**). Yet the generic term inescapably evoked also the name of a goddess. We are probably correct if we think of it in its metaphorical heyday as being a vehicle for the dual and intermingled fear-and-loathing which surrounds all taboos. On the one hand, 'Venus' was used with genuine reverence and fear as symbolizing female reproductive power; on the other hand, as in the couplet quoted above, it was mere salacious innuendo, part of the smutty verbal currency of the bar-room. *Porca Madonna*, they say in Italy: 'piggy Madonna'.

By association with their mollusc contents and their own often suggestive shapes, sea shells too were 'Venus'. The goddess is discreetly alluded to even in the Linnaean Latin name of the cowrie referred to earlier, *Cypraea moneta*. She was associated with two islands – Cythera and Cyprus – and Homer called her 'the Cyprian': thus *Cypraea*, the Cypriot designation of the cowrie, which was held sacred to Venus and called by Pliny the 'shell of Venus'. Eighteenth-century naturalists at the time of Linnaeus actually classified 'Venus-shells' according to the greater or lesser degree to which they resembled the vulva; by transference, 'vulva' became a technical term in conchology for a part of the opening of the sea shell. Perhaps the most dramatic of these shell–vulva assimilations was in ancient Japan, where one neolithic idol was a giant sea shell suspended from a rope. In the words of Mircea Eliade (in *Images et Symboles*, 1952) it was 'a monstrous vulva'.

More evidence of a similar kind may be found in the epic of Portuguese expansionism *Os Lusíadas* (1572). Its author, the poet Luís Vaz de Camões, in reference to Venus's other island called sea shells *conchas Citereia*, 'Cythera shells', while the guava was *mirto de Citereia*, 'myrtle of Cythera'. The guava is a member of the same family as the myrtle, which in ancient Rome was sacred to Venus. The Greek *mýrton*, myrtle berry, also means 'clitoris'.

These thinly veiled and flowery classical references in *Os Lusíadas* are at the same time sexual *double-entendres* (and see **Guava** in the Lexicon for more blatant evidence of the guava's prevalence as a vehicle of sexual metaphor).

By now it should come as no surprise to learn that our succulent old friends the pigs were sacrificed to Aphrodite. I'm not going to tangle with pigs again, except to note that the generic deployment of 'Venus' and the diffuse use of 'pig' have much in common; also, how interesting it is that the cowrie shell should be so profoundly identified both with the pig, on the one hand, and with woman and the vulva, on the other.

The Birth of Venus myth makes no coherent physiological sense. As extended metaphor, however, it is logical, consistent, and satisfying. The half-shell supporting the woman–goddess, like the foamy sea which surrounds her, is not a contingent or accidental detail in the overall picture. It is metaphorically necessary. The shell, evidence of the generic 'Venus', might also be construed as the afterbirth of the goddess, afloat upon the broken waters.

Its identity in Botticelli's painting is the scallop, the so-called 'St James's shell' or *coquille St Jacques* carried by pilgrims to the shrine of St James, or 'Santiago', in Spain. It is the 'scallop shell of quiet' of Sir Walter Ralegh's poem *The Passionate Man's Pilgrimage*. The pilgrimages were to Saragossa, where Santiago, who was also known as 'the Moor-slayer',★ was reputed to have seen the Virgin Mary in a vision. Santiago's emblem was the scallop shell, which with its powerful and immemorial associations of the sea, and female sexuality and fertility, shows every sign of being a pagan survival. With its patina of Christian symbolism, it irresistibly associates Santiago with the Virgin Mary of his vision, and we shall see how natural, almost inevitable it is that the 'Moor-slayer' and the Virgin should have been associated. At the same time, it associates the Virgin Mary herself with the pagan goddesses and fertility cults of the eastern Mediterranean. In particular it associates her with 'foam-born' Aphrodite. Botticelli cannot have been unaware of these associations when he planted his pagan Venus upon a 'Christian' scallop shell.

To this day, pilgrims to Saragossa take home with them a souvenir which shows the Virgin Mary on a scallop shell. Marina Warner, author of a study of the Virgin, *Alone of All Her Sex*, found this souvenir 'startling'. An earlier commentator would probably have said 'profane'. There is nothing new, however, in the idea that 'the Virgin Mary' is only a comparatively new name for a much older goddess, and in the second century Apuleius wrote in *The Golden Ass* that all goddesses were really one.

This is the idea to which that crude souvenir of Saragossa gives expression, and again, the metaphorical logic is impeccable. It merely takes the iconography of Botticelli's painting a logical step further, and blurts, in the face of Christianity's deep denial, the truth that metaphor insists upon – that when the theological gloss of centuries is

---

★ I doubt that it can be original to suggest that the name of the 'Moor-slayer' Iago in *Othello* may be from 'Santiago', but I haven't found it suggested elsewhere.

stripped away the Virgin Mary deliquesces into a 'drop of water', and merges with the 'foam-born' Venus.

Star of the Sea

To a modern reader, perhaps the most interesting thing about *Os Lusíadas* is a structural weakness of the poem – the subtle confusion which it displays between classical myth and Christianity, Venus and the Virgin. Essentially it is the same confusion which, as I argued earlier (see pages 64–6, 76–7ff), was shown by two other poets – Milton and Tennyson – in their treatment of the myth of the Hesperides. At its root is an uncertainty over the meaning, and the status, of the metaphor of Venus.

Camões casts the pagan goddess Venus in the role of the protectress of Portugal and Portuguese imperial expansion. In itself, there is nothing surprising about this. Like Botticelli, Camões was an artist of the Renaissance and the classical revival; he was following, as commentators have observed, his classical model, Virgil's *Aeneid*. There is a second obvious point to be made, however. Camões, in Maurice Bowra's characterization of him, was 'no Pagan, but a Catholic, proud to be a subject of a Christian king'. Moreover, empire was at the cutting edge of Christianity. The Portuguese adventurer-heroes of his poem were, in the Spanish term, *matamoros*, Moor-slayers, owing, Bowra wrote, 'much of their dignity to their championship of the Christian cause against Moors and idolatrous Indians'.

The ruling metaphysic of *Os Lusíadas*, then, is Christian; its apparatus is classical, 'pagan'. Camões fails, however, to reconcile the two. There is a disparity between them, a disjointedness. As Bowra noted, he is 'inconsistent on this point. He gives at least two explanations, and they are irreconcileable.'

The reason for the inconsistency is not hard to find, for we *know*, as Camões himself did, that the whole Portuguese imperial adventure was in fact steeped in the Christian beliefs of the day, and that imperial Portugal's true perceived protectress was not Venus, but the Virgin.

Since the Middle Ages, Jerome's etymology for the Virgin Mary/

Miriam, *stilla maris*, 'drop of the sea', had been superseded by the image of *stella maris*, 'star of the sea'. Commentators argue that the change came about as the result of an entrenched copyist's error, a learned explanation, like the one above for 'foam-born', which is 'lost in lexicography'.

The 'star of the sea' was identified by mariners with Venus (and with the Pole Star, too). At a stroke, the simple vowel-change from *stilla* to *stella* put the sailors, wherever in peril they were on the world's seas, under the protective eye of the Virgin; it marked an expansion of the Christian as distinct from pagan gloss upon reality. Did all this flow from the slip of a scribe's pen, a Latin pun? We are surely right to think of the shift to *stella* rather as having been insisted upon by a ground swell of popular etymology. That is to say, if there was any slip of a medieval pen, it was also, and primarily, an unconscious 'Freudian slip'.

The Portuguese sailed into the Indian Ocean and Pacific under the starry sign of *Sancta Maria*, or the Virgin Mary, whose name still figures among the Portuguese vocables of the Pacific languages. The most vivid example of its marooning known to me is in Malay, in which the cannon, that chief weapon of early colonialism, is *mariam*, 'taken evidently, though unconsciously', wrote Crawfurd in 1852, 'from the Portuguese name of "the Holy Virgin"'. The transference of meaning Virgin–cannon is surprising; the broad association of the two is less so. The name of the Virgin was frequently invoked in battle as one of the most commonly used 'field words' distinguishing an army from its opponent. In the Thirty Years War, for example, the watchword of Tilly's army at the Battle of Leipzig was 'Sancta Maria' and to this day, in modern Beirut, Christian militiamen carry 'pictures of the Virgin Mary on the butts of their M-16 rifles' (Robert Fisk, *Independent* Magazine, 1990).

The echoically derived *mariam* is a dreadful comment on the unholy alliance of imperial conquest with religious belief: the Malays associated the Christianity of the *matamoros* with their weapons of war. *Mariam* is also evidence of the violent culture shock of empire, a shock which worked both ways. It was felt not only by the subject, colonized peoples but by their conquerors, too (see for example the Lexicon, **Cannon**, (3)). The early colonizers went, under the Virgin's protection, intending to convert and if necessary kill; but amidst all the nameless newness of the Tropics, what they found lying in wait for them, and what they returned with, were images of Venus, or more precisely, a pagan, sensual experience for which 'Venus' was the readiest semantic coefficient. In the expansion of the European empires the empire of the senses was also expanded; so were the boundaries of Babel, as languages collided and merged in new permutations.

In *Os Lusíadas* we see this unconscious subversion of the Christian outlook in action. In the 'Venus' episodes of the poem, such as the sensuous and obliquely erotic 'Isle of Love' episode, it is not the fact that Camões was imitating Virgil that strikes the reader so much as the sense that something is going on in the poem of which the poet seems more or less unaware; he is telling us one thing, but somehow conveying another. As with Botticelli's painting, so it is with *Os Lusíadas*. In Camões's powerful, and powerfully sensuous, descriptions of a world that the Christian ethic had penetrated only thinly, or not at all, we can never quite shake off the uneasy suspicion, even when we are on the Isle of Love, that his Venus is really the Virgin in disguise, or rather, the Virgin in nothing at all.

Psychologists will find nothing surprising in this shadowy identification, this trespassing over the boundaries of the sexy and the sacred. It is a psychological commonplace, and a commonplace, too, in the experience of men away at sea, or at war, or both, in danger far from their wives and homes. It is a commonplace, perhaps, of the male psyche.

Men have always taken with them to war a dual vision of womankind, the cherished private photograph, on the one hand, and the pin-up on the other. The photograph will be of the wife or girlfriend, the girl next door, Penelope waiting patiently for Odysseus. She may equally be identified with Vera Lynn or the Virgin Mary. The pin-up, on the other hand, will embody – whether as Betty Grable, Calypso or Circe, Samantha Fox, or Venus – a sex-starved, arguably 'whorish' vision.

The uneasy pagan–Christian composite 'Venus' of *Os Lusíadas* is a composite of homesickness and sexual longing, of a chaste, faithful, protective wife (the protectress of Portugal), and a woman of supposed infinite sensuality and sexual 'availability'.

A recent book of travels in the Pacific (1992) was aptly called *Transit of Venus*. Ostensibly, the title refers to the purpose of Cook's first voyage of 1769, which was to study the transit of Venus across the sun. In the event, astronomy was upstaged by the astonished discovery of Polynesian sexuality. Cook would devote only a couple of lines of his journal to observation of the planet, and 'the real Venus observed', remarks the book's author, Julian Evans, 'was in those mythical anecdotes, of freedom and desire, that men are always astonished to relate about women'.

More evidence for the view that in the overflowing life-forms of the Tropics the Europeans found echoes of myth and metaphors for unrestrained sexual experience comes from 1768, when, the year before Cook, the French explorer de Bougainville landed on the Pacific island of Otaheite, or Tahiti. If de Bougainville had had his historical way, Tahiti would today be known by the name he gave it, 'New Cythera', another thinly veiled reference to Venus which may strike the historian of taste as unremarkable, conventionally of its time; to the student of metaphor, however, its conventionality – almost, we could say, its *inevitability* – is the most interesting thing about it.

De Bougainville additionally compared 'New Cythera' – with its guiltless sexuality and (from the European perspective) its unnamed lushness – with prelapsarian 'golden' Eden. Today, 'New Cythera' is a historical curiosity; but as witness to that once-perceived 'namelessness', there is the flamboyant tropical shrub still called 'bougainvillaea'.

'New Cythera' further illustrates the momentum behind the generically allusive Venus-metaphor, and its psychological range, all the way from the subtlest of sublimations to the smoking-room story. Commentators on *Os Lusíadas* have tried to identify the original model for the 'Isle of Love'. As metaphor, however, it and 'New Cythera' are effectively identical, both with one another and with 'Venus'. The terms resume an aspect of the European experience of the 'South Seas', and, on the psychological plane, they name a place in the mind, that mythical male resort of uninhibited sexual desire which sailors dream about at sea and brag about on shore-leave:

'Twas on the good ship Venus
By God you should have seen us
The figurehead was a woman in bed . . .

The garbled two-way traffic, eastwards and westwards, of words, ideas, and things associated with 'the Virgin' and 'Venus', was central among the millions of meanings which colonialism, like metaphor itself, traded, confused and 'carried over' the discrete categories of rational thought, the boundaries both of language and the world.

PART TWO
Lexicon

A

Abortionist 'Angel maker' (French: *faiseur d'anges*). 'Louise was apparently planning, rather precipitately, to visit a *faiseur d'anges* – an abortionist – in some distant town' – Francis Steegmuller, in a footnote to a letter of 1846 from Gustave Flaubert to his mistress Louise Colet. It is paralleled by the German, *Engelmacher*, although one dictionary (Cassell's) defines this, mistakenly I think, as 'baby-farmer', i.e. a wet nurse. It certainly means 'abortionist' in '... "he's got fewer scruples than a backstreet angelmaker" ...' from Philip Kerr's *March Violets*, set in 1930s Berlin.

Abuse Modern Greek for a car is *ámaxi*, formerly a horse-cab. *Ámaxâs* is a coachman or cab-driver. Abuse is *exàmaxís*, 'out of the cab', so associating it with an enraged and abusive taxi-driver.

Adam's apple In Greek it is *karoúdi*, a walnut.

Adultery In Greek it is *klepsigamia* (thief union, or thief marriage), and in Papua New Guinea Pidgin it is *plei nogut* (play no good).

Aids New transferred names for Aids are still in the making, but the pattern so far seems to correspond exactly with the transferential naming of other dreaded diseases that have preceded it (see **Chinaman/Chinese** (3) for leprosy, and see **Syphilis**). Thus, while in Africa generally Aids is known from the drastic weight-loss that is a feature of the disease as 'Slim', it also has local names identifying the disease with another country, even suggesting that it originated there.

In Tanzania, for example, a name for Aids is 'Juliana', after the name of a dress fabric worn by women in neighbouring Uganda.

Aircrew, air hostess Papua New Guinea Pidgin for a pigeon, *balus*, is also an aeroplane. An aircrew, or any member of it, is *boskru bilong balus* (boat's crew – i.e. sailor – belong aeroplane).

Airport The pidgin *peles balus*, or 'pigeon place [or homeland]' is refreshingly different. 'There is, currently, a stylistic and emotional Esperanto of airport lounges, a vulgate identically inexpressive from Archangel to Tierra del Fuego' (George Steiner, *After Babel*). The English words or phrases airport, no problem, passport, hotel, telephone, bar, soda, cigarette, all more or less associated with air travel, were in a list of seventeen universally used English words compiled by *The Economist* in 1986.

Albatross, alcatraz The name of the albatross testifies to the quasi-mythic confusion over the identity of species before Linnaeus – 'confusion', that is, if you look at the situation from a Linnaean point of view. Nor did it magically end overnight with the publication (in 1735) of the *De Systema Naturae* of Linnaeus.

In 1795, for example, the French naturalist François Levaillant dismissed the condor as a traveller's tale: 'It would appear that each traveller, having wished to speak of the condor, all have seen it; some in Peru, others in the South Seas, others still in Africa, etc.; finally, one has encountered it everywhere.' The condor was not a traveller's tale, however. It existed, and, under threat, it still does. Here is an example, though, of how hard it was, where species were concerned, to disentangle fact and fiction two centuries ago.

Another example is the penguin. In *William Wilson*, Edgar Allan Poe has a chapter called 'Albatross and Penguins'. The penguins in Poe stand tall enough to be mistaken in the evening twilight for men. No one would mistake a penguin for a man in any kind of light – it isn't tall enough. But the now-extinct bird called the great auk was a lot taller, and its name was penguin (the Celtic *pen gwyn*, 'white head').

'Penguin' has not only been popularly transferred to another bird, but to another hemisphere: the greak auk was a bird of the northern hemisphere, the penguin is a bird of the southern. Poe's bird was the great auk.

'Penguin', then, continued to be used generically rather than specifically well into the nineteenth century, and so did 'albatross'. The English 'albatross', French and Spanish *albatros*, is said to be formed from the Latin *albus*, white, and *alcatraz*, Spanish for the frigate bird (which is black). So 'albatross', which English seamen once called the 'Cape Sheep' (after its whiteness, its size, and the Cape of Good Hope), literally means 'white frigate bird'.

As a matter of record, no albatross is entirely white, not even the great white albatross, whose wings are mottled with brown. And there is even a species called the black albatross. The logo of the now-defunct publishing imprint, Albatross Books, which in the late forties competed with Penguin (the battle of the books, often, is a battle of the birds), was a black bird with white wing-tips.

An *alcatraz* is also a pelican, presumably the bird it originally named, since Spanish gets *alcatraz* from Portuguese *alcatruz*, 'bucket'; in Arabic, the pelican is *sakka*, a water-carrier (the association is with the bucket-like lower half of the pelican's beak, which holds more than its belly can). And the pelican, large and white like the albatross, is also called a sheep, not of the cape but of the sky (the Hindi, *gaghan-bher*).

Finally, *alcatraz* names yet another high-flier, the gannet, or solan goose, which in French is colloquially *le fol*, the madman (from its foolish habit of perching on ships' rails, where it is easily caught; it is foolish in its nesting habits, too).

Buried in all this is a mini-history of navigation and empire. From the first great European navigators of the early colonial period, the Portuguese, the word *alcatraz* metaphorically used to mean pelican evidently started on Spanish lips to mean something like 'high-flying, ship-following, scavenging bird'; then Spanish, with French and English following in its wake, apparently singled out the most impressive of those birds and turned the '*alca-*' to '*alba-*'. One doesn't imagine someone solemnly sitting down and putting *alcatraz* and *albus* together. Probably the name came from a casual merging together of *alcatraz* and the Latin *albatus*, 'clad in white'. It may even be that *albatus* is a stronger candidate than *alcatraz* as the immediate forefather of 'albatross'. But who knows?

It was probably the pelican, but it might have been any or all of these various bird-species, that gave the name to the island, later the high-security prison, of Alcatraz, in San Francisco Bay. Alcatraz was strictly for the birds, and to break out of it one needed to be a bird-man. The prison's name, to Spanish ears, carries other echoes – of *alcahaz*, a bird-cage, and *alcázar*, a castle.

The two most famous albatrosses in literature, Coleridge's in *The Rhyme of the Ancient Mariner* and Baudelaire's in *L'Albatros*, both date from a period in which the albatross, along with many other species, had yet to settle down into the space reserved for it by science, and both poems draw a certain strength from this mythic vagueness, this atmosphere of floating hearsay. It is doubtful if a poet today, when the albatross in flight is shown in television close-up, could get away with Baudelaire's pure white, dandified albatross – which (or whom) Baudelaire presents as his own kind of captured bird-man of *alcatraz*. He is thought to have been influenced by Poe's image in *William Wilson* of the dandy-like penguins protecting the high-flying poet, the albatross.

Coleridge in his poem was inspired by an account of 1719 of the shooting, by a melancholy and superstitious sailor, of 'a disconsolate black Albitross' [*sic*] that hovered about his ship and seemed to bring it bad luck. It's always possible, of course, that it was a black albatross, but it's far more likely to have been a frigate-bird. Coleridge, perhaps wisely, nowhere in his poem specifies what colour his bird is.

Alcohol   See **Drink**, **drunk**, **Minum**.

Algebra   The Spanish *algebrista* means both an algebraist and a setter of broken bones.

Alley-way   'Bowel' is a metaphor, through French *boyau*, from Latin *botellus*, a sausage. The tangled interior byways of a town or city are likewise its 'bowels'. *Boyau* also has the idiomatic meaning of a narrow alley-way or a communication trench in warfare, exactly paralleling the Chinese expression, 'sheep's intestines', for a complex interlocking system of narrow, winding pathways. *Boyau*, addition-ally, is the inner tube of a bicycle tyre.

Alphabet   (1) The Spanish *cristus* is the cross printed at the beginning of the alphabet – as indication that all book-learning is *ad maiorem Dei gloriam*, or AMDG, 'to the greater glory of God'. By extension, *cristus* is the alphabet itself, and *no saber el cristus* is to be illiterate or, less kindly, pig-ignorant.

(2) Latin for the alphabet, or ABC, is *elementa*, which, it has been suggested (although Müller doubts 'whether in real earnest'), derives from the consecutive letters LMN.

American   Only a subtle difference of stress differentiates the Greek for an American, *Amerikanós* from the sometimes envied, sometimes despised Greek-American, *Amerikános*.

Angel   See **Abortionist**, **Giraffe**.

Annihilation   See **Sausage**.

Apple   See **Block** (2), **Eye**.

Arctic   See **Great Bear**.

Asparagus   Popular etymology domesticates obscure words of foreign origin, unfriendly on the eye and complex of pronunciation, and turns them into user-friendly words which offer the additional bonus that they tend to explain themselves and their origins (usually wrongly) in mini-story form. This is the English of greengrocer's shops, where walnuts are 'wallnuts', coconuts once were 'cokers', *hautbois* strawberries were 'hotboys', and so on.

'Asparagus' doesn't come naturally in English, but it persists. It is, and was even when the Romans used it, a Graeco-Roman word, Greek in its basic elements, but Latin in its '-*us*' termination.

Even the learned Mr T. S. Eliot had to confess that, although his theatre cat's real name was Asparagus, '. . . That's such a fuss / To pronounce, that we usually call him just Gus.' And for centuries the genius of the English language has been begging that it be called something closer to home.

As far back as 1791 John Walker could write 'The corruption of the word into *sparrow-grass* is so general that *asparagus* has an air of stiffness and pedantry' ('grass' abbreviates 'sparrow-grass', and is not a separate laid-back Americanism as is sometimes supposed). By all the usual rules 'asparagus' in English should have died the death by now, but like grass itself it makes its regular seasonal appearances, 'being meanwhile constantly restored', writes Bloomfield, 'by those who know Latin'.

Interestingly, the Roman etymologist Varro was uncertain whether the word was Roman or Greek in origin, but with his usual confidence he gave an etymology for it: '"Asparagus shoots" because they are gathered from "rough" [*aspera*] bushes and the stems themselves are rough, not smooth.' Varro was fond of these rough places. He traced *apri*, wild boar, from there too, probably correctly (although the asp is a better candidate); but with 'asparagus' he was almost certainly wrong. One would expect the word to have metaphorical origins, but if so, no one seems to know what they were.

I did once meet a Dutch asparagus-grower, however, who insisted it was from words for the sprinkling of holy water (the 'spray' or 'sprinkle' brushlike-effect of the asparagus shoots when either growing or cut into bunches). This is promising if inconclusive territory. The immediate problem, of course, is that the word 'asparagus' was in existence as such before the Christian Church. Somewhere at the back of that Dutch grower's mind must have been Psalm 51: 7, 'Purge me with hyssop, and I shall be clean: wash me, and I shall be whiter than snow' (King James Bible). In Latin it is *Asperges me hyssopo et mundabor*.

From the psalm in Latin we have the English name of the church implement, the 'aspergill', 'a kind of brush used to sprinkle holy water' (*Oxford Dictionary*). That is Church Latin, but with antecedents in classical Latin, for example *aspergere*, to sprinkle or *aspergo*, a sprinkling. From this came the English 'aspersions', slanders which today are 'cast' but were originally 'besprinkled'.

Aspergo is a better candidate as a forebear of 'asparagus' than Varro's *aspera*, if they too are not related. And it may be, indeed, that we are back in spicy, spiky territory (see pages 99–101); the great lavender or spike was once called *aspic*.

The Latin of Psalm 51 produced different results in Spanish, in which the expression of the idea 'aspergill' owes nothing to the *asperges* (or asparagus) but everything to the hyssop. It should be made clear that the hyssop was not itself the purgative but the sprinkler, or aspergill, with which it was administered: its twigs were used for sprinkling in Jewish rites (which of course pre-dated Christianity). Logically enough, then, the Spanish *hisopo* names not only the hyssop itself but the aspergillum or any sprinkler, and in Latin America it is a paintbrush.

In Paraguay, somewhat surreally, *hisopo* has the extra meaning of 'dishcloth', which not only conjures up pictures of the Doom family in *Cold Comfort Farm* doing their washing-up with a small bundle of twigs, but gives a new meaning to 'Purge me with hyssop, and I shall be clean: wash me, and I shall be whiter than snow'. Logically, the brand name *hisopo* for washing-up liquid or a detergent should go down a bomb in Spain, or anyway in Paraguay.

Astronomy, Terms in See **Great Bear**, **Milky Way**, **Pole Star**, **Southern Cross**.

August See **September**.

Avocado pear In Jamaica it is a 'bottleneck' (from its shape).

B

Baboon Facetious Afrikaans slang for the baboon is *Adoons*, or the beautiful Greek god Adonis. A stupid person is also an *Adoons*.

Baby The Greek *drákos* is a dragon, an ogre, and an unchristened baby.
  See also **Eye**.

Backside (1) A person's backside, the American slang 'bosom of the pants', or 'parking place', in German is 'the four letters of the alphabet' (*die vier Buchstaben*). A euphemistic reference, like the British World War I army slang term for an unpleasant character, *four-letter man*, i.e. a SHIT. After 1918 it was taken to refer to HOMO, a homosexual. Four-letter words, in Jamaican English, were 'forty-shilling words', from the fine once levied for speaking them in public.
  (2) In Jamaican English, *bunchy*, which is also used of bunches of bananas.
  (3) Almost inevitably misunderstandings between whites and natives surrounded this word in the pidgin language of the South Seas. The natives got *baksait* from the whites, but adapted it to mean 'back of' (as in 'go to the back' or 'at the back'), not buttocks, which were *as*.
  See also **Dancing** (*fandango*), **Home**.

Bad The German adjective *schlecht*, meaning bad, originally meant good.

Bag and baggage In German *mit Kind und Kegel*, 'which today means, word for word, "with child and ninepin"; – *Kegel* is really here an otherwise lost word meaning "bastard"' (Bloomfield).

Kegel is also a cone in geometry. In the Austrian novelist Thomas Bernhard's *Correction*, the house which Roithamer is building for his sister is described as a *Kegel*; translators differ as between 'cone' and 'skittle'. But the word also endows the house with a sense of illegitimacy, and one critic (Robert Craft) remarks that, 'the latent incest motive cannot be understood without the sexual symbolism of the "female", Matriushka-doll, skittle'.

Bernhard's character Roithamer, incidentally, is modelled on the philosopher Wittgenstein, who designed a house in Vienna for his sister.

Baker's dozen (i.e. thirteen) In Spanish, *docena de(l) fraile*, friar's, or monk's dozen. The religious orders in the Middle Ages seemed to have enjoyed special privileges where bread was concerned, such as the bread made from the finest flour called in France 'canon's bread'. Also, monks or friars were often the bakers.

See also **Friday the thirteenth**.

Balaclava helmet In French *un passe-montagne*, or a 'pass [over the] mountain'. In Spanish, *pasamontañas*.

Bald, bald-headed (1) In 1883 a certain Herr Huebel, an administrator of the Royal German consulate in Apia, Samoa, included the following among locally gathered examples of pidgin usage which he sent to the German comparative linguist, Hugo Scuchardt: '*You no save* [i.e. savvy] *that fellow white man cocanut belong him no grass?*' or 'Don't you know that baldheaded white man?' Scuchardt commented: 'Cocanut for "head" was originally facetious . . . However it has become integrated like the jocular metaphor *testa* in Gallic and Italian vulgar Latin.' (The Latin *testa*, meaning earthen vessel, pot, pitcher, urn, is the origin of the Italian (*testa*) and French (*tête*) for 'head'.)

(2) Of US slang terms the most original is 'like heaven', because on a bald head, as in heaven, there is no parting.

(3) The Spanish *clara*, the white of an egg, also means a bald patch and, colloquially, a short interval of fair weather on a rainy day. The

Chilean Spanish, *luquete*, is an unploughed patch of land, and a bald patch.

See also **Beard** (3), **Octopus**, **Office, In the** (squid). For more on grass, or *gras*, see **Hair** (2).

Ballot box   French: *une urne* (primary meaning, 'a funerary urn'). To go to the polls is *aller aux urnes*. Also in Italian (*urna*, and *andare alle urne*), and Spanish, *urna*. The urn, incidentally, got its name when the Latin *urina* still meant only 'water' and not specifically 'urine'. *Urinare* was 'to be plunged into water', like an urn, and a *urinator* was a diver.

The Spanish *cántaro*, a 'large, narrow-mouthed pitcher', is also the 'vessel into which votes are put'.

Barbecue   See **Confusion**.

Barge   (1) The Spanish *chata* means both a river barge and a bedpan, which a barge rather resembles.

(2) French: a mud-barge or mud-dredger is a slut (*marie-salope*).

Basket   'Don't put all your Basques in one exit', goes the double pun on the proverb. But half of it may be semantically implicit *in* the proverb. In 'basket', from the French *basquette*, is the possible hint that the basket is so called because it was perceived to be typically Basque. The origin of *basquette* is officially unknown – the 'Basque' etymology is not in the French dictionaries; but I think of the basketwork-bats that the Basque game of *pelota* is played with, and I wonder.

That is the least of my wonderings, not so much about the *word* 'basket' as the *idea* of a basket. When I lived in Greece I knew an eccentric old farmer whose nickname was *Kouroúnas*, from *kouroúna*, crow. *Kouroúnas* always wore black, and always had a wicker basket containing a few eggs, or other produce – sometimes twigs for kindling, like a crow carrying his own nest with him. Thus his nickname. It has a parallel in Greek myth. The god Apollo, called away to Delphi, gave a crow the task of keeping an eye on the girl he left behind him. The girl's name was Coronis.

The crow's flight is proverbially straight, but the crow itself is associated with crookedness. The ground-idea behind 'Coronis' – from Greek *koróni* – is that of something bent, crooked, like crow's feet or a crowbar (some commentators on *koróni* refer to the crow's hooked beak). From *koróni* we also get *corona*, crown. The earliest crowns were not of gold or silver; they were wreaths, garlands, chaplets plaited from slender, pliable branches. Early crowns looked like birds' nests, or baskets.

But back to the old man, *Kouroúnas*. To translate his eccentricity into French, he was a *corbeau* (crow) with a *corbeille* (basket). There is no official link between *corbeau* (from the Latin *corvus*, a raven) and *corbeille* (from *corbis* and its diminutive *corbula*, little wicker basket). I am kicking against the etymological pricks. My problem is that I *expect* there to be a metaphorical link between baskets and birds' nests, and *expect* that link to be reflected in etymology. A rudimentary peasant basket looks like a crow's nest. We can connect crows and crowns – any metaphorical links there may be between nest-building and basket-making are more tenuous. If the one didn't actually inspire the other, however, surely the more or less fanciful *resemblance* between the two cannot have escaped the early basket-makers?

A crow's nest is a 'congeries', which in its original Latin meaning is a heap of wood. The *Oxford Dictionary* relates it to the verb 'to congest'. The Latin *congestus*, a collecting, a gathering and heaping together, was especially used of birds building their nests, and Russian has a verb – *vit* – which is used in the sense of coiling, curling, winding, or, more specifically, of birds circling or nest-building.

Latin *gerrae* – wattled twigs, or wickerwork – are associated with 'congeries'. It is tempting to suggest a possible connection also with *grex*, a flock, and that interwoven mass of people, that crowd, or congeries, which we still call a 'congregation'. Even if we resist that temptation, however, we have the legitimate etymological connection *congerro*, a companion or playmate, which is a metaphor from *gerrae*, and in the background the Greek *gerron*, wickerwork or anything made from it, especially a shield.

In this cluster of words we see the ghost of a metaphor – a perceived connection between birds' nests and wickerwork, in the first instance, and then between wickerwork and the woven fingers of friendship.

Bat   (1) In French a 'bald mouse' (*chauve-souris*).

(2) The nickname of the South African Parachute (or *Parabat*) Battalion is 'the Bats'. The tower they practise jumping from is the *Aapkas*, the ape-box or ape-cupboard.

See also **Box** (*liklik bilak bokis*).

Beard   (1) In Italy a beggar or tramp is simply 'a beard' (*barbone*).

(2) Also in Italian a poodle is 'a beard' (*barbone*) or 'little beard' (*barboncino*).

(3) In Jamaica, a Rastafarian who does not wear the customary Rastafarian beard and/or dreadlocks is a 'clean-faced man' or 'baldhead'.

Beauty   (1) The Italian *vago* is beautiful with the additional sense of 'vague, ill-defined, wandering, erring, ambiguous'. Leopardi's use of it is spot on when he writes in *Le Ricordanze* (Memories) of the '*vaghe stelle dell'Orsa*', 'the beautiful [or wandering, or vague] stars of the Bear [the constellation, the Great Bear]'.

(2) In Russian,

by the word *krasotá* [beauty] we mean only that which pleases the sight. And though latterly people have begun to speak of 'an ugly deed', or of 'beautiful music', it is not good Russian.

A Russian of the common folk, not knowing foreign languages, will not understand you if you tell him that a man who has given his last coat to another, or done anything similar, has acted 'beautifully', that a man who has cheated another has done an 'ugly' action, or that a song is 'beautiful' ... forty years ago, when I was young, the expressions 'beautiful music' and 'ugly actions' were not only unusual but incomprehensible.

(Tolstoy, *What Is Art?*, 1898)

(3) The Japanese *wabi* is the flaw or irregularity that enhances the elegance of the whole. *Shibui* is the beauty of ageing.

(4) *Kolleh* (Yiddish) – 'every bride is beautiful, every mother's child is beautiful, every lumpy ashtray your child brings back from summer camp is beautiful' (Leo Rosten, *The Joys of Yiddish*).

Bedbug   See **Chinaman/Chinese** (3) and **Office, In the** (drawing-pin).

Bedpan   See **Barge** (1) and **Pelvis**.

Beef (the meat)   *Bullamakau* (Papua New Guinea Pidgin). Scuchardt: 'The origin of *bullamacow* is anecdotal. It is said that one of the early seafarers, Cook I believe, had left "a bull and a cow" on one of the islands and that these words conflated as one with the meaning "beef".' A British consul in Fiji, Edgar Layard, reported hearing *small fellow bullamacow* used of mutton.

Beggar, tramp   See **Beard**.

Belong   This word and its variants *bolong, belung*, is used in Papua New Guinea Pidgin as an all-purpose possessive. In context it has a comical ring to the European ear. We might wish to patronize, but the real joke is on the colonizing Europeans with their deeply ingrained sense of possession and property, who imposed this concept of 'belonging'. Scuchardt comments: '"Mine" and "yours" played no role between master and slave, but the word *belong* was certainly among the first and most frequently repeated words perceived by Oceanic peoples from the mouths of the Whites.'
    See also **Fight, White man**.

Beret   See **Lazybones**.

Berries   French slang for berries is *œufs de homard* (lobster's eggs), the exact reverse of the English idiom whereby a hen lobster carrying her eggs is described as 'berried' or 'in berry'.

Beyond, Back of   In German *wo sich Fuchs und Hase gute Nacht sagen* (where fox and hare bid one another good-night) describes a remote, isolated place, which the French call *au diable* ('to the devil').

Bicycle   *Wiliwil* (Papua New Guinea Pidgin): The verb 'to cycle' is *ron long wiliwil* ('to run on wheel-wheel').
    See also (for bicycle tyre) **Alley-way**.

★

Bidet   The word entered English from French. Before the invention of the bidet, the primary meaning of *bidet* was 'pony'.

Bill (in a restaurant)   Spanish *dolorosa,* which as an adjective means 'sorrowful, painful'.

Billiards   Spanish: *guerra*, or war. The Russian *blúza*, from the French *blouse*, a blouse, is a pocket in billiards.

Binoculars   See **Twins** (4).

Bird   The Eskimo for 'young bird', *aitortungiark*, means literally 'beak open'.
   See also **Voice**.

Birth certificate   Age-paper (Jamaican dialect).

Birthmark   In German, *das Muttermal*, 'mother-sign' or 'mother-mark'. In French a birthmark can be *une envie*, which apart from its primary meanings of 'desire' and 'envy' also corresponds to the English 'agnail' or 'hangnail', a small piece of skin hanging loose near a nail. *Envie* meaning 'birthmark' thus has the sense of a deformity of the skin. But it also happens to break down into *en vie*, or 'in life'.

Bishop (in chess)   See **French Revolution** (1).

Black Maria   (1) In France *un panier à salade*, literally 'a salad basket'. The basket is the wire one – like the cage in which those in the Black Maria are contained – in which washed salad leaves are drained, but *salade* in French also has the sense of 'a bad lot' or 'bad business'.
   (2) In Germany the Black Maria is *die grüne Minna* or *der grüne Heinrich*, the green Minna or green Henry. *Schwarze Marie* – Black Maria – was the German name for a heavy naval gun of World War I. Doubtless from this, 'Black Maria' was the British soldier's name for any big German high-explosive shell, or its explosion, until 1916, when 'coal box' came to be preferred (because the shell, exploding, sent a torrent of black mud into the air).

(3) In Jamaica 'John-Crow Jacket', because of the black-painted van and the bird's black plumage.

(4) In Greek, *kloúva*, which is also a dog-catcher's van. *Klouví* means 'cage'. *Jaula*, cage in Spanish, is also familiarly a police cell or 'lock-up', which in French slang is *un ours*, a bear. In Puerto Rico, *jaula* is the Black Maria that takes you to the cell.

Black market An archaic Spanish term for the 'BM' is *straperlo*, being a combination of Strauss, Perez, and Lopez, originators of a gambling game in which the house always wins.

Blas See **Gas**.

Block (of houses) (1) French: *Pâte de maisons*.

(2) Spanish both for a block of houses and a city, town, or village square is *manzana*, whose primary meaning is 'apple'. The double meaning of *manzana* is thought to be the probable origin of New York's nickname – the Big Apple.

It was once suggested that New York should be called by a name incorporating elements of the names of all its boroughs: 'Brimaquonx.' It didn't catch on.

Bloody hell! Perhaps the most baroque ways of saying this are in French Canadian, '*Tabernacle à deux étages sans un escalier de sauvetage, hostis!*' (Two-storey tabernacle without a fire-escape, communion wafer!) and '*Par le pis-pis du Pape coupé en tranches et frit en poêle!*' (By the Pope's penis cut into slices and fried in a frying pan!). The communion wafer is also a feature of Spanish swearing (*hostia*).

See also **Hell, Go to**.

Blotting paper See **Office, In the**.

Bluestocking See **Chatterbox** (3), **Prostitute** (3).

Blue tit In Cornish, *pen-paly*, or velvet head.

Boar See **Ice** (3).

Boaster   Papua New Guinea Pidgin *bikmaus* (bigmouth) also means 'codfish'. In the film of *Mary Poppins* Julie Andrews tells the little boy, Michael, when he gapes at her, 'Don't be a codfish' – the same 'bigmouth' idea.

In Australia the verb 'to boast' is virtually unknown. An Australian boaster is a *skiter* (from Scottish). In France a boaster is *un mangeur de petits enfants* (an eater of little children) or a *m'as-tu vu*, a 'did you see me'.

Body odour   In South American slang *grajo*, a rook (the bird).

Bogyman   See **Coconut** (4), **Devil**.

Book   The Norwegian *bokflom*, or 'book flood', is a standard term for the annual deluge of books published in Norway just before Christmas.

See also **Box**.

Bottle   In the political demonstrations of summer 1990, Chinese students demonstrated against China's elder statesman, Deng Xiao-ping, by breaking hundreds of little bottles. Deng was born Dung Xixiang – he later changed his name to Xiaoping. In one etymology, *xiaoping* means 'little bottle' (*xiao* is 'little'). In another etymology, *ping* means 'peaceful'.

Bottle-opener   See **Can-opener**.

Bowler hat   French: a melon (*melon*; also *chapeau melon*, or 'melon hat'). Spanish slang for a bowler is *pongo*, a mushroom or fungus.

Box   In Afrikaans, the puff-ball mushroom is colloquially *oumeidsnuifdoos*. It is a perfectly horrible word, a product of apartheid whose literal meaning is 'old coloured woman's snuffbox'. But it is also horribly accurate. When it is ripe, the puff-ball encases millions of seeds which are released like a cloud of dust – or snuff – when the mushroom's outer casing is broken. The puff-ball 'with its dark brown contents . . . recalls a snuffbox . . . used by old native women'

(Smith, *South African Plants*, 1966), and it is also known in South African English as 'ape's snuff', 'devil's snuff', or 'monkey bomb'. The dark brown recalls, as well as snuff, the old woman's skin colouring.

The word's accuracy goes further – some might think too far. Later in the season, when it is overripe, the puff-ball's dusty contents deliquesce into slime, and then it is reminiscent, not of dry and dusty snuff, but rather of the other, slang significance of *doos* (box), which is 'vagina'. 'Box' in American slang also possesses this double meaning, whose origin presents something of a puzzle, as does its parallel existence as *doos* in Afrikaans.

'Box' to refer to the vagina and, by extension, to a woman, has a dry, functional, dismissive ring, and it is in that faintly contemptuous sense, I think, that the word is now used or understood.

Ask around (and hope to be invited back). Some people will suggest that box to mean 'woman' must be from another American usage, box to mean 'guitar', after the similarity of the woman's shape to the guitar's. Others will say it's the other way round – that the guitar is called a 'box' because a woman is (but an accordion, or 'squeeze-box', is also a box). Most, however, will speculate vaguely that box to mean 'vagina' or 'woman' must have something to do with the box being a receptacle, with the additional sense of disposability: the box, after all, is what one throws away when one has extracted its contents. And indeed, origins apart, this is the sense in which 'box' today is used as well as understood.

Etymologically, then, 'box' in this sense would be 'jocular'. But it's not much of a joke, is it? Nor is it metaphorically satisfying. When one visualizes and imagines in more detail one is in fact at a loss to find anything at all in common between the range of associations conjured up by 'vagina' and those of the usual sense of 'box' to mean a hard, rectilinear, sharply cornered container.

'Box' in this latter sense is a metonym, a particular instance employed as a generic name. Not all boxes are made of boxwood. It is a metonym of very long standing. Quintilian in the first century remarked that caskets were called *pyxides* (i.e. made of boxwood) 'regardless of their material'. Through the German *Büchse*, box, *Buchs*, box-tree, and *Buche*, beech-tree, 'box' is related to 'book' (beech-bark was the material of primitive books; we still talk of a book having 'leaves'). French has borrowed this English 'box' to mean a garage, but there the metaphor does satisfy: a box is just what a car's garage is, but it isn't a woman. Words, however, may acquire an independent momentum which pulls perceptual psychology in its wake, and behind this offensive 'box' to mean 'woman', I believe, lies a now-forgotten metaphor based on a further meaning of 'box' which has fallen by the wayside.

I suggest that the slang meaning of 'box' didn't originate as a bar-room vulgarity but as a piece of name-poetry. Uprooted from that poetry, set adrift from its metaphorical origins, the sense of a word that may have begun as clannish but not necessarily disrespectful male code has been beached on a false metaphorical correlation with the surviving, primary sense of 'box', and so come to seem an ugly and insulting obscenity.

Dictionaries of American English date 'box' to mean 'vagina' from its first recorded published use in 1954. This interpretation tends to be reinforced by a look at the explicit and exhaustive *American Thesaurus of Slang*, published in 1952, which gives a number of meanings for 'box' (guitar, accordion, etc.) but not this one.

An earlier, hidden and unofficial history of the word is however suggested by *The Book of Pidgin English* by John Murphy. It was first published in 1943, eleven years before the earliest date given in the American dictionaries.

The Papua New Guinean Pidgin English equivalent of 'box' is *bokis*, clearly a version of 'box' introduced by American and/or English settlers during the colonial period. In PNG Pidgin, *bokis* is a box of any kind, including a coffin. It is also 'a square, box-like fish about nine inches long which inflates itself when danger is imminent'. A *bilak bokis*, or black box, is a flying fox (although Todd, 1984, suggests that *bokis* also means 'fox') and a *liklik bilak bokis*, or little black box, is a bat. Crucially (and this tends to knock Todd's 'fox' on the head), *bokis* is also a term for 'the external female genitals'.

Comically, *bokis* with its range of meanings could give rise to some unfortunate misunderstandings between colonials and their houseboys. Murphy felt it necessary to advise colonial administrators and others in New Guinea and the Melanesian islands in the 1940s: 'If you are referring to a suitcase or a trunk belonging to a woman don't say *bokis bolong misis*. Similarly a woman will not refer to *bokis bolong mi*. A man can refer to *bokis bolong mi* or *bokis bolong masta* with impunity.'

The native pidgin speakers did not independently and coincidentally evolve this additional significance of 'box' but took it over wholesale from the settlers. I also believe that the taboo slang sense of the Afrikaans *doos* was calqued, or copied, into that language after acquaintance with the American (or, almost certainly, American-English) double meaning of 'box'.

A Dictionary of American English (1936) gives as a secondary meaning of 'box': 'A cavity made in the trunk of a tree, usually a maple tree or pine, for collecting sap or turpentine.' The *Natural History of Florida* (1775) goes into more detail: 'A hole is cut in the tree on the side most exposed to the solar rays ... This hole is called a box, and the turpentine is dipped out of it.'

A 'box' in this sense resembled a deliquescent, overripe puff-ball mushroom. It was originally an English term. The *Oxford Dictionary* dates it from 1720. Today it has altogether died away, surviving only vestigially, I suggest, in the sense of 'box' to mean 'vagina'. It isn't at all surprising that this slang sense has been traced back officially only to 1954: my guess would be that it goes back a good deal further. 'Box' was doubly unlikely to surface in the dictionaries or anywhere in print – it was not only a taboo word but originally it belonged to what etymologists call 'cant', that is, 'the secret or peculiar language or jargon of a class, sect, or subject'.

In this instance, 'the class' was formed of timber workers, who during the imperial and colonial periods were particularly numerous in New Guinea and Melanesia. The natives learned their 'Sandalwood English' from these workers, whence, I suggest, the pidgin *bokis*.

Boxing-ring   See **Guitar**.

Brain   *Kru* (Papua New Guinea Pidgin) as well as brain means the vital meat of a seed which feeds the shoot, and the shoot itself. A mushroom is *kru bilong graun*, 'brain from the earth'.

Branch In Eskimo, the branch of a tree is also the flipper of a walrus, *issarutak*. An arresting metaphor, and a spot of local colour from the great white wastes. But 'branch' itself originally meant 'claw' or 'paw' (as in, for example, Late Latin *branca ursina*, 'bear's foot').

Brass hats In French, the big vegetables (*les grosses légumes*). A French military decoration is colloquially a 'banana' (*banane*), while in Greek *sardélla*, anchovy or sardine, is also familiarly the word for a military stripe, or chevron.

Brassière The French *brassière* was originally only a life-jacket. A strapless brassière is *un balconnet* (little balcony), and a prominent bosom is colloquially said to be *sur le balcon* (on the balcony).

Brave/brazen The Cameroons pidgin *drai ai* ('dry eye') when used of a man means 'brave', when used of a woman means 'brazen'. Also *trong ai* ('strong eye'), with the same meanings.

See also **Partridge**.

Breast See **Milk**.

Bribe, A (1) In Italian a bribe is the 'little envelope' (*la bustarella*) in which it is handed over. Also, a *tangente*.

(2) In Mexico and Central America, a bribe is a bite (*una mordida*).

(3) In French *un pot-de-vin* ('pot of wine').

(4) A bribe comes more cheaply in the Cameroons, where it is *smol wata* ('small water').

Bricklayer See **Rolling-pin**

British, British forces See **'I say . . . !'**, **Lobster**, **Menstruation** (1).

Brothel See **Foreigner** (2), **Prostitute** (2).

Brother (1) In Papua New Guinea Pidgin 'brother' and 'sister' are *barata* and *sista*, from the English. But it is more complicated than that. 'A woman's sister is her *barata* and her brother is her *sista*. On the other hand, a man's brother is his *barata* and his sister his *sista*. The terms . . . also include cousins. Cousins of the same sex are *barata*, of different sex – *sista*' (Murphy).

(2) 'In Malay the experiences which may be logically defined by us as "offspring of the same parents" are classed together, and for such an experience is used the word *sudara*. In English we form no such class; we form two classes, according to the sex, and speak of a *brother* or a *sister*. Now, it would be manifestly absurd to say that a Malay does not know his brother from his sister; it would be no less absurd, however, to say that English-speaking people are unable to form the general idea conveyed by the Malay word' (Bloomfield).

(3) German, similarly, although it has words for 'brother' (*Bruder*) and 'sister' (*Schwester*), also has *Geschwister* 'for experiences which in English would have to be analyzed into *brothers and sisters, brothers or sisters, brother and sister, brother and sisters, brothers and sister*, as the case might be' (Bloomfield). It has roughly the sense of the English church word 'brethren' which extreme feminists sometimes object to as sexist. *Geschwister* might make them think again.

Brum   The inhabitants of Birmingham, in the English Midlands or 'Black Country', affectionately refer to it as 'Brum'. Birmingham, in its heyday, was a thriving centre of industry, a hive of activity turning out the wide variety of products called, collectively, 'Brummagem'. It was noisy work: the 'Brum', formed from the root 'Birm-', catches that noise, what writers sometimes call the droning 'bourdon note' of a big industrial centre.

The French *bourdon* is a bumble-bee and, figuratively, the drone on a set of bagpipes. Church organs in English have 'bourdon-stops' to produce a deep droning noise. In German, the metaphorical basis for the same range of associations is not the bumble-bee, but the blue-bottle, called in German a *Brummer*. Thus, the big lorry called in English a 'juggernaut' and in French a *mastodonte de la route* (mastodon of the road) is called in German a *Brummer*, a bluebottle fly, which in a small room on a hot summer's day also produces a disproportionate noise.

In colloquial German, a hangover is a *Brummschädel*, a 'grumbling', 'growling', 'droning' or 'buzzing' skull.

Children teach us, or we teach children, that the noise of an engine is 'brum-brum', and one of my editors tells me that motor bikes were once known in South African English as 'brum-brum ponies'. In Carl Hiaasen's *Tourist Season* (1986) motor bikes are described as 'skull-buzzing'.

Brussels sprouts   In German they are 'rose-cabbages' (*Rosenkohl*).

Bullet   Bolivian slang for a bullet is *mora*, which otherwise and elsewhere in the Spanish-speaking world is only a mulberry or blackberry. The analogy seems to be not just with the berry's shape but the resemblance between the colour of its juice and the blood which the bullet spills. In Chile, *mora* is blood sausage or black pudding (by analogy, again, with mulberry or blackberry). *Morado* as a noun is a bruise, and as an adjective, purple or violet. *Morapio*, sacred blackberry or mulberry, is a familiar term for red wine (sacred possibly because it's used in communion).

Bullfrog   The word 'bullfrog' is an American coinage, and French gets its bullfrog also from North America. *Ouaouaron* was picked up by the French Canadians from the Huron Indians.

Butter-fingers   The French equivalent is *mains de merde*, shit hands, which has a parallel in the English (north country) 'cack-handed' (shit-handed).

Butterfly   See **Crab-lice**.

Buttons (and stars)   In the Oregon Trade Language, or Chinook jargon, of the United States, *tsiltsil*, or *chilchil*, meant either buttons or stars.

'When [Sir William Herschel] began to observe, it was almost unheard of that a star should be seen without "rays" or "tails". Henry Cavendish happening to sit next Herschel at dinner, slowly addressed him with, "Is it true, Dr Herschel, that you see the stars round?"

"Round as a button," exclaimed the doctor, when the conversation dropped, till at the close of dinner Cavendish repeated interrogatively, "Round as a button?" "Round as a button," briskly rejoined the doctor and no more was said.' (*Dictionary of National Biography*)

C

C The cup of the hand, *caph*, in Hebrew, and the sign of the cold tap in English. But the unwary Anglo-Saxon traveller cupping his hand under the C-tap where the Romance languages are spoken is liable to get it scalded. It is one of the simplest object-lessons in the story of Babel, learned by thousands of holiday-makers every year. In Italy (*caldo*), Spain (*caliente*), and France (*chaud*) 'C' stands for the hot tap.

Café coronary Wry medical slang, of US origin and with an undertow of black humour characteristic of doctors, for choking to death or nearly to death on food, sometimes mistaken by lay witnesses (for example, other guests in the café) for a heart attack, or coronary.

Human beings are the only animals that can choke to death on their food, because the larynx is lower in the human throat than it is in the animals, and the airway and the food channel merge at that point into one. But if the larynx were not lower, speech would not be possible. The café coronary is part of the price we pay for spoken language.

Calico In French Canada *cheurtine* or *chatine*, a corruption of the English 'shirting'. 'Calico' is a corruption of Calicut, the city in India.

According to *The Leisure Hour* (1873) the calico trade was important in the development of pidgin English between the Chinese and the British: '. . . as to termination syllables double e is the most common, such as *makee*, *talkee*, *walkee*, *muchee*, *showee*, *piecee* etc. This last corruption of our word piece is very commonly used, and derived from a piece or bale of calico, which is the staple import of British manufactured goods. As these are of different qualities, the trader endeavours to impress upon the Chinese buyer that his shirtings are number one, or A1. Hence remarks of quality have advanced from "numpah wan piecee silk" to "numpah wan piecee man" (a rich or honest trader), or "numpah wan piecee woman" (a beautiful woman).'

See also **Turkey** (Calicut).

Canada '... said to be from the Iroquois language, meaning a village of tents or huts; some think it comes from the Kree word Kanatan, which signifies something neat and clean. There is, however, another explanation that I have not yet seen proposed by any writer upon the subject ... The mountain gorges were called, by the emigrants to California in the famous '49 [i.e. the Gold Rush], Canadas, the canada, or gorge being often spoken of, especially by the Mexicans who went to San Francisco at that time' (John McLean ['Robin Rustler'], *The Indians of Canada*, 1892).

In the French mind the experience of the French-Canadian settlers has made the word 'Canada' virtually synonymous with the Great Outdoors. Anything wildly outdoor is liable to get the adjective 'Canadian' tagged to it. Thus an estate car, station-wagon, or shooting-brake is *une carrosserie canadienne* (roughly, 'a Canadian carriage'), while *canadienne* pure and simple is a windcheater or sheepskin jacket and the type of canoe called a kayak. In similar vein, it is probably because of French Canada that a child's woolly suit of clothing, or a choc-ice, is an *Esquimau*, and certainly in English-speaking Canada a choc-ice was an 'Eskimo pie'. Since the non-politically correct 'Eskimo' became taboo, however (to be replaced by the metonym 'Inuit'), an Eskimo pie has become 'Canada pie'.

It is from canoeing that we get what is perhaps the single most important 'outdoor' French-Canadian contribution to metropolitan French, from which it has also entered English. This is the word *portage*, a conceptually cute term which we might best translate into English as 'carry-age' (which is doubtless why it hasn't been translated, and the French-Canadian original is retained).

Eskimo (or Inuit) has the same concept. In Canadian Eskimo it is *itibjak*, which is the act of skirting an obstacle in the river (rapids, a waterfall, etc.) by carrying one's canoe overland to a point past the obstruction. This is a *portage*, but, more subtly, the word refers not only to the skirting of the obstruction but to the obstruction itself. Thus one canoeist may say to another: 'Between point A and point B there are so many *portages*.'

The Apache word for a waterfall is 'whiteness moving downward', and in Oregon Trade Language it was *tumwata*, 'pounding water' (*tumtum* was the heart) while rapids were *skookum chuck*, 'powerful water'. *Portage*, by contrast, is a remarkably businesslike way of looking at rapids or waterfalls; but then, if you are canoeing on white water you have to be businesslike.

In 1880 Dunn commented wryly that the Académie Française in Paris had 'extended hospitality' to the word, but had given as an instance of it: 'From Quebec to Montreal there are so many "*portages*".

'While thanking the Academy for having thought of us,' Dunn commented, 'it must be pointed out that if there were any *portages* between Quebec and Montreal, it would be necessary to *portager* [the verb] trans-Atlantic steamers, which would present certain difficulties.'

That is to say, there are *no* waterfalls or similar obstacles on the St Lawrence River between Quebec and Montreal. Oddly enough, however, it *appears* as if there are. McClean (see above) wrote that: 'Quebec is called by the Indians of the Gulf of St Lawrence, Kepec, which means, being shut, from the fact that in looking up the river at some distance it appears as if it were closed.'

If the French-Canadian *portage* was eventually to enter English, there were English words that the Quebecois had spoken for so long that they thought them to be French. One such was the word for the dry biscuits which they made from their *fleur* (see page 113) called *crackers*, said by Dunn last century to have been a word of such long standing in French Canada that the French Canadians 'reach old age without thinking that the word is English'. Dunn adds that at a trial in Montreal involving the ownership of a parrot, a witness swore that it must belong to his French-Canadian neighbour because one of its words was *crackers*.

For other French-Canadian words and expressions see **Bloody**

hell!, Calico, Dusk, Fox, Great Bear, 'I Say . . . !', Snow (2),
Tree, trees (2).

Cannon   As a reading of *The Conquest of New Spain* by Bernal Díaz
will show, the cannon was the most potent weapon in the arsenal of
empire, not only because of its actual destructive power but because
of the superstitious terror it evoked.

(1) In the Patwa dialect of St Lucia in the Caribbean cannon-balls
were associated with lizards, specifically the grey lizard called *maboüya*
'which has a terrifying cry' (Breton, 1665). Du Tetre (1654) wrote
that '*Maboüyas*, which is a name that they communally give to
whatever inspires horror . . . are grey, unpleasant, puffed up, and
hideous to look at . . . Their usual haunt is the branches of trees.'

The people of St Lucia naturally therefore associated the *maboüya*
lizard with the cannon of the colonizers 'which wreaked such carnage
among these savages'. Thus cannon-balls were identified with lizards,
'these poor people believing that all the *Maboüyas* of France were
bursting from the cannon's mouth to destroy them'.

(2) Stedman (1796) wrote that in the Saramaccan Creole of Guyana
(South America) 'canon powder' [i.e. gunpowder] was *mansanny*.
Scuchardt thought he must have made a mistake: 'Although there is
talk of a barrel of *mansanny* . . . I presume this means canon, for
otherwise *man-sani* means the male sex organ.'

(3) The European soldiers were also terrified in their alien tropical
surroundings, especially by night.

The light of the burning match [to fire the cannon], like the rattling of the
bandoliers, often gave untimely warning of attack. In the West Indian
expedition the soldiers of General Venables often mistook the fireflies for the
matches of Spaniards . . . The sentinels who gave the alarm declared that the
Spaniards were advancing to attack them, and that they heard a sound like
the rattling of bandoliers. But on examination the sound turned out to be
caused by the land-crabs . . . knocking their horny legs together.

(C. H. Firth, *Cromwell's Army, A History of the English Soldier
During the Civil Wars, the Commonwealth, and the Protectorate*, 1912)

Can-opener   The Javanese for a bottle- or can-opener is *badut*, whose primary meaning is 'clown, comedian, jokester'. The Canadian Eskimo for a tin can, *ipuitok*, means literally 'has no handle'.

Cantankerous Greek slang for a cantankerous person, *strimmeno-antero*, means literally 'twisted bowel'.

Canticle In Greek a canticle is *akathistosimnos*, literally 'chairless hymn', a hymn you can't sit down for.

Capuchin In Italian the Capuchin order of monks and nuns lends its name to the nasturtium (*fior capuccino*), endives or other salad leaves (*barba di capuccini*, or Capuchins' beards), and the marsh-harrier (*falco capuccino*).

See also **Coffee** (1).

Carefree See **Sausage**.

Carrot Carrots are 'Mormon currency' (US slang).

See **Tobacco** (1).

Casual wear The German *Räuberzivil*, 'robber's civvies', equates casualness with criminality, as does the description of Baudelaire's dress sense in the Goncourts' *Journal* for October 1857: '*sans cravate, le col nu . . . en vraie toilette de guillotine*' (without a cravat, bare-necked . . . truly dressed for the guillotine). A cravat, incidentally, was originally a Croatian. The Hravati, Napoleon's Croatian mercenaries, wore cravats.

See also **Evening dress**.

Cat (1) 'The Sanskrit margara, cat, might seem to imitate the purring of the cat; but it is derived from the root *mrig*, to clean, margara meaning the animal that always cleans itself' (Müller).

(2) The Spanish *gata*, cat or she-cat, is also, familiarly, a woman from Madrid, a servant or maid (in Mexico), a hill-cloud in meteorology (presumably because the cloud slinks over the hill like a cat), and, in Chile and Peru, a crank or handle. A *gatada* is a movement or act typical of a cat. *Gateado* is catlike, but also streaked or striped.

(3) The Spanish verb *gatear* (whose root is *gata*, see above) is to scratch or claw. In South America generally it has the slang sense of looking for sexual adventure, while in Mexico (see *gata* above) it means to make love to servants.

Catfish　See **Moustache**.

Catholic, Roman　Papua New Guinea Pidgin: *Popi*.
　See also **Foreigner** (1).

Caucasus, The　'Such is the variety of dialects spoken in the Caucasian Isthmus, that it is still called by the inhabitants "the Mountain of Languages"' (Müller).

Cep　In the eighteenth century the Swedish naturalist and classifier of the natural world, Linnaeus (who made a number of mistakes in his classification of mushrooms) observed in his *Flora Lapponica* that in Sweden only foreigners considered mushrooms fit for eating. An interesting example of this is the Swedish name for the *cep* mushroom, the *Karl-Johanes-svamp*, after the Swedish king Charles the Sixteenth, formerly Napoleon's General Bernadotte. In 1818 he was elected to the Swedish throne, whence he drew the attention of Swedes to the succulence of the *cep*. The Bernadottes were a Gascon family; Gascony is renowned for its *ceps*.

Chair　In France a wing-chair is *un fauteuil à oreillettes* (an armchair with little ears).

Champagne　I like the Malay word for champagne, which is simply *puff*. In French a swizzlestick is a 'champagne whip' (*fouet à champagne*).

Chanterelle　Wasson remarks that this golden-brown mushroom with a gilled yellow underside (the whole tinged with just a suspicion of red) 'carries today [1957] more names by far than any other wild mushroom of Europe'. Its Latin name, given by Linnaeus, is *cantharellus cibarius* (literally, 'a little drinking cup used only for meals', i.e.

only when eating). According to the French philologists Bloch and Danzat the common French name derived from Linnaeus in the eighteenth century, but Wasson, pouring scorn on the idea that French peasants followed a lead given by a Swedish naturalist, points out that Jean Bauhin, in his *Historia Plantarum Universalis*, written *circa* 1600, gave *chanterelle* as being in common use around Montbéliard in eastern France.

'Clearly', writes Wasson, 'the mycologists Latinized the word as they found it' (more probably, however, the French had earlier 'Frenchified' it from the Latin).

Names for the chanterelle derive from its colour and from its shape – an irregular hollow like a battered and bent drinking-cup.

(1) In Russian chanterelles are *lisichki*, 'little foxes'.

(2) In Lithuania the russet colouring of the mushroom and the idea of it as a drinking-cup are both recalled in *lapèlaižis*, 'the fox-licked one' (foxes, like squirrels, eat mushrooms, and after a rainstorm a fox might well lick water standing in a chanterelle's hollow; the word also carries a suggestion that the mushroom is russet in colour *because* a fox has licked it). ·

(3) In Old Czech (fourteenth century) a chanterelle is simply *liščí húba*, 'fox's mushroom'.

(4) In Latvia we move into a new area of association with *gailene*, from *gailis* (Latin, *gallus*) a cock, again with a suggestion of russet (the bird's feathers) but a suggestion, too, of the cock's wattle, which the mushroom's shape resembles. In Dutch and Italian the latter suggestion is uppermost, with *hanekam* (cockscomb), and *gallinaccio* (turkey-cock).

(5) In Germany and Austria the ornithological connections persist, with *Eierschwamm* (egg mushroom) 'suggestive of the scrambled eggs that these mushrooms resemble and with which in Austria they are often prepared' (Wasson).

(6) In Bulgaria a chanterelle is a 'duck's foot' (*pachi kraka*), 'a happy figure of speech, as will be perceived by any mycophile who recalls the color and shape of the webbed foot of a duck, idly suspended in air or water' (Wasson).

(7) In Catalan, *rossinyol*, 'said to be derived from *ros, rossa*, an adjective that describes to a nicety the red-gold colour of the lovely mushroom' (Wasson).

(8) And at this point, the word chanterelle at last proves a poisoned mushroom, as Wasson falls victim to the dizzy sickness that finally afflicts almost all who write about words – the tantalizing, maddening perception of profound but unprovable affinities which may be real, or may not: 'These ornithological ties, always masculine, are curious. Does not *chanterelle* itself suggest singing and *chantecler* [chanticleer, the cock]? Are we not in the presence of an eruption, subtle and unconscious, of the old erotic theme, by way of the cock's comb, the gobbler's wattles, the crowing chanticleer, the virile *rossinyol* [nightingale]?'

The old erotic theme? Perhaps. But to quote George Steiner (*After Babel*), 'What we can say best of language, as of death, is, in a certain sense, a truth just out of reach.'

Chatterbox   (1) French: a word-mill (*moulin à paroles*). The same idea exists in Spanish, in which *molino*, mill, also means a 'restless, noisy fellow' and, colloquially, 'mouth'.

(2) The Javanese for 'to talk incessantly', *ablak*, means also 'to flap the wings', while *chachalaca* (Mexican Spanish) is a grouse or any bird that cries continually as it flies and, colloquially, a chatterbox. 'Chatter' in English has the primary sense of bird noise, and 'chatterbox', when it isn't used of children, tends to be applied only to women.

(3) The Spanish *bachiller/-era*, means, as an adjective, garrulous, and as a noun, a graduate and someone who talks too much. The primary meaning of the feminine is 'a loquacious woman', and second, 'a bluestocking'. See also **Prostitute** (3).

(4) The Estonian *krap* for a tittle-tattler or scandalmonger has the primary meaning of 'wooden cowbell'. The Spanish *badajo* is both the clapper of a bell and an idle talker (*badajear* is to talk nonsense).

(5) The quarrelsome-sounding German *Quasselstrippe*, a chatterbox or prattler, is also an ironic colloquialism for the telephone.

(6) The Greek *saliáris* for a chatterbox is 'slobberer'.

(7) In Romany, a lawyer is *rokrenguero*, 'talk, or talking fellow', related perhaps to the Gaelic *racaire*, a chatterbox, while Norwich (see also **Potato**) is *rokrengueriskey gav* (1873), 'talking fellow town' or 'lawyers' town'.

(8) The House of Commons (which is packed with lawyers) is in Romany *ryoriskey rokkaring keir*, literally 'the gentlemen's talking house'. A parrot is *rokrenchericlo*, 'talking bird'.

(9) In classical Rome, a chatterbox, particularly a talkative woman, was a *lingualacca*, a sole. A chatterbox, like a sole, was all *lingua*, tongue.

Chestnut   (1) The Spanish *castaña*, chestnut, is also a chignon hairdo, a bottle, jug, or jar in a chestnut shape and, for reasons I can't even guess at, an abandoned mine. In Mexico, *castaña* can mean a valise or satchel.

(2) The Greek *kastaniá*, a chestnut tree, also means a collapsible picnic-box.

(3) In World War I, chestnuts meant bullets both to the English soldiers and the French (*châtaignes*).

Chignon   Elision from French *châtaigne*? See **Chestnut** (1).

Child, children   (1) 'Poor man's gold' (Caribbean). In a version of the same idea, the Greek *akliros* means, as well as childless, poor or unlucky.

(2) *Pikinini* or *pickaninny* for a baby, in various pidgins and creoles, is from Portuguese *pequeno* (small, little), and its use under colonial rule appears to fall in with the pattern of patronizing child/servant words glanced at in **Waiter**. See also **Civilians and soldiers**.

(3) In Estonian, the final child in a family is *kraabikakk*, whose primary meaning is 'the last small loaf made from the dough left in a kneading trough'. The last child in Cameroons pidgin is known as the *was bele* (literally 'the wash belly', or 'wash womb'). A younger sibling is a *folo bak*, which Todd analyses as the English 'follow back' calqued from local vernaculars. Presumably because younger children tend to follow older children about.

(4) 'Infant' is related to the Latin *infantia*, inability to speak. *Infans* is 'dumb, speechless'.

For other perceptions *of* children see **Baby**, **Crawling**, **Eye**, **Fox**, **Hair** (1), **Nipple** (2).

For perceptions of phenomena, grown-ups, foreigners, etc. *as* children see **Christmas** (2), **Civilians and soldiers**, **'I say . . . !'**, **Pidgin**, **Waiter**.

Chinaman/Chinese (1) Modern English usage requires 'Chinese'; *Chinaman* is felt to be racist, and it was barred from use by the BBC in, I believe, the early 1970s. Perhaps the origin of the feeling that the word is derogatory is the song 'Ching ching Chinaman', but in fact it is a literal translation of the Chinese for a Chinese, *djing-kuo run*, or 'China man', and as such, as the philosopher W. V. Quine points out, 'it departs from the usual patterns of the English language precisely in order to conform to the way in which the Chinese refer to themselves'. ('China', however, is not a Chinese but a foreign word; *djing-kuo* translates roughly as 'centre of the world' or 'Middle Kingdom', as China was once referred to.)

(2) Undoubtedly derogatory, if obscurely so, is the Japanese for a Chinaman, *chanchanbōzu*, from the supposed resemblance of a China-man's head to a poppy capsule (which is round, with a fringe suggestive of a 'coolie's' bamboo hat).

(3) The Mexican *albarazado*, *-ada*, meaning the offspring of Chinese and half-breed parents, in metropolitan Spanish means 'affected with white leprosy'. To the Hawaiians, also, leprosy was 'the Chinese disease'. The colour 'Chinese white' is still found in paintboxes. A similar identification of the Chinese with dirt and disease is in the Japanese term for the bedbug, 'the Nankin[g] insect'.

See also **Foreigner** (2), **Tibet**.

Chinea In the Italian festival of the Chinea a symbolic gift of a horse or mule, and a tribute of gold, were offered to the Pope. It started in Naples in the thirteenth century under Charles of Anjou, King of Naples. The horse and gold were usually handed over on 29 June, the eve of the feast day of St Peter and St Paul.

Chinea is an abbreviation of the Italian *acchinea*, which derives in turn from the French *hacquenée*, from the London borough of Hackney once famous for its horses. Against protests from Pope Pius VI, the Kingdom of the Two Sicilies decided against the continuation of the Chinea in 1788.

Choc-ice   See **Canada**.

Cholera   A colloquialism for cholera among British soldiers in India was 'Corporal Forbes', close to, and surely derived from, the Latin *cholera morbus*.

Christmas   (1) The literal meaning of the Romany *mul divvus*, Christmas Day, is 'wine day'.

(2) South American anchovy fishermen observing enormous changes of temperature in the waters of the Pacific Ocean possibly triggered by 'rushes of highly saline water' dubbed the phenomenon *El Niño*, 'The Child', because it occurs, when it does, just after Christmas and the birth of the Christ-child (*The Times*, 19 September 1989).

See also **Book, Xmas**.

Circumflex accent   In Spanish the *acento circunflejo* is familiarly *capucha*, the hood of a woman's cloak or a monk's cowl or hood.

Civilians and soldiers   (1) Semantically, the relationship between soldiers and civilians, and soldiers and their officers, is marked by condescension, and bears many features similar to the relationship between waiters and their customers (see **Waiter**). Officers in the old (Tsarist) Russian army called their men *ryebyáta*, their 'children'. The same idea is present in the English (also French and Italian) word, the poor bloody 'infantry'. Foot-soldiers are 'infants', without minds or articulate voices of their own.

(2) Interestingly, the same perception exists in reverse, in the condescending French term used by soldiers of civilians, *pékin* or *péquin*, related, via Provençal, to the Portuguese *pequeno*, 'small' or 'little'. The term was popularized by Provençal soldiers at the time of the French Revolution, and in Provençal *péquin* has the sense 'sickly, puny, weak'.

(3) According to Victor Hugo, however (*Choses Vues*, I, 1840), *pékin* was exclusively a *wartime* term. In peacetime, the French civilians patronized the soldiers as *tourlourous*. An onomatopoeia from the bugle-call, it can be traced back to sixteenth-century French as *turlureau*, and is still found today in the *too-ra-loo-ra* refrain (often

followed by 'laddy') of many folk-songs. Littré (1873) called it a
sailor's term for soldier-boys, and certainly it has maritime associations.
In the West Indies, there is a small crab commonly found on beaches
and called, variously, *tourlourou*, *touroulou*, *tootletoo*, etc. In St Lucian
Patwa, says Delphinis, it is *touloulou*, and it names 'a red coloured
beach crab living on the landward side of the beach'. This is the same
word originally with the same meaning, metaphorically transferred.
The first known recorded use of it as a metaphor for a crab was in
1686. It later returned to metropolitan French (first recorded use,
1834) as *toutletou*, even more reminiscent than before of 'tooting' and
bugles, but now meaning only the crab.

The metaphor is fairly straightforward. The crab is red in colour,
like a soldier's uniform. With its claws held before it like drumsticks
it scurries about the beach like a soldier-boy in the barrack-square, in
response to a bugle-call.

See also '**I say . . . !**'

Clay   *Sitrongpela graun* (strong or strongfellow ground; Papua New
Guinea Pidgin).

Clay pigeon   Incomprehensible to me (and to the journalist Bernard
Levin, who has put his incomprehension eloquently into print) is the
French slang term for clay-pigeon shooting, *ball-trap*. The title of a
TV film broadcast over Christmas, 1989, *Ball-Trap on the Côte
Sauvage*, hinged on this incomprehension. Standard French for a clay
pigeon is the banal *pigeon artificiel*. The American gangster Legs
Diamond was known as the Clay Pigeon, because he survived injuries
in many a shoot-out.

Clear (the table, etc.)   Layard to Scuchardt, example of Fijian usage:
Capsize that big fellow pellate and give master small fellow pellate (i.e. Clear
that big plate and give master a small one). The use of 'capsize' for clearing the table is particularly apt, since the dirty plate shortly thereafter was sunk in the washing-up water. But this is an accidental
bonus, as 'capsize' was used in many different contexts. Its use,
Scuchardt comments, 'remind[s] us that seamen were the first English
teachers for the islanders'.

Cloud (1) In nineteenth-century English sailors' slang a bank of cloud or fog on the horizon giving a fictitious resemblance of land was called a *fly-away* or *Cape fly-away* (because the 'land' disappeared, or flew away, as the ship came closer to it). Also a *Dutchman's cape*. A related idea, perhaps referring to distant cloud at sea, is the Norwegian *blane* meaning primarily 'a faraway point on the horizon that has a bluish appearance'. But it can also refer simply to the horizon, or to a patch of blue in a cloudy sky (see 3, below).

(2) 'Certain clouds elliptically parted, considered a sign of fine weather after rain' (Smyth) were called *Noah's Ark*.

(3) The *Magellanic Clouds*, 'great cloudy looking spots in the southern heavens, which are found to consist of a vast number of *nebulae* and clusters of stars' (Smyth) were called *Sacks of Coals*. The same term was used of the patches of deep blue sky in the Milky Way near the South Pole. Of any patch of blue sky, however small, it was said (and it sometimes still is) that it was 'enough to make a Dutchman's breeches'.

(4) The Norwegian *bleik*, as well as meaning 'a thin layer of clouds', can mean the bleaching of clothes or a place where clothes are laid out to bleach in the sun.

Club-foot *Pied équin* (equine, or horse's foot; French).

Coal (1) Nuts of coal in French are sparrow's heads (*têtes de moineau*).

(2) Coal in Romany – *wangar* or *wongar* – also meant money. A miser, *wongar-camming mush*, was literally 'one who loves coal'.

(3) The Germans call hydroelectric power 'white coal' (*weisse Kohle*).

Cockroach (1) In Swahili, a cockroach is colloquially *mdudu wa choo*, the lavatory insect. This is thought to be why *mende*, the conventional Swahili for cockroach, is also one who practises sodomy.

(2) In Japanese, by contrast, cockroaches seem to be associated with the kitchen. From the poem *Cockroach Story* by Anthony Thwaite:

> *Aburamushi* is the name for him
> I suddenly remembered, wondering
> What *abura* means: *mushi* is 'insect' or
> A dozen other things in Japanese . . .

Abura means oil, fat, grease, or sweat. The Japanese *aburamushi* means the oil or sweat insect.

(3) That Japanese 'oil', however, may refer to the insect's waxy faeces. Jacob Bontius explained in 1631 that the Portuguese called the cockroach *cacalacca* ('shellac-shit'). Citrus fruit are coated with wax for shininess and preservation, and 'the most commonly used wax is shellac, made from the excreta of the Asian lac beetle' (*The Times*). From the Portuguese the Dutch got *kakkerlak* for cockroach, a term which they also used of half-castes.

Coconut (1) Just as the Eskimo languages abound in finely shaded words for ice and snow, Swahili subtly distinguishes between seven stages in the development of the coconut, all the way from the first forming of the fruit on the stem, *upunga*, to *nazi kavu*, a coconut in which the nutty part is dry and separating from the shell. The latter is equivalent to the Malayalam *koppara*, whence the Portuguese, and Europe generally, got 'copra', the dried kernel of the coconut exported for its oil. This has been connected with the Hindi verb *khapnā*, 'to dry up', but by others ultimately with the Sanskrit *kharpara*, skull. It doesn't seem too fanciful to see a resemblance between the dried-up coconut and the head-hunter's withered trophy, and the coconut is elsewhere 'jocularly' identified with the skull. (See **Bald, bald-headed**, 1.)

(2) Yule and Burnell note the frequent identification of the human head with the coconut and wonder whether the 'coco' of 'coconut' might not have originated with the Spanish *coca*, a shell, like the French *coque* primarily identified with an eggshell 'but used also for the shell of any nut'.

(3) However, 'The etymology of this name is very obscure', they dutifully note, and go on to give 'the more common' one, whereby the coconut got its name by identification of the nut with a monkey's grimace or other grotesque face, doubtless helped along by an association of it with the monkeys that lived in the trees. By this reasoning, the coconut is also a monkey-nut, or the name might translate literally as 'funny-face nut' – the resemblance of the face (two eyes and a nose) being seen in the three marks at the nut's stem. A writer called García noted in 1563: 'We have given it the name of *coco*,

because it looks like the face of a monkey, or of some other animal'
(see also **Monkey-head mushroom**).

(4) Among the meanings of *coco* in modern Spanish are bogyman,
face or grimace, coconut and, familiarly, head. For a time the idea
was in circulation that the nut resembled an ape (1598); in Spain,
coconuts were shown to children to frighten them with the threat of
the apelike form hidden inside the outer husk, whence, perhaps, the
meaning of *coco* as 'bogyman'.

(5) In Arabic (*al jauz-al-Hindī*), and in Greek (*indikon káruon*) the
coconut is 'the Indian nut'; this is also how Marco Polo refers to it
and how the coconut was generally known in the Middle Ages.

Coffee (1) In Italy (and elsewhere) milky coffee with a head of
whipped cream or bubbly hot milk is *un capuccino*, because its appearance resembles the garb of the Capuchin order of friars. (For similar
reasons, in France, a small gingerbread cake covered in white icing is
une nonnette, a young, or little nun.)

(2) For decaffeinated coffee, *Muckefuck* is the Germanization of the
French *mocca faux*, dating from the Franco-Prussian War of 1870–71.

Commons, House of   See **Chatterbox** (8).

Condom   Yiddish *Schmeckeldecke* is literally 'cock [or penis] ceiling'.
A Scottish Gaelic euphemism for condoms, *ruisgean measan gaol*,
means literally 'peelings from the fruit of love'.

Confetti   See **Office, In the**.

Confusion   The Russian for confusion, *katavásiya*, has as its primary
meaning 'a hymn for two choirs' (from Greek *katavásis*). A figurative
Spanish term for confusion or disorder, *pachamanca*, has as its primary
meaning 'barbecue'.

Cooking   In Greek cookery one doesn't 'brown' food; one 'makes
it rosy' (*rothízo*). *Rothokókkinos* (rose-red) is 'ruddy' of a person and
'browned' of food.

Copra   See **Coconut** (1).

Crab   See **Civilians and soldiers** (3), and **Palindrome**.

Crab-lice   *Papillons d'amour*, 'butterflies of love' (French).

Cracked (of wall, plaster, etc.)   In French, *lézardé*, or 'lizarded'. In the Channel Islands, there is a protected species of green lizard, *Lacerta viridis*, that lives in the walls of Guernsey Castle. When the walls are repointed, cracks are left especially for them to hide and live in.

Cramming   A crammer's in France is *une boîte de bachot*, a baccalaureat box, and cramming in Russian is *dolbruzhá*, whose first meaning is a mallet, or heavy chisel. The Japanese *kyoikumama* (pejorative: literally 'education mama') is a woman who pushes or crams her children to succeed in the highly competitive Japanese education system. Doubtless she bears some responsibility for the suicides every year among Japanese students who fail to make the grade, or who fear they won't make it.

Crawling   The idea of 'on all fours' is inherent in the Spanish *andar a gatas* (roughly, 'to go like a cat'), used in particular of crawling babies. The Greek verb *árkoúdícho* is the same idea, except that the comparison is not to a cat, but to a bear.

Creator   See **Rolling-pin**.

Crow   See **Basket**, **Walnut (wall?)**, **Welsh**.

Crown of Thorns   See **Porcupine** (1).

Crying   The colloquial Japanese *beso* is 'the appearance of the face when about to cry'.
 See also **Brave/brazen**, **Wake**.

Cuff-links   See **Twins** (3 and 5).

D

Dancing The Spanish *fandango* is related to *fondango*, arse. *Fostró*, foxtrot, is a riot or brawl in Venezuela. In Eskimo, *momerpok* is 'to dance the Eskimo way', while *mominguarpok* is 'to dance the white man's way'. *Gavotte* is from Provençal *gava*, a goitre. It was originally a dance of mountain people, and mountains – where iodine is washed away from the soil – often fall within the so-called 'goitre belt'.

See also **Money** (2) and **Whirlpool** (2, waltz).

Dancing cheek to cheek Crab exchange (US slang, 1950s).

Dandelion (1) The French *pisse-en-lit* (or the Spanish *orinacamas*) corresponds exactly to the English dialect 'pissabed'. Dandelions are a diuretic. The Spanish also call the dandelion simply *amargón*, from the adjective *amargo*, 'bitter'.

(2) Their leaves have serrated edges, whence dandelion (from French *dent-de-lion*, tooth of lion; in Spanish *diente de león*). There is a place in Kent called Dent-de-Lion but pronounced dandelion. In German, likewise, it is *Löwenzahn*, 'lion-tooth'.

This widespread way of naming the dandelion puzzles me. Why name a common plant indigenous to Europe after the supposed resemblance of its leaf-shape to the teeth of an African animal? A shape which gardening books, anyway, compare rather to a lance. It is the lion's-mane appearance of the flower itself that is striking, not the toothed leaves. The name came perhaps from the crusaders – it certainly doesn't seem to be based either in local peasant observation or, like many flower-names (bestowed by the monks), in religion. Perhaps, given 'pissabed', it is a later 'polite' name for the flower.

(3) The Spanish plural, *dientes de león*, has the super-transferential sense of spaced indentations in general, the indented edges of tools, ornaments, the 'scalloped' hems of tablecloths, etc.

(4) There is a story, which I have been unable to track down to its source, of an American professor of literature researching Shakespeare in the English Midlands, pointing at a dandelion and wanting to know the dialect name for it. 'Golden lad', he was told. And then at a dandelion in seed, or 'dandelion-clock' (which the Germans call a 'feather-crown', *Federkrone*). This time he was told, 'A chimney-sweep'. If the story is true (one wants it to be), we have an insight into the song from *Cymbeline*: 'Golden lads and girls all must, / As chimney-sweepers, come to dust.'

Daredevil   The Norwegian *brand* means also a beam or log, a beam with carved ornaments on a gable or the stem of a ship, a big, burly man, and (perhaps most relevantly in ballads) a sword.

See also **Theatrical terms** (4).

Death   See **Life** and **Rose** (3).

Decorations (military)   See **Brass hats**.

Dentist   *Dokta bolong tis* (Papua New Guinea Pidgin).

Desert   In Afrikaans the Kalahari Desert is familiarly known as *Dorsland*, or, in South African English, 'Thirstland'.

Devil   (1) It was from the French Revolution that French got its laconic description of the executioner as *le Monsieur de Paris* (the gentleman from Paris). *Monsieur*, as in Lawrence Durrell's novel of that name, is also the Devil. In French-Canadian, *Charlot* ('Charlie') is the hangman or the Devil, and in England the hangman's noose was once 'the Devil's neckerchief'.

(2) A similar identification of the Devil and the executioner exists in Greek, in which an executioner (and a dog-catcher) is *bógias*, close

to the English 'bogyman' or 'bogy', defined by the *Oxford Dictionary* as an object of terror and, as a quasi-proper name, the Devil. Another familiar Greek word for the Devil is *exapódos*, which means 'six feet' (i.e. like an insect or – perhaps back to 'bogy' again – a bug), similar to the Spanish *Patas*, paws or feet, or the Devil. The Devil in Greek is also *triskataratos* ('the thrice cursed').

(3) In Romany the idea of the Devil, *beng* or *bengui*, is mixed up with the idea of mud, *pangka* in Sanskrit. Borrow comments: 'According to the Hindu mythology, there is a hell of mud; the bengues of the Gypsies seem to be its tenants.'

See also **Gallows** and (for another kind of bogyman) **Coconut** (4). See also **Stormy petrel**.

Diarrhoea (and **dysentery**)   (1) In Malay, *buang* is 'to throw away'; *ayer* is water. Diarrhoea is *buang-buang ayer*. For dysentery simply add the word *darah*, blood.

(2) In Afrikaans diarrhoea is *Appelkoossiekte*, or 'apricot sickness', because apricots were the first spring fruits which the early Cape farmers produced. They suffered from griping pains and diarrhoea and rightly blamed the apricots.

(3) The Jamaican and generally West Indian term for diarrhoea, *belly-work*, has exactly the same idea behind it as the Latin American Spanish *obradera*, diarrhoea, from *obra*, work.

(4) The Japanese *akahara*, dysentery, is literally 'red belly'. In Papua New Guinea Pidgin, more bluntly, dysentery is *pekpek blut* ('shit blood').

Dictionary   In Cuban and in River Plate Spanish (Uruguay and Argentina) a dictionary is humorously a *mataburros*. Formed on the model of the heroic *matador* it is translatable as 'slay-donkeys'. One remembers Samuel Johnson's description of himself as a dictionary-compiler as a 'harmless drudge', a sort of donkey. *Matadero*, a slaughterhouse, is also figuratively 'drudgery' in Spanish.

A killing business, but *mataburros* for dictionary probably refers not to the effort of compiling or even reading one, but the effort of carrying it, enough to kill a donkey (see also **Drink, drunk** (3)).

In Spanish, any hefty tome, whacking great book, doorstop from

Valhalla, etc. is a *mamotreto*, which is otherwise any sort of lumber including a large, cumbersome piece of furniture, any large, useless or shapeless object, or a car that has failed its MOT, i.e. an old crock.

Dirty old man (1) In Vietnamese a dirty old man is *ba moui lam*; its literal meaning is thirty-five – the supposed age of the man in question.

(2) In Latin America, a *laucha* is a mouse, a thin person, and a dirty old man.

Dishcloth See **Asparagus**.

DIY In German an amateurish and botched attempt at DIY is *ein Fremdeingriff* (a strange encounter).

Dog Caribbean slang for a dog is 'bruk-kitchen', or 'broke-kitchen', because dogs break into the kitchen. South African slang for a mongrel is 'Kaffir dog', while in Greek it is *kóproskili* ('shit dog').

Dog-catcher See **Black Maria** (4), **Devil** (2).

Doggerel In French it is toy-flute verse (*vers de mirliton*). *Mirliton* is also a cream puff.

Door See **Pearl** (2).

Drainpipe trousers Cameroons: *trausa wei i get pensel fut* (trousers which it got pencil foot).

Drawing-pin (thumb tack) See **Office, In the**.

Dresser See **Theatrical terms** (5).

Drink, drunk (1) In The *Rubáiyát of Omar Khayyám* Edward Fitzgerald wrote:

> And lately, by the Tavern Door agape,
> Came stealing through the Dusk an Angel Shape

Lexicon: **Drink, drunk**

> Bearing a Vessel on his Shoulder; and
> He bid me taste of it; and 'twas – the Grape!

In the notes to his own translation of *The Rubáiyát*, John Bowen wrote (1976), 'The pitfalls which beset the unwary translator of Persian poetry are exemplified by Fitzgerald's evident misreading of *pĭrĭ*, an old man, for *pĭrĭ*, a fairy, which led to the strange metamorphosis of an old drunk into an Angel Shape.'

Too much alcohol more often transforms an Angel Shape into an old drunk with a Milwaukee goitre (beer belly).

(2) In South Africa *witblits*, or 'white lightning', is slang for cheap spirit distilled from peaches or grapes, and 'tiger's milk' is the generic term for any strong liquor (like 'wolf juice' in Canada).

(3) Strong drink in Spain (*mataburro*, 'donkey-slayer') has something in common with the dictionary (see **Dictionary**).

(4) The Swahili for liquor distilled from bananas, *moshi*, has the primary meanings of smoke, steam, soot, or lamp-black, which recalls the South African English *Cape smoke* for cheap Cape brandy, and the English 'steaming', a slang term for 'drunk'.

(5) In New Guinea Pidgin, *longlong* is 'insane, demented, stupid', while *long* on its own is an all-purpose preposition meaning 'by' and 'on' and everything in between. 'Drunk' therefore is *longlong long wiski*.

(6) Nansen reports of the Eskimos:

When the Europeans first came to the country the natives could not at all understand the effects of brandy. When Christmas approached, they came and asked Niels Egede when his people were going to be 'mad'; for they thought that 'madness' was an inseparable accompaniment of the feast, and the recurring paroxysm had become to them a landmark in the almanac. They afterwards ascertained that it was due to this liquor, which they therefore called *silaerúnartok* – that is to say, the thing which makes men lose their wits.

(7) In French a drink with strong alcohol content is a 'push-to-crime' (*pousse-au-crime*).

(8) 'When Henry Hudson discovered the river which bears his name his men made the red man drunk, and this circumstance has

been preserved in Manhattan, [which means] the place where they got drunk' (John McLean, *The Indians of Canada*).

(9) And the following morning, there's the hangover, colloquially in German a *Katzenjammer*, literally 'cats' lamentation' but with a suggestion of howling misery (see also **Brum**).

See also **Minum**.

Drone (of bagpipes, etc.)   See **Brum**.

Drop (Just a)   French: a tear (*larme*). In Dutch a drop of milk in tea is 'a cloudlet' (*wolkje*).

Dummy (in card games)   In Spanish, *el muerto* (the dead body); also in French (*le mort*); in Russian *bolván*, wig-block.

Dusk   In Greek, the dusk is metaphorically *lykóphŏs*, 'wolf-light', which I have also heard in Austria (*Wolflicht*). In French it is *entre chien et loup* (between dog and wolf) – the dogs have knocked off barking for the day: the wolves are about to start howling. There was an English saying 'dark as a wolf's mouth', where 'mouth' may originally have been the wolf's *month*, the perpetual dusk of January.

In French, dusk is also *l'heure du berger*, the shepherd's hour, when *l'Étoile du berger*, the shepherd's, or evening star, Venus, steals into the sky. It sounds 'romantic' (and 'the shepherd's hour' is held to be auspicious for lovers), but of course dusk, when the wolves were about, was exactly when the shepherd (with his dog) had to be at his most watchful, and when things were 'between dog and wolf' in another sense.

It is, all in all, an edgy time of day. In Latin it is *crepusculum*, and in English once was 'crepuscle'. It and other derivatives – like the adjective 'crepuscular' – have now fallen largely out of use, as has 'the gloaming', a word of Scandinavian origin corresponding in literal meaning, though not in richness of association, to the French-Canadian *la brunante*, 'the browning', which sounds like something from cookery. 'Crepuscle', to English ears, is a bit creepy, and 'the gloaming' has echoes of gloom and glumness.

Crepusculum also carries a sense of doubt. *Creperae*, in Latin, were 'doubtful matters', 'because dusk', Varro tells us in one of his strongest etymologies, 'is a time when to many it is doubtful whether it is even yet day or is already night'.

Dysentery   See **Diarrhoea** (1 and 4).

E

Earth The Japanese for the planet earth, *chi*, is also a stretch of countryside and the blank space at the bottom of a page, while Papua New Guinea Pidgin has the lovely idea of *peles* or *ples daun*, 'down here place' or 'down here where we live'. Also *dispela graun* (this fellow ground).

Earth in the sense of 'soil' is in the Cameroons *doti*, from English 'dirty' reinforced by Twi *dote*, 'soil, earth, clay'.

Egg In Spanish, the adjective for fried (of eggs) is *estrellado, estrellada*, which means 'starry'. To fry eggs is *estrellar* which otherwise, colloquially, is to dash to pieces or shatter, and, as a reflexive verb, to fall and break one's neck.

See also **Fool**, **Testicles** (2).

Egg whisk In German a 'snow broom' (*Schneebesen*) because the whipped-up white is like snow.

Elephant (1) Semantically, we perceive elephants in terms of their ivory (Greek *èlephos*). In Sanskrit, however, *hasta* is 'hand' and *hastī*, meaning 'the creature with a hand', is 'elephant' (the trunk being the 'hand'). Whence the Hindustani *hāth* and *hāthī*, with the same meanings. From the Hindustani comes the Anglo-Indian *hatty* for an elephant. (Whence Colonel Hatty, the elephant in *The Jungle Book*.) Tennyson, in *Merlin and Vivien*, wrote of elephants' 'serpent hands'.

(2) The Roman etymologist Varro in the first century BC wondered why the elephant was known as the *Luca bos*, in which *bos* is 'ox' but

Luca, speculatively, had the sense 'Libyan (i.e. 'African'), or 'Lucanian' (from the southern Italian area of Lucania) or, possibly, 'light', from *lux*.

It is curious that Varro didn't refer to the elephants in the triumphal march after Caesar's conquest of Gaul (58–51 BC). Suetonius wrote that Caesar 'ascended the Capitol by the light of forty elephants on the right and left bearing lamps [*lychni*]'. Andrea Mantegna, in his painting commonly known as *The Elephants* (c. 1500–1506), showed three elephants (preceded by an ordinary *bos*, or ox) with garlands on their heads and tall flickering torches mounted on their backs. If this doesn't provide an etymology 'light oxen' it does at least suggest that Caesar was following the logic of such an etymology.

See also (for more on light), **Great Bear**.

English Channel   In France *une manche* is a sleeve; *La Manche* is the English Channel. (For other 'sleeve' metaphors see **Office, In the** (squid) and **Penguin**.)

Epilepsy   In Greek *seliniasmós*, 'moon sickness'.

Estate car   See **Canada**.

Evening dress   *Klos singsing* (Papua New Guinea Pidgin). A *singsing* is a ceremonial gathering with singing and dancing. French slang for a tuxedo or any short jacket is *pet-en-l'air* (fart-in-the-air, which approximates to the English 'bum-freezer'). In German to get dressed up is to put on one's 'peel' or 'skin' (*Schale*).

See also **Casual wear**.

Executioner   See **Devil**, **Gallows** (2).

Eye   'The pupil, *pupilla*, is the spot in the middle of the eye in which is located the power of seeing: because small images are apparent to us at this spot, they are called "pupils". Little boys are said to be "darlings", *pupillus*. Many even call this spot the "little girl", *pupula*: the pupil, *pupilla*, is called this because, like the little girls, it is pure and undefiled' (the sixth-century encyclopedist and etymologist Isidore of Seville).

Steiner (in *After Babel*) tentatively suggests that this eye–child comparison (found in English when a child is called 'the apple of [someone's] eye') may be a 'semantic universal', or one of those 'key anthropomorphic metaphors' which the Neapolitan philosopher-philologist Giambattista Vico (1668–1744) suggested as a common feature of all languages. It has been traced, writes Steiner, 'in all Indo-European languages, but also in Swahili, Lapp, Chinese, and Samoan'. These metaphors are essentially the same from language to language. In each case the eye, or the pupil of the eye, is named after a child or baby. Thus, noting Isidore's remark about 'little girls', above, the modern Greek *kóri* means maiden, girl, virgin, daughter, and the eye's pupil, which can also, however, be *mavrádi*, otherwise 'black spot'. The Greek *mátia mou* ('my eyes') is figuratively 'darling', 'my dearest'.

In Barbados and Guyana the 'baby' is the pupil of the eye, 'the small image of oneself reflected in the pupil of another's eyes' (Cassidy and Le Page). 'The baby' is also the 'eye' or the softest part of a grain of corn, a newly developed ear of corn, and the bull's-eye of a target.

Against this image of the eye as tender and vulnerable, there is another of the eye as sharp, for example the Malay, *mata*, eye, but also the blade of a knife or sword. The same metaphor may opaquely connect 'espy' and the French sword, *épée*. Associations of sharpness, including that of the eye, are touched on in the main text (see page 100).

Eyes of her The bow of a ship was called by its crew 'the eyes of her'. Chinese junks, and boats in the Mediterranean, had eyes painted to either side of the bow to ward off 'the evil eye'. The custom is still fairly widespread in Greece, but even where there are no painted eyes the same expression is used of the bow, the hawse-holes to either side of it, and, sometimes, the outermost part of a bay, as in 'There are the eyes of her'.

Eyebrow See **Tree, trees** (4) and **White man** (2).

F

Fart   See **Evening dress, Fritter, Petticoat, Puff-ball, Sexual intercourse**.

Fickleness   See **Office, In the** (cuttlefish, or squid).

Fight   In South Seas pidgin the English word *fight* is used in a wide variety of apparently disparate contexts. The former British consul Edgar Layard gave some examples to Hugo Scuchardt: 'To the question: "Did you dust that mat?" Vanno answered: *Yes, I fight him. What for you leave pin in clothes belong-a-you?* said Vanno, *Him fight my finger.*' Fights, in the usual usage of the word *fight*, were frequent among the seamen and others with whom the indigenous natives came into contact, and the word's prevalence in pidgin reminds us, says Scuchardt, 'that the contact between the races was often not very amicable'.
   See also **Belong, Clear**.

Finger   In French a bandaged finger is a 'doll' (*poupée*), the source of the English 'puppy'.

Fish   (1) In nineteenth-century English sailors' slang, the side of a split fish without the bone was called the *flag-side*. The sailors' word for the movement of fishes' fins was *fluffit*.
   (2) In Cameroons pidgin a certain kind of fish is popularly called a *brok marach* (or break-marriage), because it has so many bones that it reputedly causes quarrels between husbands and wives. As in the English phrase, 'I've a bone to pick with you.'
   See also **Chatterbox** (9), **Sole**.

Flag of convenience   *Bandiera ombra* (shadow flag; Italian).

Flea   See **Office, In the** (drawing-pin).

Flower   The mariner's compass on maps and charts was known in the nineteenth century as the *flower* or *flower of the winds*. *Flowering* was the name given to 'the phenomenon observed usually in connection with the spawning of fish, at the distance of four leagues from shore. The water appears to be saturated with a thick jelly, filled with the ova of fish, which is known by its adhering to the ropes that the cobles [low, flat-floored fishing boats] anchor with while fishing' (Smyth).

Fluff   See **Theatrical terms** (7).

Flurry   The nineteenth-century nautical meanings of flurry were (1) the convulsive movements of a dying whale and (2) a light breeze shifting to different points of the compass, causing a little ruffling on the sea (Smyth). 'And now abating in his flurry, the whale once more rolled out into view; surging from side to side; spasmodically dilating and contracting his spout-hole, with sharp, crackling, agonized respirations. At last, gush after gush of clotted red gore . . .' (Melville, *Moby-Dick*).

Flying fox   See **Box** (*bilak bokis*).

Fool, A   In the Spanish Caribbean and Central America a fool, twerp, etc., is *pendejo*, which means pubic hair. In Chile, *un huevón*, 'big egg'.

Foot   (1) In Papua New Guinea Pidgin a foot is *leg*, or *lek*, and a footprint also is simply a *leg*. A toe is *pinga bilong lek* (finger belong leg).
   (2) In French, *pied* (foot) is used in a variety of slang expressions, among them *pied-de-biche* (bitch's foot), for a bell-push or the treadle of a sewing-machine, and *pied-de-poule* (chicken's foot) for the textile pattern called in English 'hound's-tooth'.

(3) *Le foot* is French for football, and *footing* is walking. In Latin American Spanish, also, the pseudo-English *footing* (plural *footings*) is a hike or a walk.

Football hooligan   In Italy, football hooligans are *tifosi*, derived, according to the Italian novelist Alberto Moravia, from 'typhus' (Italian, *tifo*). 'The lust for violence shown by the *tifosi*, their Nazi salutes and the attention given to their behaviour by the newspapers and television, seem to him [Moravia] to foreshadow a new barbarian era' (Patrick Marnham, *Independent*). The applications of *tifosi* have since spread, so that it now means fans in general. Well-behaved motor-racing fans at Monza are also *tifosi*.

See also **Lout**.

Foreigner   (1) France was formerly Gaul, which the Romans identified with *gallus*, a hen. The old Celtic name for France was assimilated with *gallus*, to the point where France's emblem for itself became 'chanticleer', the cock. We still associate hens with France, as in the 'French hens' of the Christmas song. Frenchest of all French hens are the patriotic *poules* of the Bresse region, whose markings are a tricoloured red (the comb), white (the plumage), and blue (the lower legs and feet). France is France's later name for itself, from the name of the German tribe, the Franks, and a straw poll of languages would almost certainly find that 'Frank' – spread by the Arabs and the Romans – is the most common word for a foreigner, and 'Frankish' the commonest designation of 'foreignness'. Lingua franca was the mercantile pidgin of the Mediterranean, and from Ethiopia to Thailand, *franca* can be found as the Arabic-based *farang*. In Malaya and the Indian archipelago it was *franchi*, as in, for example, *for-franchi*, 'the European disease', for syphilis.

Greece was invaded by the Franks, and in Greek there is a whole complex of variants on 'Frank' to mean 'foreign'. *Frankikos* means Frankish, Catholic (as distinct from Greek Orthodox), and West European (Western Europe is *Frankia*); *frankos* is a Frank and a Catholic; *frankópappas* – or Frankish priest – is a Catholic priest; to convert to Catholicism is *frankepho*; *frankostáphilo* – or Frankish grape – is the redcurrant, and *frankósiko*, or Frankish fig, is the prickly pear;

and finally, the system of writing Greek in Roman letters, as I am trying my best to do here, is *frankochiótika*.

(2) Another surprisingly widespread word, and rather a nasty one, is *kanaka*, originally, according to the *Oxford Dictionary*, Hawaiian for 'man'. It was once in use in English, and is still, I understand, in use in Australia. The dictionary defines it as 'A native of the South Sea Islands', but in fact it is an ugly, pejorative word meaning something between 'native' and 'nigger'. In various forms and spellings it remains in use throughout the Pacific basin, and even further afield. In the Pacific, it is in regular use as *kanak*: '. . . with a sly perversity the Melanesians had stolen the Pacific word for "nigger" from the French; they called their country Kanaky, so the French had to call them "*Mélanésiens*" . . .'(Julian Evans, *Transit of Venus*, 1992).

In Ecuador and Peru, on the Pacific seaboard of South America, *canaca* means a Chinese, but also a brothel-keeper. In Chile it also means 'brothel', while by association with Chinese skin colouring, *canaco* has come to mean pale or yellow in Chile and Ecuador.

Perhaps nastiest of all, the word has somehow entered German, in which *Kanake* is an abusive slang term for a foreigner, immigrant labourer, refugee, and so on. It is back in vogue with the rise of the German right; for example, 'We East Germans are no Kanakas' (*The Times*, 4 February 1993).

(3) 'Horde' appeared in European languages after AD 1241, when the Mongol Horde entered Poland and Hungary. It was originally *urdū*. Hindustani is also called 'Urdu' because it is the *zabān i urdū* (the language of the camp), and Hindustani retains *urdū* to mean both a nomad camp and a body of armed, not necessarily hostile men. Persia suffered most from the Mongol invasions, but somewhat surprisingly *urdu* in Persian strikes no terror but is only 'a camp' (*urdugah* is a camp-site).

In Russian *ordá* quickly established itself to mean a wild and terrifying, hostile and essentially foreign mob. In Poland the word acquired an 'h' (*hórda*) but otherwise kept the Russian sense. And in countries further west, in the languages of countries themselves uninvaded by the Mongols but horrified by the calamity of the invasion, the Polish *hórda* with its added 'h' and its air of dread entered French, German, Dutch, Swedish, and English.

See also **Aids, Chinaman/Chinese, 'I say . . . !', Syphilis, Us and them, Walnut (wall?), Welsh**.

Formal wear   See **Evening dress**.

Forty   See **Rose** (2 and 3).

Fox   The French *renard*, fox, is from Old High German, *regin-hart*, which approximately translates as 'strong in counsel, rule, intelligence'. Old French for a fox was *goupil*, from the Latin *vulpes* or *volpes*. The great popularity in the Middle Ages of the German epic known in English as 'Reynard the Fox' gave modern French *renard*. In the original epic, Reynard symbolized the Church; as understood and adapted in medieval France, the fox of the epic came to typify peasant wiliness. Given the original epic, however, it is interesting that Christian associations (usually, however, those of being a bad Christian) continue to cling to fox-metaphors.

In French Canada, a *renard* is figuratively someone who over the entire period of Easter doesn't once go to communion. A similar idea exists in Greek in which the adjective *akoinóntos* means both 'unsociable' and 'not having received the sacrament'. And perhaps this idea of unsociable behaviour underlies the archaic English verb 'to fox' (it exists also in French, as *renarder*) to describe, not someone who has not drunk communion wine, but someone who has drunk too much of the unsanctified stuff. It means 'to vomit', and especially to vomit after drinking.

The unsociable 'loner' quality of the fox is also noted in the Japanese *aramikake* or *aramisaki*, literally 'the god who shuns human society'. Attitudes to the fox parallel those to red-headed people (see page 110–11), sacrificial victims simultaneously revered and reviled, shunned and perceived as shunning. The Egyptian god, Set, had red hair, and the Egyptians sacrificed to him 'red-haired men who were burned and whose ashes were scattered with winnowing-fans . . . for the express purpose of making the corn turn red or golden' (Frazer, *The Golden Bough*). The Egyptians hunted these red-haired men on their foreign excursions, and the rural rite of fox-hunting has every appearance of being a sacrificial fertility rite on exactly the same lines.

In Romany, the language of those ancestral social outsiders, the Gypsies, a fox is *weshen-juggal*, literally 'dog of the wood'. The fox seems to be important to the Gypsies as a symbol of their own wandering way of life. Borrow derives the Romany *chavo*, child, from the old French hunting term *cheaus*, fox-cubs (could this be the origin of the French term of endearment *chou*, cabbage?), and he quotes a Romany rhyme:

> Kek man camov te jib bolli-mengreskoenaes
> Man camov te jib weshenjugalogonaes
>
> (I don't want to live like a baptized person [i.e. a Christian]
> I want to live like a dog of the wood [a fox])

which like the figurative use of *renard* opposes the idea of the 'good Christian' with that of the pagan fox. The Gypsies perhaps tended to avoid Leicestershire, their name for which was *Weshen-juggal-slommo-mengreskey tem*, 'fox-hunting fellows' country'.

See also **Chanterelle** (1–3).

Foxglove The Spanish foxglove, *dedalera* (from *dedal*, a thimble) would accommodate one finger only, as would the German one, *Fingerhut* (literally 'finger hat'). It was the latter name, with its single digit, that suggested the botanical name *digitalis* to the German botanist Fuchs (1542). Fuchs, rather extraordinarily, is German for 'fox', and the name he bestowed on the foxglove is more commonly known today as the drug digitalis (found in foxgloves) used in treating heart conditions.

The foxglove, big enough only for a human finger, will however hold a fairy's whole hand, and the etymology 'folk's glove' (i.e. the fairy folk) has been suggested. But it may also be believed to hold a fox's paw, and in Norwegian the flower is 'fox-bell', with no suggestion of fairies at the bottom of the garden. In Anglo-Saxon, too, it was the foxy rather than folksy *foxes glofa*.

France, Frankish, the French See **Foreigner** (1) and **Walnut (wall?), Welsh**.

French Revolution, Effect of on language (1) In the French Revolution the queen bee of the hive (*la reine*) was solemnly and neutrally renamed *l'abeille pondeuse*, the laying bee. *Reine* for queen bee has since returned, but the feudal queen in French chess and card games is still only *la dame* (the lady), the castle is still only the tower (*tour*), the bishop still the madman (*fou*), and the jacks, no longer young princelings but still only servants (*valets*). *Pion*, pawn (see also pages 83–4), is modern French slang for an assistant schoolmaster.

(2) The revolutionaries revised the calendar, starting the year in September and renaming the months according to the seasonal weather. September was *Vendémiaire* (22 September to 21 October), followed by *Brumaire* (October), *Frimaire* (November), *Nivôse* (December), *Pluviôse* (January), *Ventôse* (February), *Germinal* (March), *Floréal* (April), *Prairial* (May), *Messidor* (June), *Thermidor* (July), and *Fructidor* (August). These names bestowed from on high survived until 1805, having already by then been wittily translated into English (and arranged by rhyme) as Wheezy, Sneezy, Freezy, Slippy, Drippy, Nippy, Showery, Flowery, Bowery, Wheaty, Heaty, Sweety.

(3) The revolutionary months were divided into three weeks of ten days each. The five days left over in the year were set aside as national holidays. The philosopher A. J. Ayer commented: 'Perhaps some lack of a sense of humour was shown in their being respectively dedicated to Virtue, Genius, Labour, Opinion, and Reward, but then a sense of humour would probably be a handicap to anyone who was engaged in obliterating every feature of a former regime in the interests of social progress' (*Spectator*, 8 July 1989).

(4) The Parisian quarter of Montmartre was renamed, unsuccessfully, Mont Marat, after the revolutionary leader. The name 'Montmartre' is itself an instance of the move in French (see pages 96–7) from the pre-Christian 'Mars', the Roman god of war, to the Christian saints Martha or Martin or, in this instance, the word 'martyr'. It was, earlier, *Mons Martis*, the mount of Mars, but three saints are said to have been martyred there in the third century.

(5) The French Revolution gives modern politics the notion of the left and the right wing, 'red' to mean 'revolutionary', and 'white' for the old guard. The first pejorative uses of 'élite' and 'élitism' also date from the revolution. For a time it spawned the belief that French, the

language of liberty, which Montaigne a century before had believed to be dying out, would become the new world language. In the event, the only universal language bequeathed by the revolution was the metric system, devised by the revolutionaries. It spread throughout the world, even, eventually, to diehard England.

(6) Carlyle's characterization of Robespierre as the 'sea-green incorruptible' has entered English. But Carlyle was being heavily ironic. The colour 'sea-green' was emblematic of changeability, like that of the sea, or, in politics, of pragmatic expediency hypocritically masquerading as principle. It has come, however, often to be understood in the opposite sense, as a real, not veiled, compliment. Thus the journalist, Robin Oakley, writing in *The Times* (31 July 1990) about the IRA murder of Conservative MP Ian Gow: 'It was typical of his sea-green incorruptibility that he then upset his friends among the Ulster Unionists by lending his support to the campaign for Conservative candidates to stand in Northern Ireland seats, saying national parties should fight across the nation. Principle once again came before convenience.' But Ian Gow's upset Ulster Unionist friends would have believed that he had, in this matter, shown himself to be sea-green by putting convenience before principle.

(7) Neal Ascherson, on the European 'revolutions' of 1989: 'Revolution, insurrection, revolt: none of these terms fitted, except in the Romanian case. Our language here needed a word like *Aufstand* or *powstanie*, in German or Polish, with their connotation of a "standing up" after long prostration' (*London Review of Books*, 14 June 1990).

Uprising?

See also **Civilians and soldiers** (2), **Devil** (1), **Gallows** (3).

Friday the thirteenth   In Islam, words for Friday reflect the fact that it is the holiest day of the week, for example the Malay *Juna'at*, literally 'congregation'. It is the day Muslims prepare themselves for, but on which Christians get prepared (for Sunday). In Greek, Friday is *paraskeví*, preparation. In the Spanish-speaking world the equivalent of the unlucky 'Friday the thirteenth' is *Martes trece* (Tuesday the thirteenth).

The unluckiness of Friday for sea travel has been extended to its unluckiness for any journey or enterprise, especially when combined with the number thirteen. One reason for this seems to be that Friday is a blessed day in Islam, full of stored-up blessedness. A Moslem says: 'I will prepare myself for Friday and then, please God, you will see what you will see.' As a result, the unfortunate Crusaders always got it in the neck on Fridays. Their priests tried to restore morale by insisting that, so far from being an unlucky day, Friday was the best in the whole week: on Friday, mankind had been ransomed from eternal damnation [i.e. Good Friday]. This view was adopted officially in the later Middle Ages, when Philip II of Spain made a practice of sending out his expeditions on a Friday. I must check on the Spanish Armada; but my bet is that it sailed both from Spain and from the Low Countries on Fridays. What is more, the Spaniards artificially fixed Tuesday the Thirteenth as an unlucky day, which it still is.

(Robert Graves, *The Crane Bag and Other Disputed Subjects*, 1969)

Did the 'preparation' of the Greek *paraskeví*, Friday, mean primarily preparation against attack?

Friend   See **Basket**, **Twins** (2).

Fritter   French: *pet-de-nonne* (nun's fart). Jamaican for a codfish fritter is *aachibombo*. *Aachi* is codfish, *bombo* is buttocks, or vagina. In Spanish the fritter, *buñuelo*, gave its name to a famous film-director.

G

Gallows (1) Russian slang for the gallows is *glagol*, the word for the fourth letter of the Cyrillic alphabet. The shape of *glagol* – Γ – is exactly that of the Greek capital gamma, or of the gallows. A crane (hoist) is also *glagol*.

(2) The crane we call a 'derrick' was originally a gallows. 'Derrick' preserves the (originally Dutch) name of a hangman who worked in London around 1600. 'Gibbet', a gallows, is also the projecting arm of a crane; it is related to the 'jib' of a sailing-boat.

(3) The French *potence*, a gallows, was originally only a bracket. During the French Revolution and the Terror the guillotine was colloquially 'the great widow' (*la Veuve*). Camille Desmoulins wrote that 'She has had at least half a dozen husbands, and she had to bury them all'. Victor Hugo wrote (in his novel *Quatre-vingt Treize*): '*On couche avec, on ne la féconde pas*' ('Men sleep with her, but she doesn't get pregnant'). 'On days when it stood idle, the guillotine was covered with a white sheet. Like an altar' (Jan Kott, *New York Review of Books*, 12 October 1989).

(4) In the United States, a pair of braces is still referred to as 'galluses', i.e. gallows, originally a Scottish word.

(5) In Anglo-Saxon times, when criminals were hanged, a wolf was sometimes hanged with them, and the Anglo-Saxon *varagtreo*, gallows, literally means 'wolf-tree'.

See also **Devil** (1 and 2).

Gannet (solan goose) See **Albatross**.

Garage See **Box**.

Gas 'The most famous individual formation [of a word] is the word *gas*, invented about 1600 by the Dutch chemist Van Helmont. He believed that gas was a phenomenon related to the idea which the Greeks expressed by *chaos*, which in Dutch receives nearly the same pronunciation as *gas*, and he used also a term *blas* (a fairly regular derivative from the Dutch verb *blazen* "to blow") for an aerial radiation from the stars' (Bloomfield).

The word 'gas' took off, 'blas' didn't.

Gavotte See **Dancing**.

Germans, The See **Walnut (wall?), Welsh**.

Ghost In Romany, a ghost is figuratively *bavol-engro*, 'wind-fellow'. English has 'ghost' from the first English printer, Caxton. He learned his trade in Flanders where the word was *gheest*. In the disputes over spelling early this century it used to be said that 'rhinoceros' without its 'h' would lose its horn. Similarly, it could be argued that 'ghost' is the more ghostly for that spectral, silent 'h'.

Giraffe The phrase 'thought to be' occurs often in the story of 'giraffe', which entered English from the Arabic *zarāfa* or *zurāfa*, thought to be from the Ethiopic *zarat* (the Arabs are thought to have encountered the giraffe for the first time in Abyssinia). The Ethiopic word, in its turn, may derive from an ancient Egyptian word *sr* (the vowels of ancient Egyptian are unknown). *Sr* may (or may not) have had something to do with the animal's swinging motion.

It isn't much to go on, but somehow this hazy vagueness is appropriate. Of all the animals in the bestiary, perhaps the giraffe is the one which most seems like a mythic, imaginary being, come true in reality.

Historically, it's been seen not as one animal in its own right so much as an improbable composite of several animals. According to an Arabic account of AD 1022, 'In Persia the animal is called camel-bull-panther [*ushtur-* or *shutur-gāw-palank*], because it has something in common with each of these three.' And a Persian text tells us: 'Its hands [fore legs] and neck are like those of a camel, its skin is like that of a leopard, its teeth and hoofs are like those of an ox.' Other accounts compare parts of the giraffe to the stag (its head and skin), a gazelle (its tail), an antelope (its horns), and even a cock (its back). In English it was known (from the Greek) as the 'camelopard'.

After this menagerie it is refreshing to come across an old Persian popular etymology analysing the Persian *zurnāpa*, giraffe, into components which make it mean 'having legs shaped like a tallboy's', or as the Japanese say of lanky furniture, 'with butterfly legs' (*chōashi*). *Zurnāpa*, however, is probably *zarāfa* in Persian dress.

How imaginary is this animal (from *The Book of Imaginary Beings*, by J. L. Borges)?

The Kilin is said to have the body of a deer, the tail of an ox, a single horn, and to be covered with fish-scales. Its horn is covered with flesh, indicating that while able for war, it covets peace. It does not tread on any living thing, not even on living grass. It symbolizes gentleness, goodness, and benevolence. It is said to have appeared just previous to the death of Confucius, and it will appear whenever a benevolent sovereign rules; it was a mythical animal of good omen.

Allowing for the distorting and exaggerating effect of myth-making 'Chinese whispers' over a great distance in space and thousands of years in time, that fairly approximates to the traveller's-tale descriptions, above, of the giraffe.

According to a monograph published in 1928, *The Giraffe in History and Art*, by Berthold Laufer, 'When live giraffes were first transported into China in the fifteenth century under the Ming dynasty, they were taken by the Chinese for the Kilin (*k'i-lin*), a fabulous creature of ancient mythology . . .' In Japanese, the giraffe is *hyōda*, 'panther-camel', but also, after the Chinese myth, *kirin*.

The myth may have some distant foundation in reality. From fossil remains, the giraffe is known to have existed on the territory of China in primeval times. It has been argued that myths of monsters and giants may be based on the perplexed discovery in ancient times of the fossil remains of mammoths, whales, and so on. By the same argument, the Kilin would be an ancient Chinese folk-memory of the giraffe elaborated into a myth – when the giraffe again came to China in historical times, the myth was waiting for it. But who knows?

Who knows, either, whether the *zaráfa*, with its angelic, peaceful nature, is related to the angel-name *seraph*? But in the Middle Ages it was thought to be, and as late as 1607, in the *Historie of Four-Footed Beastes*, the giraffe is still called *serapha*, an 'Englished' version of *zaráfa* which may indeed (or may not) have something to do with 'seraph', the back-formation from 'seraphim'.

The giraffe, like the Kilin, was traditionally a beast of good omen, and they were sometimes presented as goodwill gifts. The Sultan of Turkey gave one to the Signoria of Florence in 1487. Among many paintings in which this herald of the Renaissance was immortalized were an *Adoration of the Magi* in the school of Pinturicchio (1454–1513) and two paintings by Andrea del Sarto (1486–1531).

In 1826 Mohammed 'Ali, Pasha of Egypt, gave a giraffe to the King of France. She caused a sensation. Thousands queued to see her, giraffe-songs were composed, and giraffe-motifs swept French fashion. She delighted Parisians for almost twenty years.

The following year, 1827, the Pasha gave one to King George IV of England. It survived a few months in Windsor Park, then died.

Gods, The   See **Theatrical terms** (8).

Goitre   See **Dancing** (gavotte), **Turkey** (*güegüecho*).

Gossamer   German *Sommerfäden*, 'summer threads', refers to the fine floating threads spun by young spiders and usually seen at their most numerous in the autumn. This is the time that geese are in season, and 'gossamer' is thought originally to have been 'goose summer', the same period of the year called in Dutch *kraanzomer*, or 'crane summer', because then the cranes are flocking and flying south.

Grammar school   So called because Latin and Greek were taught there. The word 'glamour' was derived in the Middle Ages from 'grammar'. The possession of learning, or grammar, was thought to be magical and mysterious. 'Glamour' in its modern sense was popularized by Sir Walter Scott.

Graveyard   In Yiddish *das guten Ort* or 'the good place', because the graveyard was where you were at last at peace and beyond persecution. 'The good place' also refers to a woman. Thus to the question 'Where have you been?' the answer, '*Das guten Ort*' could mean either 'to the graveyard' or 'with a woman'.

Great Auk   Shell UK's first six oilfields were named in alphabetical order after water-birds: Auk, Brent (the Brent goose), Cormorant, Dunlin, Eider, Fulmar. The first, Auk, was discovered in the northern North Sea in 1971 and began production in 1975, in a joint venture by Shell UK and the American firm Esso. One of Esso's American employees had never heard of the auk and, seeing AUK on documents, took it to mean A-UK (United Kingdom). What, he wondered, would happen as further oilfields were discovered – B-UK, C-UK, etc. – and F was reached? This is the true version of a story whose apocryphal version – still told by oilmen today – is that A-UK, B-UK, etc. was the original idea.

For more important information, see **Albatross**.

Great Bear, Constellation of the   Millions of people must have looked up at the northerly night sky, as I did as a child, and wondered why the constellation popularly called the Plough is also, and more 'properly', known as the Great Bear (*Ursa Major*). The resemblance to a plough is easy to see: the Romans called its seven stars the *Triones*, the 'plough-oxen'. Or it could be imagined as a wagon, which is what Homer called it in the *Odyssey* – a now-archaic English name for it was 'Charles's Wain', and in Spain it's still called *carro*, or 'cart'. We can also see the resemblance to a 'cauldron' (*chaudière*) as the early French Canadians called it, or 'the Big Dipper', as it's still called in the United States. We can even see why in parts of India the constellation is the Elephant, with the ploughshaft imagined as the trunk, and the Pole Star a mouse crawling into it.

But a Great Bear? Why? Puzzlement deepens when one realizes that the Arctic, and so the Antarctic too, is named after this supposed resemblance to a bear (the Arctic's name is from the Greek *arktos*, 'bear', after the northerly constellation).

According to Müller, 'the name of the Arctic regions rests on a misunderstanding of a name framed thousands of years ago in Central Asia; and the surprise with which many a thoughtful observer has looked at these seven bright stars, wondering why they were ever called the Bear, is removed by a reference to the early annals of human speech'.

From the Sanskrit root-verb *ark* meaning to be bright or make bright, Müller traces *rik*, a song of praise or hymn, *arkah*, a ray of light and, by extension, the sun, and *riksha*, meaning both bright and bear. He admits that a 'doubtful point' is the uncertainty which attaches to the exact etymological meaning of *riksha*, bear. 'We do not see', he says, 'why of all other animals the bear should have been called the bright animal', and conjectures that it was 'either from his bright eyes or from his brilliant tawny fur'.

This once-perceived 'brightness' of the bear is a puzzle to the modern mind. One can only conjecture. There is a hint of brightness in the old German bear-name, *Goldenfusz*, 'golden-footed'. Is it from the bear's paw dipped in the golden honey of a beehive? A more substantial straw may be clutched at in the writings of Varro, who at one point wonders about the origin of the Latin adjective *Luca*, *Lucas*, or *Lucans*. According to one source, it was from *Lybici*, 'the Libyans', and therefore, to all intents and purposes, signified 'African'; according to another, it was from *Lucani*, 'the Lucanians', after the southern Italian region of Lucania. But, writes Varro, 'bears are no more Lucanian [i.e. native to southern Italy] than they are Lucan [native to Africa], though they are called Lucanian. Therefore I rather think that *Lucas* is from *lux*, "light"' (see also **Elephant**, (2)).

But it is not in dispute that Sanskrit has the same word *rikshas* for stars, the bright ones, and bears, and Müller comments that 'even if the derivation of *riksha* from *ark* had to be given up, the later chapters in the history of the word would still remain the same'. Müller's suggestion is not that either bears or stars were called bright because of some perceived metaphorical affinity between them, but that bears and stars were both independently perceived as 'bright ones', and that subsequently 'the etymological meaning of *riksha*, as simply the bright stars, was forgotten, the popular meaning of *riksha*, bear, was known to everybody'. And he adds: 'The Hindus also forgot the original meaning of *riksha*. It became a mere name, apparently with two meanings, star and bear.'

In an additional complication, *riksha*, bear or bright one, became confused with *rishi*, sage (or holy person, whence the Romany *rashi*, clergyman, or priest). From this ancillary misunderstanding the myth evolved that the seven stars of the Great Bear were the homes of the seven sages. It may be that 'bright' was used even this early of intelligence: the seven sages were 'bright', the bear was a 'bright' animal. But Müller's picture is of a myth evolving from misunderstandings and mishearings, in a game of Chinese whispers played across millennia. The Greeks and Romans inherited the ancient misunderstanding about the Great Bear. So, still more distantly, did we.

Great White Shark   The terrifying villain of the *Jaws* movies is a rerun of the great white whale, Moby-Dick, and it drew the interest of *Moby-Dick*'s author, Herman Melville, who wrote that its

white gliding ghostliness of repose . . . is most vividly hit by the French in the name they bestow upon that fish. The Romish mass for the dead begins with 'Requiem eternam' (eternal rest) whence *Requiem* denominating the mass itself, and any other funereal music. Now, in allusion to the white, silent stillness of death in this shark, and the mild deadliness of his habits, the French call him *Requin*.

In fact, French *requin* names any shark, not just the Great White. Otherwise, however, Melville's etymology is not quite as eccentric as might appear. *Requin* is certainly obscure – suggested origins include *quien*, a Norman form of *chien*, dog, and *orquin*, diminutive of orc, the killer whale. The *requin–requiem* idea gained respectability in the 1870s, when Émile Littré's dictionary recorded the view that the *requin* is so called because the shark is so efficient a killer that anyone faced with it might as well say his requiem. Melville may have read this in Littré, or heard it from French sailors – it has every appearance of being a colourfully anecdotal, but perhaps finally false, 'popular etymology'.

A later author, Georges Duhamel, found the *requiem* etymology 'very simple and fine', but 'unfortunately', Duhamel had to admit, 'the best informed experts dismiss it as a fantasy'. Fantasy or not, it continues to be influential, and to appear in dictionaries, for example the *Petit Robert* of 1967.

Requin, like the English 'shark', has the figurative sense of 'swindler, sharper' – but in English these are the *original* senses: it is shark to mean fish that is the metaphor. 'Shark' is related to 'shirk', to Italian *scrocco*, 'scrounging', French *escroc*, 'crook', and German *Schurke*, 'rascal'.

Grippe   The French for 'flu' has the sense of a disease which grips or seizes, and it dates from the epidemic in the spring of 1743. It caught on. On 10 January 1768, Voltaire wrote: 'Grippe, on a world tour, passed our Siberia [Ferney near Geneva, where he lived] and laid hold a little of my old and sickly face.'

See also **Quinsy**.

Guava   In Guatemala *guayaba*, a guava or guava jelly, is also a kiss, and has the additional meaning of political power or the presidency. A kiss (and a guava) is soft; politicians, especially in Guatemala, tend not to be. A suitably *machismo* train of association, however, equates the soft, succulent and (thought-to-be) available pretty girl (*guayabo*) in her see-through blouse (*guayabera*) with the guava. But the pretty girl tells lies (*guayabas*) as politicians do; and power, like the pretty girl and the guava, can be sweet.

That isn't at all scientific, but at least it makes some sense of the otherwise perplexing range of words with 'guava' at their root. And certainly there is evidence to suggest that the guava has long been found suggestive of the female sex organs (see page 145). I'm at a loss though to suggest why *guayaba* (guava) should have the additional meaning of 'ankle' in Ecuador.

Guitar   In German, colloquially a 'beggar's harp' (*Bettlerharfe*). In the Argentine, a word for guitar is *encordado*, which also means a boxing-ring (the 'stringed' one or thing: the guitar, the ropes round the ring). The Japanese *bachimen* (from *bachi*, 'punishment inflicted by heaven', and *men*, face or surface) is the 'place on a guitar where it is played'.

H

H   The pronunciation of the eighth letter of the alphabet is the one
respect in which English as spoken by Northern Ireland's Protestants
and Catholics consistently differs. Protestants say 'aitch' while Catholics
say 'haitch'. It's been suggested that the IRA has used this difference
in pronunciation as a litmus test to establish allegiances. In Hebrew,
H is *heth*, a hedge.

See also **Ghost**.

Hair   (1) The Spanish verb *filotear* is primarily used of corn and
means to come into ear, to ripen. But when used of a child it means
'to grow hair' – the child's fine (and often very pale) hair resembles
the filaments under the encasing leaves and around a cob of corn.
Filote is Colombian Spanish for an ear of green maize, and *estar en
filote* is, of a child, to begin to grow hair.

(2) Japanese has a useful word, *age-otori*, which my dictionary
translates as 'Looking less handsome for having had her hair done up'.

(3) A hairpin or hairclip in Spanish, *horquilla*, is also a pitchfork,
while 'a hairpin bend' is a *curva en herradura*, 'a horseshoe bend'.

(4) In Germany *ein Föhn* is a domestic hair-drier, after the warm
and unpleasant Alpine wind (*der Föhn*) felt especially in southern
Germany.

(5) 'Shampoo' is from the Hindi *chhāmpo*, from a verb meaning to
press, knead, massage.

(6) In medieval Europe a full head of long hair on a man was a
symbol of status and power, despite St Paul's dictum that long hair is
'a shame unto a man' (which is why the clergy have tended to wear

their hair short and to disapprove of long hair among the laity). In England and France, the length of the hair and the cut of the beard were high matters of state. At various times, kings and noblemen wore their hair long, or short. At the Battle of Hastings, King Harold's advance guard reported that the Normans were so closely shaven that they 'did almost seem to be priests'. After the invasion, Englishmen of every class wore their hair long as a mark of rebellion. The equation of long hair with power persists in language in words like the English 'bigwig' and the Latin American Spanish *pelucon*. In Peru it is used to mean simply 'long-haired', but in Ecuador it has the sense 'bigwig' or 'big shot', and in Chile it means 'conservative'.

For pubic hair, see **Fool**.

See also **Bald, bald-headed**, **Beard**, **Chignon** (chestnut), **Infantry-man** (*poilu*), **Moustache**.

Halcyon   See **Kingfisher** (2).

Hammock   (1) '*Hammock* was introduced into English from the Spanish *hamaca*, itself a no doubt assimilated form of a Carib word. In English it was little changed, because it happened to resemble the native words in *-ock*, such as *hassock, hummock*. In German, however, where it resembled nothing in the native stock, it was assimilated into the form of a compound *Hängematte* "hang-mat"' (Bloomfield).

(2) *Betseil* ('bed sail'; Papua New Guinea Pidgin).

Handkerchief   *Mouchoir* (French; *une mouche* is a fly). In carpentry, the idea of a neatly folded handkerchief gives *mouchoir* also the sense of a triangular bracket; *en mouchoir* is 'in triangular shape' or 'obliquely'.

Hangman   See **Devil**, **Gallows**.

Hangover   See **Brum**, **Drink, drunk** (9).

Hanky-panky   In the Napoleonic occupation of German palatinates early in the nineteenth century the French soldiers would invite the German girls back to their tents: '*Voulez-vous visiter ma tente?*'

Overheard by the Germans this became the echoic *Fisimatenten* –
hanky-panky. A German father will still say to his teenage daughter
as she goes out for the evening: *'Kein Fisimatenten heute Nacht!'* It
also has the sense of excuses, humbug, fuss, shuffling.

Hare (1) Romany, *kaun-engro*, 'ear-fellow', and in French also, like
some bats, it is identified as *oreillard*, by its long ears.

(2) As the grain was cut and the reapers approached the centre of
the field, the hare was trapped. In Ireland the final sheaf was sometimes
called 'the hare' and reapers would say, 'We'll put the hare out of it
today.' From the same observation comes the Spanish colloquial
levantar la liebre, 'to raise the hare', meaning to blow the gaff on someone or something. A hare in Spanish is also, figuratively, a coward.

(3) Hares, because they breed quickly, are associated with fertility,
and thereby, like rabbits, with rampant sexual activity. In colloquial
German a 'bed hare' (*Betthase*), oddly enough a masculine noun, is a
nymphomaniac, while in Spanish *una liebre corrida*, 'a [well-run] hare'
is a prostitute; also any experienced person or 'old hand'.

(4) In French, something which jogs the memory is a 'think-
animal' (*pense-bête*), and whatever the beast is it can't be a hare because
a memory like a sieve is *une mémoire de lièvre*, 'a hare's memory'.

Hatchet-face French: a knife-blade face (*visage en lame de couteau*).
A genius in Spanish is colloquially a hatchet, *hacho*, and the animal
called, from Spanish, the llama, is thin like a razor or knife-blade,
llama.

Hatred In a conference on hatred in Oslo in autumn, 1990, a
Muslim delegate, Moncef Marzouki, pointed out that 'the root of the
word *hate* in Arabic is the same as that for *fear*' ('Winning the Race
against Hate', *Guardian*, 19 September 1990).

Head In Russian someone with an oversized head is a *golovástik*, a
tadpole; an undersized head (a pinhead) is a *golóvka*, which is also the
pommel on a saddle and the 'best bit' of anything. (Head itself is
golová.) A similar idea existed in the Cornish *penyn*, meaning both
'tadpole' and 'the left-over end of something'. It survives in the

Cornish dialect *pednans*. A pollywog, related to 'poll', head, was English dialect for a tadpole.

Heaven (1) Old sailors' slang for a sailor's idea of heaven was a sort of permanent shore leave called *Fidler's* (or *Fiddler's*) *Green*, described by Smyth as 'a sort of sensual Elysium, where sailors are represented as enjoying, for "a full due", those amenities for which Wapping, Castle Rag, and the back of Portsmouth Point were once noted'. Perhaps the green that sailors had in mind, though, was the underwater green of seaweed rather than a village green, because the fidler, or fiddler, is 'a small crab, with one large claw and a very small one [like the arm wielding the fiddler's bow, and the arm whose hand forms the notes on its bridge]. It burrows', according to Smyth, 'on drowned islands.'

(2) Also, *Lubber-land*, 'A kind of El Dorado in sea-story, or country of pleasure without work, all sharing alike' (Smyth).

(3) Papua New Guinea Pidgin for heaven is *antap* ('on top').

See also page 5.

Hedgehog Romany, *pal of the bor*, or 'brother of the hedge'. Also *hatchi-witchu*, 'the prickly thing of the wood', from the Wallachian *aritche*, a hedgehog, and the Persian *besha*, a wood. A word for pig in Spanish Gypsy is *eriche*, also evidently related to *aritche*, and to words in other European languages (see pages 7 and 23).

See also **Porcupine**.

Helicopter Papua New Guinea Pidgin: *magimiks bolong Yesus* (i.e. Jesus). Not so different from 'egg-beater' or 'chopper'.

Hell, Go to In Norwegian, *dra til Blokksberg*, or 'go to Brocken', Brocken being a peak in Germany's Harz Mountains where witches were thought to assemble.

Hen See **Foreigner** (1).

Hold (of a ship) *Bikdaonbilo* (big down below; Papua New Guinea Pidgin).

Home   In Papua New Guinea Pidgin home is *asples* (literally 'arse place'); *as*, by extension from 'arse', also means 'source'.

Homosexual   In Italian, *finocchio*, or the fennel plant. In Spanish, *mariposa*, or butterfly. An effeminate man (in South America) is a *floripón*, a big flower, in Papua New Guinea Pidgin, a *nainsi*, and in Jamaican slang a *cut puss* (i.e. a castrated cat).

See also **Cockroach** (1).

Honeymoon   In German, traditionally *Flitterwochen* meaning literally 'tinsel' or 'spangle' weeks.

Hound's-tooth (check)   See **Foot**.

Hummingbird   (1) In French *oiseau-mouche*, or 'bird-fly' (i.e. the insect).

(2) In German *Kolibri*, and in Spanish and Italian *colibri*, better known internationally as the brand name of a cigarette-lighter.

(3) In Spanish a hummingbird is a *chupaflores*, *chupamiel*, or *chupamirtos*, 'suck-flowers', 'suck-honey', or 'suck-myrtles', and in Cajun also, *sucfleur*.

(4) In Algonquin Indian it is *no-no-caus-ee*, 'the exceedingly delicate creature'.

(5) In Jamaican English, the *god-bird* (not to be confused with *God's bird*, which is the nightingale or mockingbird), from folk belief in the hummingbird's supernatural origins and skills, and its reputation for being clever and very hard to kill. A *god-bird* is also the smallest, most petted member of a family.

Hydroelectric power   See **Coal** (3).

I

I (1) 'Germans would not be Germans, and philosophers would not be philosophers, if they did not make the most of the child's use of "I", in which they see the first sign of self-consciousness. The elder Fichte, we are told, used to celebrate not his son's birthday, but the day on which he first spoke of himself as "I"' (Jespersen).

(2) '. . . the word *je*, I. This word, at least in all languages known to me, is not to be reduced, not to be decomposed, primitive; and it expresses no sensible idea, it represents nothing but the meaning which the mind attaches to it; it is a pure and true sign, without any reference to any sensible idea' (Victor Cousin, *Lectures on the History of Philosophy during the Eighteenth Century*, Paris, 1841).

Müller comments: 'It must be admitted that the French *je*, which is the Sanskrit *aham*, is a word of doubtful etymology. It belongs to the earliest formations of Aryan speech, and we need not wonder that even in Sanskrit the materials out of which this pronoun was formed should have disappeared.'

Ice, icicle (1) In Malay ice is *ayer băku*, or congealed water; also, but less correctly, *ayer batu*, stone water.

(2) *Blink; blink of the ice*: Smyth (1867) informs us that nineteenth-century sailors would know of an iceberg ahead, hidden over the horizon, by 'a bright appearance or looming (the iceberg reflected in the atmosphere above it), often assuming an arched form'. The phenomenon was called the *blink of the ice* by the Greenlanders, 'by which reflection they always know when they are approaching the ice long before they see it'. In Greenland, Smyth added, 'blink means iceberg'.

(3) In Russian a block of something, including ice, is *kabán*, whose primary meaning is 'wild boar'. Not as inappropriate as it may at first sound. A block of ice on a swollen river has the destructive power of a wild boar charging out of the undergrowth, wreaking havoc. And even if the ice-block were stationary, anything cumbersome (like pig-iron) tends to get named after pigs.

(4) *Chandelle de glace* (ice candle) is idiomatic French for an icicle. A drop at the end of the nose is also *une chandelle*.

See also **Kingfisher** (2), **Snow** (2).

If only . . . (1) *¡Ojala . . .!* is borrowed by Spanish from the Arabic of the Moriscos, 'Would to Allah that . . .' (Portuguese *oxalá*).

(2) 'In Chinese the term for the optative mood, expressing a wish or desire, means "something unreal". In 1966 a lecturer at Sichuan University [was] beaten up for "having the audacity to suggest that 'Long live Chairman Mao!' was unreal".' (Jung Chang, *Wild Swans*, 1993)

Indian clubs French: *bouteilles de bois* (wooden bottles).

Indian file French: 'in wolf line' or 'in wolf-tail' (*à la queue loup*). Swahili for Indian file, *mpororo*, means also a line of tribal tattoo marks down the length of the nose.

Infantryman French: a pebble-pusher (*pousse-cailloux*). An infantryman of World War I was 'a hairy' or 'hirsute' (*poilu*).

Insurance The Greek for 'insurance' (*asfália*) is interchangeable with the Greek for 'fuse' (as in a fuse-box).

'I say . . . !' (exclamation) 'I say!' as an expression of shock, surprise, complaint, protest, etc. is a bit dated now, but it was once so common a tic of speech that it proved a fruitful source of so-called 'echoic', frequently heard or overheard, words to describe the foreigners who spoke them.

Thus, according to Yule and Burnell, 'The Chinese mob used to call the English soldiers *A'says* or *Isays*, from the frequency of this apostrophe in their mouths. (The French gamins, it is said, do the same at Boulogne).' A similar 'echoic' word for an Englishman is the French-Canadian *un goddam*, recorded in 1880. Further south, among the Chinook Indians of Oregon in the late eighteenth century, the British were collectively *Kinchotsh* (King George), while in the Japanese port of Yokohama, last century, the British and the Americans earned for themselves the name *Damuraisu H'to*, the 'Damn-your-eyes-people'.

Exactly the same process after the Falklands War of 1982 produced the Falklands expressions *wheneyes* and *whenwons* for soldiers and their officers, the first because the soldiers would be heard to begin a sentence 'When I . . .' while the public-school or university-educated officers would use the indefinite pronoun, 'When one . . .'

The echoic tag 'I say!' also attached itself to the French in their period of empire. During the Napoleonic expedition to Spain the Spanish called the French soldiers *didones*, after their verbal tic of saying '*Dis donc!*' ('Look here!' or 'I say!'). In lingua franca, likewise, a Frenchman was a *dido*, and in Java last century the French were called the *orang deedong*, the *dîtes-donc* or *dis-donc* people.

Nor do the Spanish escape. In Spain *coño*, cunt, is as elsewhere an all-purpose expletive. The Spanish evidently said it often enough for *coño* to have become, echoically and figuratively, a Spaniard in the former Spanish imperial domaine of Chile.

The colonizers also characterized their subject peoples by reference to their distinctive speech patterns. For the French, the Vietnamese were *mangeurs de syllabes*, 'syllable swallowers', while the Spanish verb *gerundiar*, literally 'to gerund' (i.e. to speak in gerunds, or to over-use the gerund) was particularly used in Latin America of the native Indians.

While the colonizers were saying 'I say!' all over the place, the colonized tended to repeat themselves rather by saying that they *couldn't* say. This too gained an echoic momentum. Thus, when the Panama Canal was under construction, the Americans took to referring to the Spanish-speaking Panamanians as *spiggoties*, because they kept saying that they couldn't '*speak-a-de*-English'. And the name of the Mexican province of Yucatán in the language of the local Indians meant 'What do you say?', the reply the Indians gave in answer to persistent enquiries as to the name of their country.

This may be described as peoples comprehending one another

exclusively in terms of their mutual incomprehension. Perhaps the most irresistibly comic echoic derivation is to be found in Papua New Guinea Pidgin. Like 'I say!', the English expressions 'old boy' and 'old man', also often used for surprise or mild protest, are now archaic. They were getting on a bit even in 1943, when they were employed in the Melanesian islands of the Pacific as *oleboi* and *oleman*, parodic (to an English English-speaker) versions of 'I say!', 'By Jove!' etc. in which one can almost see the ghost, snifter in hand, of a lounging colonial clubman.

But if 'old boy' has died the death in English, it hasn't in PNG Pidgin. Todd (1984) recorded *olaboi*, and glossed it 'usually an exclamation of delighted surprise'.

He translated it as 'Wow!'

Italians, The   See **Walnut (wall?), Welsh**.

Its   The possessive pronoun *its* is sometimes said to have been 'invented' by Shakespeare, in whose work it occurs several times. Müller says it 'has sprung into life since the beginning of the seventeenth century'. But it is not in the King James Bible, and Ben Jonson doesn't recognize it in his *English Grammar* of 1640. Until the end of the seventeenth century *his* was commonly put where we now put *its*.

J

Japan (1) An ancient Japanese name for Japan, dating at least from the Nara period (the eighth century AD) is *akitsushima* or *akitsusu*, 'dragonfly island', 'so called from its shape resembling the dragon-fly, or, as some say, from its abundant harvests' (Hepburn). The dragonfly is sacred to Shinto, the Japanese religion: *akitsukami*, or the 'dragonfly god', translates as 'the visible god'.

(2) A slightly different picture emerges from another ancient Japanese word for Japan, *ashiwara-nakatsukuni*: *ashiwara* is 'a tract of ground covered with reeds'.

(3) The archaic Japanese *chōka* is 'my country'. Its literal meaning is 'morning house'.

See also (for Japanese) **K** (3).

Jerkish '... I'd go even further and call him [Ivan Klima] one of the Fab Four – the others being Milan Kundera, Josef Skvorecky and Vaclav Havel – who managed to preserve Czech literature from the language of the state, known to Klima as *jerkish* (after the minimal vocabulary taught to chimps)' (Clive Sinclair talks to Ivan Klima, *Independent*, 26 May 1990).

Jerusalem artichoke The 'Jerusalem' is a popular etymology from *girasole*, the sunflower, to whose family the artichoke belongs. By extension soup made from artichokes is 'Palestine soup'.

Judge In Romany, *borobeshemeskeguero*, or 'great-sitting-fellow'. A wonderfully ponderous word for a ponderous person, not so far removed in its sense from 'bigwig' (see **Hair**, (6)). In legal jargon also, judges are always spoken of as 'sitting' – the *besh* of the Romany word.

Borrow remarks, of the Gypsies' translating the name 'Stanley' into Romany,

When they rendered Stanley by *Beshaley* or *Beshley*, they mistook the first syllable *stan* for 'stand', but for a very good reason rendered it by *besh*, which signifies 'to sit', and the second for a word in their own language, for *ley* or *aley* in Gypsy signifies 'down', so they rendered Stanley by *Beshley* or *Beshaley*, which signifies 'sit down'. Here, of course, it will be asked what reason could have induced them, if they mistook *stan* for 'stand', not to have rendered it by the Gypsy word for 'stand'? The reason was a very cogent one, the want of a word in the Gypsy language to express 'stand'; but they had heard in courts of justice witnesses told to stand down, so they supposed that to stand down was much the same as to sit down, whence their odd rendering of Stanley. In no dialect of the Gypsy, from the Indus to the Severn, is there any word for 'stand', though in every one there is a word for 'sit', and that is *besh*, and in every Gypsy encampment all along the vast distance, *Beshley* or *Beshaley* would be considered an invitation to sit down.

While we are about it, 'dock', the place where the prisoner stands, or stands down from, also looks like a metaphorical coinage of country people familiar with appearing before 'great-sitting-fellows'. It is identical with the Flemish *dok*, a rabbit-hutch, or cage. 'Dock' implies that the prisoner sees himself as already in jail even before he is sentenced.

See also (for lawyers) **Chatterbox** (7).

Juggernaut (i.e. lorry)   See **Brum**.

K

K (1) 'To a literate member of Western culture in the mid twentieth century, the capital letter K is nearly an ideogram, invoking the presence of Kafka or of his eponymous doubles. "I find the letter K offensive, almost nauseating," noted Kafka mordantly in his diary, "and yet I write it down, it must be characteristic of me"' (*After Babel*, George Steiner).

Josef K. in Kafka's *The Trial* is (arguably) falsely accused. Among the Romans, by contrast, K for *kalumnia* (calumny) was branded on the forehead of a false accuser.

(2) 'No two consonants would seem to be more distinct than *k* and *t*. Nevertheless, in the language of the Sandwich Islands, these two sounds run into one, and it seems impossible for a foreigner to say whether what he hears is a guttural [the *k*] or a dental [the *t*]. The same word is written by Protestant missionaries with *k*, by French missionaries with *t*. It takes months of patient labour to teach a Hawaiian youth the difference between *k* and *t*, *g* and *d*, *l* and *r*' (Müller, who also argues that Latin *k* sounds tend in Greek to turn into *p* sounds). 'X' breaks down into the sound '-*ks*-', and the tendency of *k* to turn into *g* can be seen in the shift from the '-*ks*-' sound of *x* in a word like 'expert' to its '-*gz*-' sound in words like 'exact' or 'exit'.

(3) '. . . a sound like briskly plied knitting needles, for Japanese is a language full of T's and K's' (Angela Carter, *Nothing Sacred*).

Kayak Nansen coupled the invention of the Eskimo canoe, the kayak (he calls it *kaiak*), with that of the Eskimo harpoon, as 'the highest achievement of the Eskimo mind'. Yule and Burnell wondered whether it was 'by an accident, or by a radical connexion through Turkish tribes on the Arctic shores of Siberia, that the Greenlander's *kayak* is so closely identical' with the Turkish *kāīk*, which they define as 'the small skiff used at Constantinople'. Whence the name of the Greek fishing-boat, *caïque*.

See also **Canada**.

Kill, To   In Papua New Guinea Pidgin *kilim* means only to strike, or hit very hard. To kill is *kilim i dai*.

Kingfisher   (1) The Peruvian Spanish *camaronero* identifies the kingfisher as a catcher of prawns (*camarónes*), whence the part of Africa called (from the Portuguese) 'the Cameroons'.

(2) But in Europe, the kingfisher is better captured by the Norwegian *isfugl*, the 'ice bird', even though, more precisely, the bird is associated not so much with ice as with the period of traditionally fine weather just before the onset of winter with its ice and storms. This is the period once called in Yorkshire 'St Martin's little summer', occurring around St Martin's feast day, November the 11th.

'Expect St Martin's summer, halcyon days', we are told in Shakespeare's *Henry VI*. In modern Greek, *alkión* means 'brooding on the sea', and it, and 'halcyon', an old English kingfisher-name, arise from the ancient (incorrect) belief that the kingfisher hatches its eggs in a floating nest of fishbones. Periods of unexpected calm are *alkionídes méres*, halcyon, literally 'kingfisher' days.

According to the myth, Ceyx, son of the day star, was the husband of Halcyone, the daughter of Aeolus, god of the winds. When Ceyx was drowned, the gods had pity on him and his wife and changed them into kingfishers. For fourteen days in winter, while Halcyone broods on her nest, her father Aeolus ensures it won't capsize by restraining the winds and keeping the sea calm.

In English 'halcyon days' is usually used figuratively, and wrongly too. But in Greece I have heard *alkionídes méres* applied specifically to this time of year, when, some say, calm seas are a reality in the Aegean, if not elsewhere.

Kiss See **Guava**.

Kite (1) The English 'kite' suggests the bird of that name, once common in the British Isles.

(2) But in German a kite (the toy) is *Drachen*, suggesting *Drache*, a dragon.

(3) In Italian and French it is *cervo volante*, and *cerf-volant*. *Cervo* or *cerf* is a stag or deer. *Cervo volante* (or *cerf-volant*), flying stag, is a stag beetle, and a kite.

(4) Malay for a kite is *wau bulan*. *Wau* means 'sail', and it's an onomatopoeia suggestive of flapping in the wind. Malayan kites originally had strips of rattan or, extraordinarily, dried leeches at their front edges, which flapped and fluttered to make a *wau* noise (a modern Malaysian kite employs audio or computer tape instead to produce the same effect).

Bulan means month, or moon. In Malaya, kites traditionally have a crescent-moon-shaped rear trailing edge (and in Malaysia, of course, as elsewhere in the tropics, the crescent moon doesn't stand on its end, as in northern climes, but lies on its back, just as the paper crescent moon of the Malaysian kite does). In Malay, then, a kite is a 'moon sail'. It can also be *wau burong*, or a 'sail bird'.

(5) Greek for a kite is *aitós*, eagle, or *khartaetós*, paper eagle.

(6) In Mexico a small paper kite is *güila*, a whore. In Costa Rica *güila* is a small spinning-top and in Chile it means rags, tatters.

Kiwi fruit (Chinese gooseberry)   In French, *souris végétal*, 'vegetable mouse'.

Knee   *Skru* (Papua New Guinea Pidgin). Any joint in the body is *skru*. An injured knee is *skru i lus* (loose screw). A kneecap in Malay is *tempurong*, a coconut shell.

Knitting pattern   In French 'the boss' (*le patron*). Also in Greek (*patrón*), borrowed from the French.

Knockout   The English and Americans 'see stars', but in French a knockout blow is one of *trente-six chandelles* (thirty-six candles); the

French say of someone who has been beaten 'black and blue' that he is *marbré* ('marbled', as in raw meat).

Ku Klux Klan

'Have you never –' said Sherlock Holmes, bending forward and sinking his voice – 'have you never heard of the Ku Klux Klan?'

'I never have.'

Holmes turned over the leaves of the book upon his knee [the *American Encyclopaedia*]. 'Here it is,' said he presently, '"Ku Klux Klan. A name derived from a fanciful resemblance to the sound produced by cocking a rifle . . .'

(Sir Arthur Conan Doyle, 'The Five Orange Pips',
from *The Adventures of Sherlock Holmes*)

A fanciful etymology, too.

L

L   The sound of 'l', in company with that of 'r', is a phonetic minefield. Lamdacism, difficulty in pronouncing one's 'l's, is closely related to rhotacism, a similar difficulty with the letter 'r', and both problems (as they seem from a Western point of view) are associated with languages of the Far East. Thus the tired Chinese-restaurant jest about 'flied lice' (for 'fried rice'). Pei remarks, 'Japanese lacks the sound of *l*, and a Japanese speaker pronouncing a foreign word with *l* usually substitutes a lightly trilled *r*. Chinese reverses this process, saying "lice" for "rice".' Roman Jakobson wrote (in *Six Lectures on Sound and Meaning*) that:

The two liquids *r* and *l* have such clearly distinct functions in our languages (cf. *ray-lay, fur-full*) that it seems strange to us that in some other languages they are simply two combinatory variants of a single phoneme. Thus in Korean this phoneme is represented by *l* at the beginning and by *r* at the end of a syllable . . . It is natural that a Korean who is trying to learn English will at first pronounce *round* with an initial *l*, *sell* with an *r* at the end, and will reverse the order of the two liquids in *rule* which will then be confused with *lure*.

In deference to these difficulties, the now-defunct and never exactly flourishing invented language of Volapük abandoned 'r' in favour of 'l'. A red rose in Volapük was a *led lol*.

Ladybird   In Russian, God's (or divine) 'little cow'. Also in archaic English dialect, 'God Almighty's cow'.

Laughter (1) Rippling laughter in French is *les rires perlés* (pearled laughter); mother-of-pearl too may be said to 'ripple'. Forced laughter is *rire du bout des dents*, to laugh with the end of the teeth, or *rire jaune*, yellow laughter, with the suggestion of a forced, sickly rictus of a smile.

(2) Laughter sounds like a sneeze (atishoo!) in the Japanese exclamation *aashiya-koshiya* expressing the sound of laughter.

Lavatory, **lavatory seat** (1) A cloyingly childish German euphemism for lavatory is *Örtchen* (literally 'little place'). In 1966 an English booklet published in German informed German football fans visiting England for the World Cup that year that there were many *hübsche Örtchen* (pretty little places, or pretty lavatories) they could travel to by bus or train.

(2) French: a lavatory seat is a 'little moon' (*lunette*), as is the wishbone of a fowl. See also **Spectacles** (1).

(3) The Greek *kouloúra* is a ring-shaped loaf of bread and, colloquially, a lavatory seat, a lifebelt, and zero.

See also **Barge**, **Bedpan**, **Pelvis**.

Lawyer See **Chatterbox** (7). See also **Judge**.

Lazybones French: mollusc, or mussel (*mollusque*, *moule*). Also in Mexico, *lapa*, limpet or scrounger. In Ecuador, *lapa* is a beret.

Left and right In the Cameroons, the left-hand side is *wuman han* (woman hand) and the right-hand side *man han* (man hand).

Lemon Lemons are so extensively used in Greece that the Greeks even have a word, *lemonókoupa*, for the empty half of a squeezed lemon.

Lentil (1) A lens is so called 'on account of its shape' (*Oxford Dictionary*) resembling a lentil's. In French, likewise, a spectacle lens is *une lentille*, a lentil, and contact lenses are *lentilles de contact*. The Italian *lente* is a lentil, a lens, the bob of a pendulum (which is also lentil-shaped) and, in the plural, pince-nez. In Greek, *phakí* is a lentil, and *phakós* is a lens, magnifier, or torch. Lentils existed before lenses did, so here is a metaphor where we can be historically sure of the vehicle (lentil) and the tenor (lens).

(2) Apart from the freckles in the main text (see pages 109–11), lentils are also the vehicle for freckle-metaphors, as in Greek *phakída*, French *lentille* again, and Italian *lentiggine*, from *lenticchia*, lentil. The idea is the same as that behind the Greek *spirí*, a grain of corn but also a spot or pimple or the bead of a necklace.

Leprosy   See **Chinaman/Chinese** (3). See also **Aids** and **Syphilis**.

Lesbianism   See **Love** (2).

Life   The Romany *merripen* means both life and death. In Spanish Gypsy, a *Merinao* is an immortal.

Light-heartedness   See **Sausage**.

Lily   'The worn-out, violated word "lily" is devoid of all expression. Therefore I call the lily *éuy* – and original purity is restored' (Russian 'Kubofuturist' Alexei Krucényx, from his *Declaration of the Word as Such*, 1913).

Lobster   The Latin *locusta* was a lobster or any crustacean, and a locust. The original broad meaning survives in the modern Spanish *langosta*, from *locusta*, which signifies equally lobster and locust. The very strange English word 'lobster' evolved from *locusta* via an unexplained 'p' for 'c': the 'p' then became an unexplained 'b'.

During the English Civil War, a resemblance was perceived between the lobster's articulated armour and the helmet worn by Roundhead cuirassiers, which had chain-mail around the sides of the face and at the back of the neck. It was called a lobster-tail helmet, and by extension 'lobster' became an abusive slang term for soldiers in general. The British Army changed its uniform, but then, in the eighteenth century, the soldiers in their red coats resembled lobsters for another reason, and the term remained in use. 'Lobster-box' became a colloquialism for an army barracks.

Most of us only see a lobster, when we can afford it, as red, cooked, on a plate waiting to be eaten. In an Irish restaurant, however, you might be surprised, as I was once at Minogue's in London, to see lobster listed on the menu as 'Dublin lawyer'. How can a lobster be a lawyer?

For a clue to that we go to lingua franca, the maritime pidgin spoken in the Mediterranean until the early years of this century. In Simonet's dictionary of lingua franca, published in 1888, lobster (*homard*) is given as *papaz*. The word is from *papas*, Greek for a Greek Orthodox priest. Different cultures with different languages, then, have at different times seen the lobster as a lawyer and as a priest.

Simonet wrote, 'I believe it is called so [i.e. a priest] due to its shape.' Simonet presumably meant the lobster's two large claws extended as though at a climax of the Greek Orthodox mass, and perhaps the swaddled appearance of the lobster's shell, like a priest's tightly wrapped and overlapped robes, the same characteristic which had caused people to call the Roundhead cuirassiers 'lobsters'. Certainly there is something about the lobster's, the priest's, and the lawyer's appearance for which the adjective 'overdressed' seems appropriate; and isn't there, too, something benedictory, priestly, about the slow *urbi et orbi* movement of a lobster's claws?

But the German linguist Hugo Scuchardt disagreed with Simonet. A lobster was lexically interchangeable with a priest, he argued, because of its colour. Scuchardt meant, not the lobster's colour when cooked, but when raw and alive, under water, as the fishermen saw it. And a lobster, alive, is not red but 'greenish- or bluish-black' (*Oxford Dictionary*). In the live lobster's 'bluish-blackness' we have an explanation which straightforwardly accounts both for the Greek Orthodox priest *and* the Dublin lawyer. Both wear black, as the living lobster does.

It is perhaps for the same reason that I have heard black London taxis (with their armoured, crustacean appearance) referred to as 'lobsters' (although this may be rhyming slang: lobster and crab, cab). From the living lobster's bluishness we get the English slang term for a policeman – raw, or unboiled, lobster – because of the policeman's blue uniform.

Opinions may differ as to just how blue or how black the living lobster is. William Barry Lord in his *Crab, Shrimp, and Lobster Lore* (1867) wrote of the 'strange metamorphosis' whereby 'the peculiarly rich blue shade of [its] shell ... changes to a bright red in the cooking-pot, and the uniform of the *police* is exchanged for that of the *line regiments*'. This perceived 'rich blue' is perhaps the chief reason why Simonet thought the *papaz* analogy to be based not on colour but on shape.

There is something else to be said about shape: the lobster, prone on the seabed, may be thought rather to resemble a worshipper than a priest. With its claws spread before it, and its bulbous curled tail behind, it looks like a Muslim praying to Mecca, and on this analogy the *homard* or *omar* (old French names for the lobster) seems to be praying, paying homage.

The blackjack used to kill newly caught fish is known to anglers as 'the priest', probably because it delivers the *coup de grâce*, although in the West of Ireland it's jocularly said that it's because it's 'the last thing the fish sees before it dies'. The *Oxford Dictionary* gives 'to be [a person's] priest' as 'to kill him' (in allusion to the function of a priest in performing the last offices to the dying). But *papaz*, the lobster, and 'the priest', may be only isolated instances of a deep and subconscious perceived connection between Christianity, with its fishers of men and its hooks and crooks, and the sea.

See also **Berries** and (for images of other animals as priests) **Octopus**.

Loneliness   In provincial Russian (1916) to live in loneliness is to live like a wolf. The Greek *magoúphis* means a solitary or wretched person and an ownerless animal.

Lout   Russian for someone who scoffs at traditional values is *kham*, or Ham, the son of Noah who mocked his father.

Love   (1) Borrow says that the Romany for 'to love', *camova*, 'is expressive of physical desire, and is connected with the Sanscrit *Cama*, or Cupid' (he also gives *cama* as the origin of the Latin *amor*, love). He adds that 'the English must not triumph over the Gypsies, as their own verb "love" is connected with a Sanscrit word *lubha* [the root of the Romany *lubbeny*, a prostitute] signifying "lust"'.

Old High German for 'love' is *luba*. The Romans had *lubere*, 'to be pleasing', which Varro related to *lubrica*, 'slippery'. The lips, by this reading, are *labia* because they lubricate, and 'lubriciousness', like 'lechery' (see page 94) has much to do with lip-licking and the libido.

(2) The idea of licking is also implicit in 'lesbianism', whose origin is usually given, wrongly, as the island of Lesbos, home of the poet Sappho. The Greek verb, *lesbiázein*, meant 'to lick the sexual organs'.

(3) The useful Tierra del Fuegan word *mamihlapinatapei* doesn't necessarily always apply to love, but probably most often does in practice. The *Guinness Book of World Records* defines it as 'looking into each other's eyes, each hoping that the other will initiate what both want to do but neither chooses to commence'.

(4) The Russian *razlyubíto* is the feeling one has for someone one once loved.

Lumber   See **Dictionary, Tree, trees** (1).

Lunch, No such thing as a free   Hospitality or generosity with an ulterior motive is in Italian *carità pelosa*, or 'hairy charity'.

M

M 'If we watch from below people walking up-hill and speaking together, the nasals *m* and *n* are heard longest.' A certain Professor Helmholtz, quoted by Müller.

Mackerel A dried mackerel in Greek, *tsiros*, is also a very thin person.

See also **Pimp**.

Madness (1) In Greek, people of disturbed mind were *nympholeptoi*, 'seized by the nymphs'.

(2) In the Chinook jargon of Oregon the adjective for 'mad' or 'foolish' was *pelton* or *pilton*, 'derived from the name of a deranged person, one Archibald Pelton, whom the Indians saw at Astoria; his strange appearance and actions made such an impression upon them, that thenceforward anyone behaving in an absurd or irrational manner was called *pelton*' (Hale, 1890, abridged by Jespersen, 1922).

(3) US slang (1950s) for madness: bubbles in the think tank, a guest in the attic, a kink in the conk.

See also **Albatross** (gannet), **Drink, drunk** (5 and 6), **French Revolution** (1) (bishop).

Magic, magpie Robert Graves tells us (in *The Crane Bag and Other Disputed Subjects*, 1969) that the *mag-* of magpie, the only bird still popularly a bird of augury in the British Isles, 'may stand for "magic"; its other name is Pie-Annet, the pie (two-coloured bird) of the goddess Annet, or Anatha, or Annis who is Milton's "Blue-faced Hag"'.

See also **Quack**.

Magnet In French, *un aimant*; as an adjective, *aimant* is affectionate, loving. In 1992, the Académie Française ruled that *aimant* in its sense of a platonic lover is defunct in French. 'The *magnet* is named from a place in Asia Minor . . .' (Bloomfield).

Mah-jong means 'the twittering of sparrows' (the clicking of the tiles). For a similar reason, the French call the game of backgammon *tric-trac*.

Maize Maize, like the turkey, originated in the Americas, and names for maize have much in common with those for the turkey. Thus, although maize is no more Turkish in origin than the turkey is, it was called 'turky' in parts of France, *gran turco* (Turkish grain) in Italy, and 'Turkish corn' in Germany and Holland. In Russia it carries the Turkish name for corn, *koukourou*.

It was the Portuguese who, in the early sixteenth century, first started maize on its international travels, and in places, as a result, it has been identified, like the orange (see page 73), with Portugal – for example, in the Congo region of Africa, where it is *masa ma Mputa*, 'the ear from Portugal'. Like the orange, it has a variety of other names hinting at supposed European origins. In Lorraine, in France, it was 'Rhodes corn', in the Pyrenees 'Spanish corn', in Tuscany 'Sicilian corn', and so on. Among the Zinacanteco Indians of Mexico, maize is referred to by terms which translate as 'the sunbeams of the gods'.

See also **Hair** (1), **Turkey**.

Masturbation In Japanese masturbation is *senzuri*, meaning a thousand slippings and slidings. The colloquial verb, *zuri*, is 'to slide down, slip down'. Female masturbation is *manzuri*, or ten thousand slidings.

Matches In Malay, *tarek api* (*tarek* is 'to pull', *api* is 'fire').

Medicine See **Quack**.

Memory See **Hare** (4).

Menstruation   (1) In colloquial French, the start of menstruation is 'The English [i.e. the redcoats] have landed' (*les Anglais sont debarqués*). 'If you don't try what I advise [a remedy to bring on the redcoats] how will you know why they are staying away?' (Gustave Flaubert in a letter to his mistress Louise Colet, 13 September 1846). Francis Steegmuller comments in a note: ' "The Redcoats have landed" is an expression of relief well known to French lovers.'

(2) In Papua New Guinea Pidgin, *sik bolong mun* ('moon-sickness') or *si mun* (see moon).

(3) In Cameroons pidgin *get flawa* or *flaua* (get flower) is to have one's first period. 'The equivalent expression in Cameroon English is "germinate"' (Todd). A girl who has had her first period, therefore, can be described as having 'germinated'.

Menu   In colloquial German *Magenfahrplan* (stomach itinerary or timetable).

Mess up, make a mess of   Papua New Guinea Pidgin *bagarapim*, which also means 'to rape'.

Military decorations   See **Brass hats**.

Milk   In Papua New Guinea Pidgin, milk and breast (or udder) are *susu*, which also means pus. *Susu* is also 'a deep, narrow fish of milky whiteness, about fifteen inches long, found under reefs and belonging to the trevally family' (Murphy). Perhaps from Malay, in which milk is also *susu*. Cajun, likewise, calls a type of fish *sac à lait* (bag of milk). In Swahili, milk is *maziwa*, related to *ziwa*, a woman's breast (there is another word for an animal's udder). The primary meaning of *ziwa* is 'lake, pond, marsh, pool'.

Milk train   The German *Lumpensammler* (literally 'rubbish collector', 'collector of odds and ends', 'rag-and-bone man') is also the last bus home.

Milky Way   In Friesland, famous for its black-and-white cattle, the

Milky Way was called the Cow Path, a name also popular in Lancashire.

Minum   The useful Malay verb *minum* means both to smoke and to drink, or both in tandem.

Miser   See **Coal** (2).

Mist, fog, etc. *Frost smoke* was the nineteenth-century English sailor's term for 'A thick mist in high latitudes, arising from the surface of the sea when exposed to a temperature much below freezing; when the vapours as they rise are condensed either into a thick fog, or, with the thermometer about zero, hug the water in eddying white wreaths. The latter beautiful form is called in North America a "barber", probably from its resemblance to soap-suds' (Smyth).

Money   (1) A Swahili slang term for money, *mbango*, means primarily a kind of wild pig with projecting tusks.

(2) The Spanish Gypsies (1873) called the Spanish coin, the *real, quelati*, 'a thing which dances', from *quelar*, to dance.

(3) The Yiddish *Oof* for money, which has passed also into English, is from the German *auf* or *auf dem Tisch*[*e*], 'on the table', from laying money on the table in gambling.

(4) In South America, paper money is colloquially *lechuga*, lettuce. The Greek *lepta*, small change, also means 'minutes' (in time) and 'thin'.

See also **Coal** (2).

Mongrel (dog)   See **Dog**.

Monkey-head mushroom

In the fungal hierarchy of the Chinese cuisine the highest rating belongs to the Monkey-Head Mushroom, concerning which Mr K. C. Wu, the former governor of Formosa, has given us curious information. This is a rare mushroom, sells at a high price, and never passes through the vulgar marketplaces. Its *parfum* is of exquisite delicacy, and it transforms any dish that it flavors. So precious is it that only the best cooks are entrusted with it . . . It is found only in the High Mountains of Central China, and the best come from the sacred range of Sung Mountains . . . They grow out of the trunks of trees, and are of the size of small monkey heads, with yellow hair, two dots for eyes, and curves that are singularly suggestive of a nose and mouth. We are told that where one grows another is always to be found, and they are considered mates, male and female. When you find one, you follow the direction of its eyes, and there on another tree is the other one. They gaze on each other in a perpetual trance. Who is the mycologist that will identify for us the Monkey-Head Mushroom?

(Wasson)

See also **Cep**, **Chanterelle**, **Coconut** (the Monkey-head mushroom sounds very like the 'Chinese whisper' of a coconut), **Puff-ball**.

Months of the year   See **French Revolution** (2), **November**, **September**.

Moon   (1) In Greek, moon is *selíni*. A shilling is *selíni*. Celery is *sélinon*.
(2) In Cameroon pidgin a crescent moon is a *hafhaf mun*.
See also **Epilepsy**, **Kite** (4), **Lavatory, lavatory seat** (2), **Menstruation** (2), **Spectacles** (1), **Water-lily**.

Mother   See **Milk**, **Nipple**, **Pregnancy**.

Motor bike   (1) German slang for a noisy motor bike is *ein Feuerstuhl* (a fire stool, or fire chair).
(2) Vatican Latin had trouble with the concept of the motor bike, but came up with the synthetic *birota ignifero latice incita* ('two-wheeled vehicle driven by fire-bearing juice').
See also **Brum**.

Motor car   (1) In 1907 the Italian prince Scipione Borghese and two companions travelled from Peking to Paris in an Itala motor car across the Gobi Desert, the Mongolian plain, Siberia, and westward through Russia towards Moscow, Berlin, and Western Europe. Most people on their journey had never before seen a motor car. In Mongolia they reasoned that the Itala must be drawn by a winged horse. 'Horsepower' had a literal sense in those days, and in that place (among the wild ponies of the Mongolian plain), which it has since largely lost.

A worried Tartar chieftain, on learning that the Itala was forty horsepower, commented that that was almost as many horses as those under his command. A Mongolian mandarin went for a ride in the Itala, chased by his cavalrymen: 'It was as though the whole ancient world was up in pursuit of that small modern thing which fled before them without horses.'

In Christian Russia it was thought that the Itala was powered by the Devil, and people ran from it and its passengers screaming and making signs of the cross. The Itala – the 'cart with no horse' – frightened horses and upset the carts they were pulling all the way from the Asian steppes to the province of Perm, so many outside one town that the local market had to go without eggs and milk.

(2) In French an unexplained noise in a car is a 'nightingale' (*rossignol*). '*J'ai des rossignols*': 'My car's making funny noises.'

(3) The British sports car of the fifties and sixties, the Austin Healey Sprite, was nicknamed 'Frogeyes' because of its prominent headlamps.

(4) *Car brand names*: In South Africa Nova means 'Don't go'. Rolls-Royce was planning an international Silver Mist – then they discovered that *Mist* is 'dung' in German. The Fiat 127 was originally the Rustica – rural-sounding in Italy, but not the best advert for bodywork in English. The idea behind Mitsubishi's Starion was star + Orion. It was taken to be a mispronunciation of 'stallion'.

See also **Tyre**.

Moustache All facial hair in pidgin is *gras bolong maus* (mouth hair, or mouth grass). A catfish is *mausgras* (i.e. 'mouth-grass', or 'mouth-hair', the catfish's whiskers). In US slang (1950s) a moustache is 'lip-spinach' or 'misplaced eyebrow'.

Mushroom See **Box** (puff-ball), **Cep, Chanterelle, Monkey-head mushroom, Puff-ball**. See also **Brain, Rain** (2).

My (possessive) See **White man**.

247

N

N The possibly watery origins of N (see page 20) seem to be
reinforced by the Hebrew N, *nun*, a fish. N is said to be the image of
a wriggling eel.

See also **M**.

Nappy The Greek *panni* ('nappy' with the consonantal sounds
reversed) is a nappy, the sail of a ship, or any piece of cloth.

Needle in a haystack In French it is to look for the sheep with five
paws (*chercher le mouton à cinq pattes*).

Nest The Romany *tas*, a nest, is also a 'cup'.

Nickel From the German, so called after 'Old Nick', because the
metal is the very devil to mine.

Nightingale See **Chanterelle** (7 and 8), **Hummingbird** (5),
Motor car (2).

Nightmare Ephialtis was the Spartan soldier who in 480 BC
betrayed the Greeks by guiding the Persian soldiers to their rear at the
first Battle of Thermopylae. In Persia he was remembered as a
historical figure. In Greece he was altogether forgotten, consciously at
least. Except that *ephiáltis* became part of the language: the traitor's
name is today the more common of modern Greek's two words for
'nightmare'.

As the result of a very similar story, French for a time had a verb *raguser*, meaning to commit an act of treachery. It derived from the name of the Duke of Ragusa, Marshal Marmont, who changed sides in a war of 1814.

See also page 13.

Nipple   (1) The Greek *rága*, *róga*, or *ráx*, all have the double meaning 'grape' and 'nipple'.

(2) The Japanese *chigobami* is 'the bites inflicted on a mother's nipple by an infant', while *chichi* is breasts, milk, or a nurse.

(3) The Latin American *chiche*, a devilled, potted fish, is a vulgar term for the nipple.

(4) In the pidgins, respectively, of Papua New Guinea and the Cameroons, the nipple is the 'eye' (*hai bolong susu*) and the 'mouth' (*bobi maut*) of the breast.

In *A Summer Birdcage*, Margaret Drabble compares nipples to jelly babies.

Nitpicker, fusspot, nag, pedant, etc.   'Nitpicker' is itself pretty colourful when one thinks about it, but so is the German *Korinthenkacker*, literally a 'crapper of currants'. 'Currant' is from 'Corinth'. A Spanish 'sultana', *esmirna*, is from 'Smyrna'.

Nothing   See **Sausage**.

November   The Eskimo equivalent of November, *akkulerutat*, comes from *akkulerôrpok*, 'when the hair of the reindeer is not yet fully grown'. (By extension it means also: 'It is not yet quite ready; it is still between.')

See also pages 91–3.

Nutmeg   The Greek *moscokárudo* means literally 'musk [or perhaps sweet-smelling] walnut'.

Nymphomaniac   See **Hare** (3).

O

Octopus   The octopus in Japan has the name *tako-nyudo*, 'bonze-octopus'. Fuku-roku-ju, one of Shinto's seven gods of happiness, is sometimes represented as an octopus, with a suitably smooth, disproportionately elongated, bald skull. The octopus then, like the lobster, is seen as a priest.

Interestingly, there is evidence of a similar vein of perception of aquatic mammals, whose brains (and therefore whose skulls) are bigger than those of their relations on land. This is a point made by Konrad Lorenz, among others. Relative to its body size, for example, the skull of the otter is bigger than that of the stoat.

Exactly paralleling the Japanese term for an octopus is the colloquial term for the swimming monkey of Gabon, the talapoin, known also as 'the Buddhist priest'.

See also (for more marine 'priests') **Lobster**, and for more about the octopus the entry following this one, **Office, In the** (octopus). See also (for tadpoles), **Head**.

Office, In the   You work for a big company, or *bikkampani*, the Papua New Guinea term first for the New Guinea Gold or Bulolo Gold Dredging Co. and then, by extension, for any large corporation. You enter your office, or paper house (*haus peipa*), to find papers strewn all over your desk like confetti.

It looks like a 'paper battle', or *khartopólemos*, which is the Greek term for throwing confetti at weddings. It might be that there is not just a paper battle but a paper war going on. *Papierkrieg*, or paper war, is colloquial German for an administrative wrangle involving lots of paperwork and correspondence. Junk mail and red tape also merit the term *Papierkrieg*, while a literary feud is the more lightweight *Federkrieg*, or literally 'feather war'.

German writers are on the whole heavy-, not featherweights, but they do wield pens. The first pens were feathers, and 'pen' — the Italian *penna* — was originally and is still literally a feather. The libretto for Haydn's *Creation* was written in Italian and subsequently translated into English by an Italian. To this day, English choral societies solemnly sing the line 'The eagle on its quills ascends the air' ('feathers' doesn't scan).

Back to your desk covered with paper. You toss some of it into File 13, US slang for a wastepaper-basket, and in doing so you reflect that the Spanish call not only a wastepaper-basket but, with a fine sense of the ridiculous, the office desk itself a *papelera*. In Spanish, indeed, the very *idea* of paper (*papel*) is a load of laughs. A *papelón*, piece of wastepaper, is figuratively also an impostor, bluffer, show-off, as well as a ridiculous act or a ridiculous state to be in. *Papelonero* is Latin American slang for ridiculous, *papelada* is a farce, and a *papelero* is a ridiculous person.

And all this paperwork *is* ridiculous. How are you going to clear it all? You wish you were an octopus with eight arms, to do it all more quickly.

No problem. Let's turn you into an octopus, or squid, or cuttle-fish. The names overlap to some extent, in scientific as well as in popular use, but in metaphor all these various cephalopods resolve into a single distinct image: that of an underwater underwriter.

Think of a clerkish underwriter of the nineteenth century, with an inkstand, quill pen, and special powder for smoothing the writing paper, which is perhaps provided by the fellow-cephalopod known as the 'paper nautilus'. If that is facetious, the rest of the picture is soberly accurate. We can even imagine our underwater underwriter as having a smooth-domed bald head and wearing shirtsleeves.

The squid was known in the nineteenth century as the 'pen-and-ink fish' or 'sea-clerk'. It has a gristly, translucent stiffener along its back, the shape of a quill pen, and its own ink, or sepia, which it ejects when it is alarmed in order to provide a smokescreen for its retreat.

Kalamári in Greek is both a squid and an inkstand. In Cornwall (still the place in Britain to catch squid) an ink-pot was a *padelynk* and a cuttlefish (also a fickle person) was a *padelynkyn*. The French naturalist Cuvier illustrated his *Anatomy of the Mollusca* with pictures of cuttlefish and other members of the mollusc family, which he drew using cuttlefish ink, or sepia. Sepia ink has even been successfully extracted from the ink-sacs of fossilized cuttlefish.

The quill-shaped dorsal plate floats on water and was called by sailors 'sea-biscuit'. Nowadays one sees it only in budgies' cages, but it was once pounded into a powder called 'pounce', used for smoothing writing-paper.

The scientific name of the squid is *Loligo vulgaris*, 'lolligo', wrote Varro, 'because it "flies" [*volat*] up' from under, originally *volligo*'. This is one of Varro's nonsensical etymologies. Our underwriter doesn't fly. *Loligo* alludes, and alluded even in Varro's day, to the fact that the squid has for centuries been popularly known as the 'sleeve' (*loligo*) after the hollowness of its tentacles, like empty shirtsleeves.

The same tubular hollowness seems hinted at in other Greek words related to *kalamári*, like *kálamos*, which is reed, cane, or pen, and *kalámi*, reed, cane, fishing-rod, bobbin, and shin-bone.

Cartoons show the octopus or squid as a pen-wielding parody of the prolific scribe (*kalamâs*) and a cartoon-like metaphor from Japan gives us the image of our underwriter as bald. To portray the octopus/squid as I am doing, anthropomorphically, conforms with Japanese traditions, one of which compares the octopus, with its smooth, domed body, to the bald, shaved head of the bonze, the Western name for the Buddhist priest (see **Octopus**).

But back to our clerk, or scribe, on whose desk, as well as all this paperwork, are all the usual office bits and pieces. There's a pad containing blotting paper, which the French call 'fog' or 'drinking' paper (*papier brouillard, papier buvard*), paper-clips, which the French in a triumph of the imagination call *trombones* (after their trombone-slide-like shape), and, most interestingly, what you call if you are English 'drawing-pins', or, if you are from the United States, 'thumb tacks'.

The American term is more expressive than the English, but neither matches the Spanish or French. A drawing-pin in Spanish (*una chinche*; more commonly, *chincheta*) and in French (*une punaise*) both have the primary meanings 'bug' or 'bedbug' (although a French 'bedbug' is more literally *punaise des lits*). And Greek also, from the French, has *pounaiz* to mean drawing-pin.

What have a bedbug and a drawing-pin in common? Are the pins called bugs for the same reason that fleas were once called 'F-sharps' in English slang, because the prick of the bug's bite (or sting) resembles a pinprick?

But think again of 'thumb tack'. It carries in 'tack' the suggestion of 'attaching', as bugs attach themselves to the skin, and the term as a whole suggests also the hard pressure and screwing motion of the thumb involved in the act of using a 'drawing-pin'. Using a thumb tack resembles the act of killing a bug, or turning an 'F-sharp' (a F-lea) into a 'B-flat' (old slang for a dead B-ug).

Or, in French, the way to kill a *puce* (flea) found in one's *pucier* (fleabag, or bed) is with one's *pouce* (thumb).

The Spanish *chinche* can also be a bore or tedious person, while *chincharrero* is any place swarming with bedbugs, but in particular a fishing-smack.

A box of drawing-pins, with the 'swarming' effect of its contents, is a sort of *chincharrero*.

Olive The Latin *bacca*, olive, was used like the English 'berry' as a unit to designate small fruit, and as such it could mean 'grape' and even 'wine'. It is related to 'Bacchus'.

See also **Testicles** (7).

Onion See **Pearl** (1).

Orchid See **Testicles** (7).

Orgasm In colloquial German *höchste Wallung*, or 'maximum bubbling'. Not dissimilar from German fury, as in, for example, *er bringt mir zur Weissglut*, 'he makes me boil with rage', where *Weissglut* is literally 'white heat' or 'passion'.

Orgy In pre-Castro Cuba, *fiesta de percheros*, or 'clothes-hanger party'. 'You entered, said a few pleasantries to your hostess, took off your clothes and put them on hangers, then spent the rest of the evening in orgiastic pleasures' (David Detzer, *The Brink*, 1980).

Oxford   Romany: *lil-engreskey gav*, 'book fellows' town'.

P

P   Hebrew *pe* (the mouth).

Palate   In French *palais* means both 'palace' and 'palate', the roof of the mouth (or *pe*; see above). The idea of a palace was associated with that of a vault, which was *palais voûté* (vaulted palace). The vault was a suitable image for the palate, which also became *palais*, from the same Latin root, *palatium*. The idea of the roof of the mouth as the sky exists in Italian, in which palate is *il cielo della bocca* (the sky of the mouth), and in Greek *ouranískos*: *ouranós* is 'sky'.

Palindrome   (1) In Greek, *karkínos*. Its primary meaning is crab, a creature which like the palindrome is just as happy going backwards as forwards. A palindrome often to be found on fountains in ancient Greece was *Nispon anomimata mi monan opsin* (Wash the sin as well as the face).

   (2) The Spanish for a palindrome, *capicúa*, is also a symmetrical or reversible number, considered lucky in the lottery.

Paper   See **Office, In the**.

Panamanians   See **'I say . . . !'**

Partridge   In Greek partridges are associated with health and courage. To be *perdíki*, to be 'partridge', is to be well again, to have recovered. To be *perdíkoula* is to be brave or bold.

Passing time   See **Pumpkin seeds**.

Peace offering   In German *Drachenfutter* or 'dragon fodder' is a colloquial name for the gifts husbands who have stayed out late, or all night, buy for their wives, who are of course the 'dragons'.

At Saturday lunch-times in German bars and cafés men can be seen drinking with their *Drachenfutter* beside them. When Germans go to the bar after work, stay out late, etc., it's known as a *Feierabend*, or 'celebration evening'. The usual *Feierabend*, in Germany as elsewhere, is Friday evening when the week's work is done. *Feierabend* is a goodwill greeting when the working day is over. It might translate as 'party time'.

Peach   In Spanish, *melocotón*, 'honey-cotton'.

See also **Rose** (4).

Pearl   (1) In Latin a pearl was *unio*, because, as Pliny writes, it is 'the unique gem', or because pearls are only found singly. From *unio* comes the family name of freshwater bivalves called Unionidae and the Middle English 'union' to mean 'a pearl of large size, good quality, and great value'. They were prized by the Romans, and Suetonius says that Julius Caesar invaded Britain in the hope of obtaining pearls. If so he must have been disappointed. The best, 'union' pearls, also called 'orient', are from the warmer waters of the Indian Ocean and South Seas. The Arabs traded in them, and Swahili owes *lulu*, meaning pearl, to Arabic.

The idea of a pearl is playfully and figuratively employed in the Swahili salutation *Hujambo kama lulu?* which my dictionary translates as 'Are you as well as a pearl [is beautiful]?' From Swahili (in which *lulu* apparently now means only 'money'), English gets the ironic expression 'a real lulu', and Lulu, the woman's name. Margaret, also meaning pearl, is from *margarita*, which Pliny calls neither a Latin nor Greek word, but barbarian (probably Babylonian). To the same root we owe the name 'margarine'.

The Romans had a notion that pearls could be drunk in suspension by dissolving them in vinegar, and Pliny records both Queen Cleopatra and a rather shocking profligate called Claudius (who delighted in eating talking birds) as having done this. In *Hamlet*, another Claudius, Shakespeare's Danish usurper-king, drops 'an union' into a cup of poisoned, presumably vinegary wine and gives it to Hamlet, who later forces the wine upon the dying Claudius with the pun, 'Is thy union here?'

The schoolboy pun on this, substituting 'onion' for 'union', isn't so far wrong. The onion is so called from its resemblance to the union, or pearl. Like the pearl it is composed of layers, or coats, laid one upon the other, and it too has a subdued nacreous glow, an opaque sheen. Pliny also has the idea of *physemae*, or 'air-bubbles' resembling pearls, which the oyster produces as it were in a false pregnancy.

(2) Oysters open and shut, like doors (folding doors in English were once called 'bivalves'), and the open shell of an oyster looks like the number 8.

An itchy bit of grit has got into my mind here, and I have no idea whether it is the germ of an etymological pearl or only a *physema*. The French oyster, *huître*, is from the Latin *ostrea*. It was once *uistre*, and according to Robert's dictionary the 'h' was added to avoid the reading '*vitre*'. *Huis*, door (as in Sartre's play *Huis Clos*), we are told is from classical Latin *ostium*, door, no relation to *ostrea*, oyster. *Huit*, meanwhile, eight, is from the Latin *octo*.

False (French or Latin) family relations? Perhaps. But that bit of grit still itches . . .

Pelican   See **Albatross**.

Pelvis   The Norwegian *bekken*, pelvis, means primarily basin, or bedpan. It also means a cymbal (the musical instrument). The Greek *lekáni*, a lavatory-pan, is also the pelvis.

See also **Barge**.

Pen   See **Office, In the**.

Penguin   The French *manchot*, penguin, means primarily someone with one arm or one hand (it is related to *manche*, sleeve).

See also **Albatross**.

Penis   (1) The Swahili *mlingoti*, meaning mast (of a boat, ship, etc.) is sometimes used in songs and jokes as a euphemism for the penis.

(2) Why a penis in Cameroon pidgin should be *mblakot*, thought to derive from the English 'black out', I do not know, except that Todd gives as an example of its use *Dem bin kot pikin i mblakot* – They circumcised the child. Is the idea that the child 'blacks out' when he's circumcised?

(3) In Papua New Guinea Pidgin a penis is *kok* and a clitoris, from the same root, is *kokeru*.

(4) The Spanish *nabo*, a penis, is primarily a turnip.

See also **Cannon** (2), **Testicles** (2), and pages 51, 88, 143–4.

Pepper   A Frenchman called Nicot gave us 'nicotine' (see **Tobacco**) and another called Peter Pepper gave the French *poivre* to mean pepper. Initially, Europe successfully picked its pecks only in Java: 'Europeans had no control over the fields of pepper trees outside Java, and Pierre Poivre's efforts in the Îles de France et de Bourbon, where he was governor (1767) only seem to have been of passing interest; the same was true of similar attempts in French Guiana' (Braudel).

Petticoat   *Follar* in Spanish is 'to fart', *follón* is a silent fart or noiseless rocket. In Colombia, *follado* is a petticoat, and in Ecuador a *follón* is a petticoat and a skirt. One starts to wonder about 'petticoat' itself. It was originally 'petty coat' and was 'a small coat worn by men beneath the doublet' (*Oxford Dictionary*). A coat, however, is no smaller or larger than the person wearing it – why call this particular coat 'petty', or 'small'? Was the 'petti-' originally nothing to do with size, but with the fact that it was the article of clothing that got farted into? The French *péter* is 'to fart', and 'petty', we remember, was once a lavatory in English. A fart, after all, is a mere trifle, a small (or *petit*) thing.

See also **Evening dress**.

Philistine

What is a philistine? In its modern usage, the word goes back to the German student movement of the early nineteenth century. A student had been killed in a brawl with townspeople, and the preacher at his funeral took as his text: 'The Philistines be upon thee, Samson.'

Thereafter, the term came to be applied to anyone who was not a student, and, by extension, to 'a person deficient in liberal culture and enlightenment, whose interests are chiefly bound by material and commonplace things'.

The term 'philistine' was popularised in England by Matthew Arnold and Thomas Carlyle. For Arnold, the philistines were the rising middle classes, whose materialistic prejudices and narrow education made them quite unfitted to succeed the old aristocracy as the rulers of the nation.

Those who call Mrs Thatcher a philistine are the unconscious inheritors of the Arnoldian tradition.

(John Casey, 'Who are the Real Philistines?',
Evening Standard, 9 July 1990)

The brawl, murder, and ensuing sermon are in fact supposed to have happened not in the early nineteenth century, but the late seventeenth, in 1689 in Jena. No one has been able to verify the story, but the word *philister* was certainly in use in Jena before that date.

The word in the modern sense probably grew out of the 'town-and-gown' dispute in Jena, but it first began to gain currency more than a century later, with the publication, in 1797, of Goethe's and Schiller's *Xenien*. Before Goethe's death in 1832, Carlyle had used 'philistine' and 'philistinism' in *Sartor Resartus*.

Arnold in *Culture and Anarchy* and other writings then gave contemporary currency to the modern, contemptuous use of the word, which can perhaps be called the German equivalent of the contemptuous French use of *bourgeois*.

According to Trotsky, Lenin said after meeting H. G. Wells: 'What a philistine! What a monstrous little bourgeois!'

Philtrum 'There is no word', wrote Bill Bryson (in *The Story of English*), 'for the indentation on your upper lip.' Ah, but there is. 'Philtrum', a form of 'philtre', a love-potion, has the specialized meaning of the groove running down from the septum, or dividing wall of the nose, to the top centre of the upper lip. According to an old story, the philtrum is the mark of the finger of the angel, telling the baby to hush, and not to give away the secrets of life before birth. The philtrum is the sign of the angel's bewitchment of the newborn child.

Picking up girls   Greek youths call it making *kamáki*. They stroll along the *paralía* at the harbour's edge, where the tourists sit outside the tavernas, and sometimes it's as easy as harpooning fish in a barrel. *Kamáki* is a harpoon.

The Greek verb *phtheírein*, 'to seduce', was also to destroy. Modern Greek *phthoreús*, seducer, is also 'corrupter', 'destroyer'.

Pidgin   The word 'pidgin', for a marginal, makeshift tongue loosely based upon and constructed out of the raw materials of another, is usually said to be 'a Chinese perversion of the English *business*', which is how the *Oxford Dictionary* defines it. Sometimes (for example in Minette Marrin's *The Eye of the Beholder*) 'pidgin' is even used in English to mean 'business', as in 'It's not my pidgin' (usually heard and intended, I think, as 'not my pigeon'). In fact, despite much research, no one knows where 'pidgin' comes from. It may even be a corruption of 'pigeon', with the idea that pidgin was used like a carrier-pigeon to send simple messages, or that it resembled bird-talk. In Papua New Guinea *pisin* means both 'pidgin' and 'pigeon'.

Certainly, however, the development of pidgin tongues is closely tied up with business (see **Calico**), and 'pidgin' has also been suggested as a corruption of the Portuguese *ocupação* (business, or occupation) or the Hebrew *pidjom*, barter. The most obscure etymology is that it is from *pidian*, a word attributed to the South American Yayo Indians in *Purchas His Pilgrimes* (1625) and said to mean 'people'. (The English were in contact with the Yayos in 1604–5, when they attempted to set up a South American colony.)

More promising and psychologically plausible, because the native peoples were seen as backward, baby-talking servants, is that 'pidgin' is a patronizing term from the Portuguese *pequeno*, 'little', or 'child'. Pidginized versions of French, Dutch, and Malay were known respectively as *petit nègre*, *baby hollands*, and *baba Malay* and the Portuguese were among the first Europeans to trade in Africa, Asia, and the Americas. And *pékin*, related to *pequeno*, was a patronizing term in French (see **Civilians and soldiers**).

Pidgin has been much reviled as, for example, 'bush English', 'a macaronic jargon', 'inferiority made half articulate', 'vile jargon', 'revolting', 'a grotesque gibberish which would be laughable if it were not almost melancholy'. We should remember, though, that in the wake of the Norman Conquest the English spoke pidgin French, and that pidginization is on the increase as modern travel results in more and more language contacts. For example Japanese, once deeply resistant to foreign influence, is now awash with imported, usually English words which the Japanese call *gairaigo* ('words that come from outside'). Just as the colonizers once found 'bush talk' comical, so we now find the English of the Japanese who are economically colonizing the Western nations.

Pidgin has a unique fascination for anyone interested in language and its development, and pidgin has also been eloquently defended. Of the many rejections of the 'funny foreigner' attitude towards it, that of Hugo Scuchardt is still one of the best: 'It is not the foreigners who break away single stones from a splendid, well-appointed palace [i.e. a European language] in order to build meagre huts, but the owners themselves who put them to such ends.'

See also **Belong**, **Calico**, **Clear**, **Fight**.

For similar perceptions of children, servants, foreigners, etc. see **Child**, **Civilians and soldiers**, **'I say . . . !'**, **Waiter**.

Pigeon-hole   In French, *trou-madame*, literally 'hole-Madam'.

Pigeon-toed   The colloquial German *über den grossen Onkel gehen* means literally 'to walk over one's great-uncle', but is a corruption from the French *grand ongle*, big toenail. It entered German in the first half of the nineteenth century as a result of the French occupation of Berlin, and it has proved so successful that there's even a colloquial verb, *onkeln*, 'to walk pigeon-toed'.

See also (for other echoic words in German) **Coffee**, **Hanky-panky**.

Pimp   In French, *maquereau*, whose primary meaning is 'mackerel'; in German, *ein Kuppler*, or 'a coupler'. *Maquereau* is also found in US slang as mac or mack (Brecht's Mack the Knife), macgimper, mackerel, magiffer, magimp, magoofer, all meaning 'pimp'.

Pince-nez   See **Lentil** (1), **Spectacles** (5).

Pit See **Theatrical terms** (9).

Poinsettia 'I ... walked through the forests among the tall red poinsettias, the Vietnamese called them the Man of Genius Tree' (James Fenton, *All the Wrong Places*).

Pole Star English seamen last century called it *gath-linn*, from the Gaelic, 'signifying ray and moisture, in allusion to its subdued brightness' (Smyth).
   See also **Great Bear**.

Police car In French an unmarked police car is *une voiture de police banalisée* (a police car which has been 'banalized', or made commonplace).

Policeman (1) The Canadian Eskimo *pokertalik* is literally 'wears trousers with stripes'.
   (2) In Romany, *gav-engro*, town or village fellow.
   See also **Lobster**.

Poodle See **Beard**.

Poppy The French *coquelicot*, poppy, meant originally a cockscomb, or wattle.

Porcupine (1) Cameroons: *chukuchukubif* (prickprick or thornthornbeef). *Chuck* – in the Caribbean it is *juk* – is from the English dialect 'chook' – to pierce – reinforced by the Fula 'chuk' – to pierce or prick – plus English 'beef'. *Chukuchuku* on its own means 'thorn'. *Chukuchuku kap* is the Crown of Thorns.
   (2) The Algonquin Indian for a sow, *koo-koosh*, is derived from the same language's word for a porcupine, and signifies a bristly, prickly animal, sharp to the touch. But the idea of a bristly pig is of course implicit in 'porcupine' just as it is in 'hedgehog'.
   See also **Hedgehog**.

Potato (1) The Romany *pov-engro* is literally 'earth thing'. Norwich is *povengreskoe gav*, potato town, and Norfolk is *povengreskoe tem*, potato country. East Anglia seems to have been important to the Gypsies. Norwich was also lawyers', or talkers', town (see **Chatterbox**, 7), and the 'town on the hill' (*chong gav*).

(2) As against the loan-word 'potato' (from Peru, like the potato itself), potatoes were once known in Burgundy (where they appeared around the late eighteenth century) as truffles – *treuffes*, or *cartoufles* (related to the German for potato, *Kartoffel*).

Poverty-stricken (1) A Russian word for 'poor wretch' (1916) is *golýsh*, apparently related to *gol*, nakedness; *golýsh* means also a pebble and a wind-egg ('an imperfect or unproductive egg, especially one with a soft shell').

(2) Borrow thought that the Romany *choveno* – poor, needy, starved – was 'perhaps derived from the Russian *Tchernoe* (black, dirty, wretched); or from the Hungarian *Csunya* (hateful, frightful); whence the *Chungalo* of the Hungarian, and also of the Spanish Gypsies'.

See also **Child, children** (1).

Pregnancy (1) I'm grateful to Marina Warner's *Alone of All Her Sex* for the discovery that the French *enceinte* (Italian *incinta*, pregnant) is far from being the rather prosaic word I always assumed it was. Literally it means 'engirdled'. I had related it to *ceinture*, belt, and vaguely assumed the word therefore had to do with the swelling of pregnancy round the midriff, something like a girdle, or belt.

Correct, as far as it goes, but I hadn't realized that the word refers to a *particular* belt – the sash or girdle worn by the Virgin Mary, *la sacratissima cintola* supposedly still preserved as a relic in Prato Cathedral. *Enceinte*, then, 'pregnant', acquires the transferential sense 'holy', or 'sacred', 'like the Virgin Mary when she was pregnant with Christ'.

(2) The Sanskrit *dohada* means the longings, often for unusual or uncharacteristic foods, of pregnant women.

(3) The German *Torschlusspanik*, literally 'door-shutting panic', is used metaphorically of women scared they're getting too old for childbirth.

(4) Jamaican slang for a pregnant woman, *belly-woman*, is also the

figurative name for the 'Mother Thomas' cutlass, a machete with a wide and deeply rounded blade, in profile having the shape of a pregnant woman's stomach.

Profiteer Norwegian World War II slang for a profiteer is *brakkebaron*, or 'barracks baron', after the people who made money by putting up buildings (especially barracks) for the occupying Germans.

Prostitute (1) The Javanese *balon*, a prostitute, means primarily a toy balloon and a light bulb. The same notion of a prostitute as a worthless plaything persists in the Latin American Spanish *maraca*, rattle, prostitute, and useless person.

(2) Much, much more sinister is the Jack-the-Ripperish South American slang expression for a brothel, *matadero*, which means primarily a slaughterhouse (but see also **Dictionary**).

(3) The Egyptian *almeh*, a prostitute, originally meant 'bluestocking'. The same prejudice seems to underlie the transference of meaning between the Spanish *tuna*, a students' music group, and the colloquial *tuna* to mean 'loose woman, amateur prostitute'.

(4) The Swahili *malaya* (from Persian), prostitute, means also 'a short garment worn by some women'.

(5) The old Greek *ieróthoulos* or *ieródoulos* carries the suggestion of sacred work, after the sacred prostitutes of Corinth.

See also **Hare** (3), **Kite** (6), **Love** (1), **Tom, Dick, and Harry**.

Protestants In the Eskimo tongue of West Greenland (much frequented by Scandinavian missionaries), Protestants are *nâggârtut*, 'those who say "No"'.

Nansen has a revealing story about a Norwegian missionary among the Eskimos, Hans Egede, who 'would now and then take children to his house, against their parents' wishes, and keep them there to learn the language from them. In this connection they made a song about him: "There has come a strange man over the great sea . . . who steals boys, and gives them thick soup with skin upon it (that is, porridge) to eat, and dried earth from his own land (that is, ship's biscuits)."'

When Paul Egede (the missionary's son) on one occasion offered a mother a present if she would let her son remain some time longer with him, she answered that 'children were not articles of commerce'.

Others among Nansen's observations shed more light on *någgårtut*. For example: 'Paul Egede records that when [the Eskimos] thought his father's sermons too long they went up to him and asked him if he was not soon going to stop. Then he had to measure off upon his arm how much of his discourse was left, whereupon they went back to their places and sat moving their hands down their arms every moment.'

An Eskimo told Niels Egede 'that he far preferred the *tornarssuk*'s or "Devil's" house', where he had often been: '"For in heaven there is no food to be had, but in hell there are seals and fishes in plenty"', and finally, 'When in 1728 a number of Danish men and women came . . . to colonise the country, many of them gave great offence to the heathens by their evil ways, so that they "often asked how it was that so many of our people were so bad . . ." And the Greenlanders looked down upon and laughed at the stupid, self-satisfied Europeans who preached so finely but practised so little what they preached . . .'

Pub (public house)   In Oregon Trade Language (Chinook jargon) a pub, tavern, bar, or any place of public amusement was a *heehee house*.

Pubic hair   See **Fool**.

Puff-ball   Its scientific name is *lycoperdon* (wolf's fart). 'Sometimes the mycologists have paid obeisance to popular terminology. For example, the name of the puff-ball, *lycoperdon*, is a learned back-formation to a non-existent Greek term that would mean "wolf's flatus". How much better it would have been to use the genuine Greek name for the same fungus, *petsis*, which harbours the same indelicate idea' (Wasson). In classical Greek, a puff-ball was simply a fart.

See also **Box**.

Puffin   See **Voice**.

Pumpkin seeds Something done to kill time in Greek is a *pasatémpo*. Roasted pumpkin seeds are *pasatémpos*.

Puppy 'Puppies' are feet, as in the US expression 'My puppies are barking' (i.e. 'my feet are hurting'). It follows that 'Hush Puppies' must be comfortable.

See also **Finger**.

Q

Quack (1) In Spanish America, where the school of 'magical realism' originated with the novels of Gabriel García Márquez and others, magic is linguistically equated with folk or quack medicine. The adjective, 'magic', is *ensalmado*. An *ensalmador* is a quack doctor or bone-setter (see also **Algebra**). *Ensalmar* is to set a bone, to treat with quack remedies, or to cure an illness by spells. *Ensalmo* is a spell, charm or incantation and a quack remedy or treatment. *Salmo* is a psalm. (*Como*) *por ensalmo* is 'As if by magic', the title of a magical realist novel by Sir Angus Wilson.

(2) In Cameroon pidgin *medesen* means as well as medicine, mechanical gadgetry and a talisman (Todd).

Queen bee (also queen in chess)   See **French Revolution** (1).

Querencia   Spanish *querencia* has the senses affection, fondness, haunt of wild beasts. It is a term in bullfighting meaning the spot in the ring at which a particular bull seems to feel happiest, most at home.

Quinsy   An old and now little-used name for the heart complaint, angina. 'Angina' derives from Latin and/or Sanskrit roots having the sense of strangulation as if by a snake (the effect of an attack of angina). Thus, for example, Latin *anguilla*, an eel (from *anguis*, snake) and the modern *anxiety* or *angst*. Anxiety also strangles. *Quinsy* might seem worlds removed from this, but it is a corruption of a Greek word (*kynos* is dog) meaning 'dog-strangler'.

*

Qwertyuiop   It looks like the name of a Mexican god, and Anthony Burgess called one of his books *Homage to Qwertyuiop*. But as every writer and typist in English knows, it is the top row of letters of the English-language typewriter keyboard. It contains, incidentally, all the letters needed to type the word 'typewriter', and one theory has it that the top row was originally so ordered for ease of demonstration by typewriter-salesmen.

Otherwise, *qwertyuiop* and all the letters of the typewriter-alphabet are arranged, not in order to make typing easier but, on the contrary, to make it more difficult. On the very earliest typewriters, the keys jammed if the 'typiste' (as 'typist' was originally spelt) typed too quickly. Accordingly, a layout was designed to make the task of laying a particular finger on a particular key more difficult. This was the *qwerty* layout, introduced in the United States in 1872.

The key period in its history and that of the typewriter itself was the 1930s. In that decade, the shift key of Remington won the day over Smith Corona's 'dual bank' of capitals and lower-case letters, IBM introduced the first popular electric typewriter (earlier prototypes had tended to electrocute their operators), and the *qwerty* layout faced stiff competition from the so-called 'Dvorak' layout commissioned by the United States Navy. In the latter layout, typing speeds were greatly increased (to the order of about twenty per cent) by grouping the five vowels and the five most commonly used consonants around the centre of the keyboard – making it possible to type, for example, 'unostentatious' with minimal movement of the fingers. But it never caught on. The *qwerty* layout, becoming standard in the 1930s, has survived into the age of the word processor.

R

R From its growling roll, R is 'the dog's name. R is for the dog'
(*Romeo and Juliet*, ii, 4). It's been suggested that one of the civilizing
influences of women upon language has been the softening of the
gruff and noisy rolling 'r', not a sound conducive to domestic peace.
French has a verb *grasseyer*, 'to speak with a strongly marked [growl-
ing] r'. The French verb carries associations of 'fattening' the sound.

   See also **L**.

Railway signal In Berlin slang a railway signal is *Hampelmann*,
whose primary meaning is puppet – specifically the wooden cut-out
puppets with jerky, string-operated arms and legs. In Russia *vyékha*,
railway signal, is slang for a lanky person.

Railway station In Russian a major railway terminus is *vokzál*,
after the English 'Vauxhall'. *Vokzál* is also a pleasure garden, which
was at first its only meaning. The Russians had pleasure gardens after
the English model at Vauxhall. When they fell out of fashion and
their sites became available, the gardens were appropriated for the
new railway system. Thus, in Russian, the identification of pleasure
gardens with railway stations.

Railway train (1) In China, last century, a *huo-cho*, or fire-chariot,
or *chi-cho* (fuel-chariot; a motor car was also a *chi-cho*) with its 'choo-
choo' sound.

   (2) In Germany *ein Zug*, which is otherwise, among other things, a
draught of air, drag on a cigarette, draw on a drink, and a move in chess.

(3) In *A Hundred Years of Solitude*, Gabriel García Márquez has a character who describes a train as 'something frightful, like a kitchen dragging a village behind it'.

(4) Australian pidgin: *fire nanto* and, for the train of carriages behind the engine, *long cart*.

Some natives were watching Government employees fixing an iron tank high over the ground on a railway line in the North – they were fixing it on a wooden frame, as is usual on railway lines, for the purpose of supplying engines with water. Some of the natives had never before seen a tank so upheld, and naturally had vague notions as to why the water was put so far out of reach. An old native acting as spokesman asked: '*What for you put him tank up high like it that way? You 'fraid blackfella steal him water! If blackfella thirsty him big one climb.*' Workman: 'Oh, no; we are putting it up here to give the injun (fire nanto) a drink.' Native: '*Ha, ha! fire nanto no got him long neck. No fear him reach that. By-and-bye when him big one thirsty him try climb up, and whitefella big one tumble out of long cart.*'

(*Evening Journal*, Adelaide, 19 January 1884)

See also **Sausage** (2).

Rain (1) Heavy downpour: *Walla-walla he tumble down big-fellow* (article in *St James Gazette*, 9 July 1888, by Edgar Layard, British consul in Levuka (Fiji) prior to 1874).

(2) In Russia a fall of warm rain is 'mushroom rain', so called because it presages good mushroom-picking the following morning.

(3) Very light rain, dew, or stagnant water in Jamaica is *jew-jew rain* (jew-jew from 'dew'). The Japanese adverb *chobo-chobo* is said to refer to the sound of falling raindrops and its literal meaning is 'dotted'.

Ravine squatters In Liechtenstein the very worst thing one can call anyone is a *Tobelhocker*, a taboo expression meaning literally 'ravine squatter'. *Tobel* is a wooded gorge or a ravine (thus the name of the chocolate resembling a mountain-range and called 'Toblerone'). A *Tobelhocker* is someone condemned for eternity to squat at the bottom of a ravine having every variety of filth rained down upon him. The expression dates from three centuries ago, when some thirty per cent of Liechtenstein's population were burnt for witchcraft and other forms of heresy. *Tobelhocker* is a curse upon those who condemned these innocents to death, and upon their descendants.

Reckoning, Day of In Jamaica, 'Ben Johnson Day'. The term's origins lie on the west coast of Africa, where in the eighteenth century Ben Johnson was a black slave-driver. He kidnapped a young girl and sold her into slavery, but was in turn kidnapped by her brothers, who exchanged him for her. When the Canadian sprinter Ben Johnson, who was born in Jamaica, was found to have taken drugs, and stripped of his Olympic title, he had met his 'Ben Johnson Day'. In Jamaica it is also the day before pay-day or any day of short provisions and austerity, and among bank-tellers the fifteenth and final days of the month, when the money is counted.

Regulars (of a bar, etc.) In German, 'the tree-trunks' (*die Stamme*). Presumably because 'the regulars' can be relied upon to be there, have fixed places, and don't move much from them.

Rice

In Cambodia, when the water is brought into the fields of seedlings, they call it the 'drowning of partridges and turtledoves'; when the first panicles appear they say that 'the plant is pregnant'; the rice field then takes on a golden hue the 'colour of a parrot's wing'. A few weeks later, at harvest-time, when the grain 'where the milk has formed becomes heavy', comes the game (or almost a game) of stacking the sheaves in 'mattresses', 'lintels', 'flying pelicans', 'dogs' tails' or 'elephants' feet'. Threshing completed, the grain is winnowed to remove 'the promise of the paddy' (the strict meaning of *paddy* is 'rice in the husk'). (Braudel)

Roller-coaster, switchback In French, *montagnes russes*, literally 'Russian mountains'. Perhaps because, as has been suggested to me, a Russian entrepreneur built France's first roller-coaster.

Rolling-pin The Greek *plástis*, a creator, is also the humble rolling-pin, and *krístis*, creator, is also a bricklayer. The idea of the Divine Creator as a semi-skilled workman is implicit in 'demiurge', originally a mould-maker, a metaphor attributed to Plato.

Rook (the bird)   See **Body odour**.

Rook (the piece in chess)   In Russian the rook is the *ladyá*, a poetic word for a boat. See also **French Revolution** (1).

Rose, roses   (1) 'It is said that the frozen Norwegians, on the first sight of roses, dared not touch what they conceived were trees budding with fire . . .' (Isaac d'Israeli, *Curiosities of Literature*).

(2) According to Mario Pei, a Greek rose is 'forty-petalled'. 'In the Middle East', he writes, ' "forty" is a sign of indefinite value', as in Ali Baba's forty thieves, forty winks for a nap, the forty days and nights of Christ's time in the wilderness, and those forty petals. But look it up in a dictionary, or look at the label on a bottle of Greek rose-water, and a rose is not forty- but *thirty*-petalled (*triandáphillo*).

(3) Pei's idea of 'forty' as a coefficient of indeterminacy seems to be backed up however by the marvellous Greek verb *sarandizo*, which means (a) to turn forty, (b) to be forty days old, (c) to be dead, (d) to have given birth.

(4) The more common Greek word for a rose is *ródon*, whence the name of the island of Rhodes and the English rhododendron, rose-tree. It is the root for a range of words including *ródi*, pomegranate, *rodákinon*, peach, and *rododáphni*, oleander (literally, 'rosebay tree'). The compact, convoluted roundness of the rose is perhaps the inspiration for *rodáni*, a spinning-wheel. The English 'rose' of a watering-can or garden spray doesn't exist in Greek, but *rodélla* does: it means a washer (in plumbing) or a round slice of anything.

See also **Cooking, L** (Volapük).

Roundabout (traffic)   (1) In Greek a roundabout is *kómbos*, which is otherwise a knot (tied or in wood), and a junction.

(2) 'Roundabout' was coined in the 1920s by an American writer, Logan Pearsall Smith. Before the word was adopted by the BBC, roundabouts in Britain were called 'gyratory circuses'.

See also **Traffic jam**.

S

Sail (1) In Russian a mainsail is *grot*, whose primary meaning is grotto; the mainsail filled with wind hollows out like a cave.

(2) One thinks of the *grot* as being a square sail running across the width of the boat. This was the sail, fitted to fill out with an astern wind, used by all the Mediterranean peoples from the Phoenicians onwards, until its replacement by the triangular and more manoeuvrable fore-and-aft so-called 'Latin' or 'lateen' sail.

The Latin sail was not a Latin (or western Mediterranean) invention at all, but Indian. Islam found it in the Oman Sea, and introduced it first of all to the Portuguese, and then to the Mediterranean as a whole. The 'Latin' in its name is a direct contradiction of these Islamic origins.

The Latin sail made it easier to slew the boat round and to steer it in changeable winds. Outside the Mediterranean, once the Canaries and the trade winds were reached, it could be lowered, and the old square sail hoisted in its place.

See also **Hammock** (2), **Kite** (4), **Nappy**.

Salad The French don't dress, then toss, their salads: they make them comfortable then tire them (*accommoder* and *fatiguer la salade*). And a mixed salad is 'plumed' (*une salade panachée*).

See also **Black Maria** (1), **Traffic jam**.

Sausage (1) There is a French tongue-twister sometimes given as a test in schools: *si six saucissons sont sans souci* ('if six sausages are without a care'). Interestingly (and oddly), sausages are equated with carefreeness elsewhere, too.

The English, for example, in unrepentant, light-hearted, devil-take-the-hindmost mood 'couldn't give a sausage', and a German likewise will say *es ist mir Wurst*, 'it's sausage to me'. The German chancellor, Bismarck, coined a noun, *Wurstigkeit*, 'sausageness', to characterize this attitude. *Wurstigkeit* may mean much the same as the West Indian 'calypso', believed by some to be calqued, or copied by translation, via the Trinidadian Creole *kaiso* from the West African (Hausa) *ba keito* ('without a human care'). Others, like the veteran calypso king Roaring Lion, deny that calypso has anything at all to do with Africa.

The Spanish shrug things off by saying they couldn't give a *mota*, a handful of earth or grass, and the Romans couldn't give a *ciccus*, which is the pithy membrane dividing two segments of a fruit. The same idea ultimately underlies the word 'nothing', the Latin *ne filum*, 'not a thread', whence *nihil*. *Ne filum* can be seen more clearly in 'annihilation'.

(2) In France – perhaps because they conspicuously *aren't* carefree, but over-careful – people who bring their own food with them to eat on railway trains are known contemptuously as *saucissonniers* ('sausagers').

See also **Alley-way**.

Scaffolding   The most obscure of Japan's *gairago*, or 'words from outside', known to me is *intoray* which sounds to the English ear like 'in-tray'. It is used in the Japanese film and television industry to mean scaffolding (for lighting, etc.), and is an elided abbreviation of *Intolerance*, the D. W. Griffith film (1916), which is a cult classic in Japan. The association is probably with the epic scale of the film, especially its Babylonian sequences, and with the technical innovations for which Griffith is remembered.

Scotland   In Romany, *juvlo-mengreskey tem*, 'lousy fellows' country'.

Sea-green incorruptible   See **French Revolution** (6).

Semen stain   In French it's a *carte de la France* ('map of France').

September Greek for a man who harvests grapes, *trigitís*, is also familiarly September. Spanish for August, *agosto*, also means a harvest.

Seraph See **Giraffe**.

Servants See **Waiter**.

Seven (1) The Canadian Eskimo *issuk* means a seven at cards, seven o'clock, and the end.

(2) Of the Romany *eft*, seven, Borrow wrote (in 1873), 'Few of the English Gypsies are acquainted with this word; consequently the generality, when they wish to express the number seven, without being understood by the Gorgios or Gentiles, say Dui trins ta yeck, two threes and one.'

Sex show 'Fish-fighting' (Philippines).

Sexual intercourse (1) The Spanish *follar* is (a) 'to blow on with bellows', (b) 'to have sexual intercourse', and (c) in its reflexive form, *follarse*, or in Chile and Mexico, *follonarse*, 'to fart silently'.

(2) *Pushim* (Papua New Guinea Pidgin), often mistaken by the white man in the South Seas for the verb 'to push', which is *siubim* (to shove). Part of the 'some thirty per centum of the friction between master and servant ... due to the former's failure to learn the language of the Territory' (Murphy, 1943). Also *pakim* (for the 'p' substitute an 'f') and *goapim*, which speaks for itself.

(3) *A Standard Swahili–English Dictionary* (1948) warns that 'Care should be exercised in using *jamii* ...' the Swahili verb 'to copulate', because its primary meaning is 'to gather together'. The noun, *jamaa*, means 'family, society, company, assembly, gathering'.

Shadow cabinet *Gobierno fantasma* (Spanish).

Shoelaces One of my favourite metaphors is the Spanish verb *desmajolar*, which is both 'to pull up plants [especially vines] by their roots' and 'to loosen, or untie, one's shoelaces'. It is a vivid and clear

picture of metaphor in action, and it gives a vivid word-picture of the
end of the peasant's day. Coming in from the vineyard, and taking his
boots off, he wearily realizes that he is effectively doing all over again
what he has been doing all day, as his calloused fingertips fumble with
an obstinate knotted tangle, whether of vine-roots or shoelaces. The
picture reminds us of the closeness to nature and the 'multidisciplinary'
nature of peasant life, that experiential mix, essential to poetry, which
T. S. Eliot characterized as 'Spinoza and the cooking'. 'Of the
intimacy of this knowledge [i.e. peasant knowledge of nature]', wrote
George Bourne in his *Change in the Village* (1912), 'in minute details,
it is impossible to give an idea ... The peasant did not merely
"reside" in [the countryside]; he was part of it, and it was part of him.
He fitted into it as one of its native denizens, like the hedgehogs and
the thrushes.'

Desmajolar is a clue to this homogeneous closeness, one of the key
conditions of metaphor-making.

Shopping bag   Cameroons pidgin for a holdall bag is *wuman i bele*,
literally 'woman she belly' (Todd).

Show-off, A   In French, to show off is *faire de la broue* (make froth).
In Italian, the self-conscious 'he-man' who likes to show off his
rippling pecs, chest-hair, etc. is colloquially a *fusto*, a barrel.
   See also **Boaster**.

Sidesaddle   To ride sidesaddle in Spanish is *montar a la inglesa*, 'like
an Englishwoman'.

Silly season   In German, *Sauregurkenzeit*, 'pickled cucumber time'.
Also used of a lull in political activity or a slack financial period.
French: *morte-saison*, 'dead season'.

Sin   In the Cameroons a sin is a *bad*. A mortal sin is a *big bad*; a
venial sin is a *smal bad* (Todd).

Sincere   Examples of calquing (ideas from local cultures, expressed
in a foreign language – in this case English) are the Cameroons *gud hat*

(good heart) and the Papua New Guinea Pidgin *bel klin* (belly clean), both meaning 'sincere'.

Sister   See **Brother**.

Slang   French slang for slang is *langue verte*, 'green language'.

Sleet   See **Snow**.

Sleeve   See **English Channel, Office, In the** (squid), **Penguin**.

Slowcoach   *Agteros* (Dutch/Afrikaans) means literally 'hindmost ox'.

Smoking   In the earlier days of tobacco in Europe, smoking was described as 'drinking'. The custom was to inhale through the mouth, and exhale through the nose.

See also **Minum, Tobacco**.

Snow   (1) The Eskimo word for snow in general is *aput*, but the Eskimos have many different words to distinguish different kinds of snow. Snow that is for melting into water is *aniuk*. Newly drifted snow is *akelrorak*. Wet snow is *massaktok*, and snow mixed with water, *massak*. The first snowfall is *apingaut*, and so on. A snow block for building an *iglu* (or snow house) is *auverk*, and snow houses joined by the same porch are *walereit*.

(2) In French Canada, a blizzard of fine snow is colloquially *une poudrerie*, a metaphor of long standing which Dunn calls 'a masterpiece of our language'. Literally, and originally, a *poudrerie* was a gunpowder factory. French-Canadian sleet is 'rotten snow' (*neige pourri*) – rotten in the sense that a fruit is said to be rotten – and thin ice is 'rotten ice' (*glace pourrie*).

(3) The Greek *tolípi*, a lump of raw wool, is also figuratively a snowflake or a puff of smoke.

Soap   'It is often the case that English words which the natives have made palatable for themselves are mistaken by missionaries and other

Europeans as native words. Thus G. Brown, a Methodist missionary, translated "to wash" in the language of the Duke-of-York [island] group by *tobi* until, by chance, he ordered a boy to wash a piece of cloth without soap and figured out that *tobi* is Engl. "soap"' (Scuchardt).

Sodomist   In Papua New Guinea Pidgin, *fakhimas* (active partner) or *aismalang* (passive partner).
   See also **Cockroach** (1).

Softly, softly   In Liberian English a *sofli sofli* is a lemur believed to be so strong that it can choke monkeys to death. As in the English saying, 'Softly, softly, catchee monkey.'

Sole (the fish)   In Greek *glóssa*, or 'tongue', which a sole resembles.
   See also **Chatterbox** (9).

Soul   (1) *Dewel* (Papua New Guinea Pidgin; from 'Devil'). *Dewel* also means shadow, ghost, image, reflection. The Holy Ghost is *dewel takondo*.
   (2) The Spanish *anima*, soul, is also the bore of a gun. *Animas* are bells ringing at sunset.

Southern Cross   In figurative Spanish the Southern Cross is the *altar mayor*, the 'main altar'.

Spaniard   See '**I say . . . !**'

Spectacles, A pair of   (1) In French *lunettes*, or 'little moons'; a lavatory seat is also a *lunette*, and so is the wishbone of a bird.
   (2) The German for spectacles, *Brille*, is a corruption of the Latin *beryllus*, the precious stone beryl. It would be pleasant to think that the Provençal *bésicle* was derived from *bis-cyclus* (bicycle), as has been claimed, but it too is a corrupt descendant of *beryllus*. Another French dialect form, *berniques*, is variously said to be analogous to the English 'barnacles' to mean spectacles, derived from *binocles* (pince-nez, literally 'two-eyed'), or related to 'binnacle', the illuminated box of a ship's compass.

(3) In Chinook Indian jargon, spectacles are *dolla seahost*, 'dollar' or 'silver' eyes.

(4) The Spanish *gafas*, grapples, or clamps, also means spectacles.

(5) A lorgnette is called in Spanish by the plural *impertinentes*, from *impertinente*, intrusive, fussy, uncalled for, impertinent.

See also **Lentil** (1).

Squid   See **Octopus** and **Office, In the**.

Squirrel   (1) 'In *squirrel* . . . some people imagine they hear something of the rustling and whirling of the little animal. But we have only to trace the name back to Greek, and there we find that *skiouros* is composed of two distinct words, the one meaning shade, the other tail; the animal being called shade-tail by the Greeks' (Müller). The squirrel is shaded by its tail as if it were carrying a parasol.

(2) In Romany, *ruko-mengro*, or 'tree-fellow'.

Still life   French: *nature morte*. Also Greek *nekrà thésis*. Dead nature.

Stomach   Canadian Eskimo for a reindeer's stomach is *aggarusek*, literally 'a bag into which berries are put when they are being gathered' (for a related idea, see **Shopping bag**). Nansen reported that one of the Eskimos' greatest delicacies was the contents of a reindeer's stomach:

If a Greenlander kills a reindeer, and is unable to convey much of it home with him, he will, I believe, secure the stomach first of all; and the last thing an Eskimo lady enjoins upon her lover, when he sets off reindeer-hunting, is that he must reserve for her the stomach of his prey. It is no doubt because they stand in need of vegetable food that they prize this so highly, and also because it is in reality a very choice collection of the finest moss and grasses which that *gourmet*, the reindeer, picks out for himself. It has undergone a sort of stewing in the process of semi-digestion, while the gastric juice provides a somewhat sharp and aromatic sauce.

Nansen adds that on special occasions a reindeer's stomach 'is served up with pieces of blubber and crowberries'.

Stormy petrel

In France the names for the stormy petrel are associated with the devil: *oiseau du diable*, *satanique*, and so on. They are said to come from hell to fly over the bodies of those who have been lost at sea ... A pleasanter tradition suggests that they embody the souls of drowned sailors, invoking the prayers of the living on their behalf. The stormy petrel is St Peter's bird – Italian *Petrello* means 'little Peter' – because the saint walked upon Lake Gennesaret (Matthew, xiv. 29), and this is what the bird appears to do, for it flies just above the water with its feet hanging down as though touching the waves. Alternatively, in England the bird is sometimes called Mother Carey's chicken.

(Newall)

Stove   Greek for a slow-burning stove is *salamándra*, 'salamander'.

Strawberry filter   Among television crews, this is slang code meaning that while the appearance of filming an interview is gone through the camera is actually empty of film. An interview using a 'strawberry filter' is done purely to flatter the vanity of the interviewee.

Stye (i.e. in eye)   In French *orgelet* (a diminutive of *orge*, a grain of barley).

Sunflower   Spanish: *giganta*, 'giantess'.

Sunstroke   French: *coup de bambou*, 'bamboo blow'.

Swizzlestick   See **Champagne**.

Syphilis

... infection [in fifteenth-century Europe] spread like wildfire. Each country blamed its neighbour. The French called it the 'Italian disease', the Germans blamed the French, calling it 'Malade Frantzos' [so did the Spanish, calling it *gálico*, French]. The English called it the 'French pox'. Spread to the east from Europe is credited to Vasco da Gama and other Portuguese navigators. We learn of the disease in India as early as 1498 and in Canton seven years later. The Japanese word 'mankabassam', i.e. syphilis, means literally, 'the Portuguese sickness' . . . St Denis became the patron saint of syphilitics. That he is also patron saint of France and Paris is noteworthy. Of all the names accorded to the disease in its earliest years, those referring to its French origin predominated.

(R. S. Morton, *Venereal Diseases*, 1966)

The Malays as well as the Japanese laid the blame for syphilis at the door of the Portuguese. (See **Foreigner** (1).)

T

T   See **K** (2 and 3).

Taboo   The Eskimo *aglingortok* means 'to tire of following [the rules of] taboo'.

Tadpole   See **Head**.

Tap (i.e. for water)   In the European languages, taps are named after one or other of the many different varieties of animal, bird, and so on, depicted in stone at the mouth of a spring. The water emanated from the creature's mouth, or snout, in Spanish its *jeta*, which is colloquially a tap in the Spanish of Aragon.

Thus, in France, a tap is a *robinet*, or a robin, while in Germany it is *hahn*, hen, which corresponds to the now-archaic English 'cock', still found in 'stopcock', and *poule*, chicken, which is found in the Jura and elsewhere. In other French-speaking areas, the equivalent is *cran* (dialect for *grue*, crane), or *chèvre*, goat. In Spain it is *grifo*, the mythical griffin, and in the Spanish Antilles and Latin America a group of standpipes is called collectively a *griferia*.

Taxi-driver   See **Abuse**.

Tea   In the early years of tea-drinking in Europe (from about the late seventeenth century) the tea trade with China (whence the English 'cha', 'char', and 'tea') was associated with criminality. From *The Leisure Hour*, 1873:

With a parcel of tea which we lately purchased there came a curious piece of Chinese advertising. It is a native tea merchant's bill or circular, printed on red paper sprinkled with gold leaf. It bears the announcement in 'pigeon English', that 'Tong-Wo-Sun-Kee never makes or ships LIE TEA' ... this 'lie tea' is not so much an adulteration of other than tea leaves, as it may be a mixture of good fresh leaves with what have already been infused. The latter are chiefly bought for a mere trifle at the large tea-drinking establishments, and dried in the sun. The writer has seen acres of ground in the vicinity of Canton, Macao, Shanghai, and other places, where the leaves were spread, sometimes on mats, and sometimes on the bare soil, to shrivel up ... When mixed with fresh tea this 'lie tea' is shipped at a much lower price than usual, but very little of it is consumed in England. Germany has been its principal destination ...

Perhaps this was why, in Germany, tea-dealers were considered 'immoral members of society, lying in wait for men's purses and lives', and why in Holland tea (or lie-tea) was ridiculed as 'haywater' (Isaac d'Israeli, *Curiosities of Literature*).

The expensive Chinese variety of tea, *oolong*, is from the Chinese *wu*, black, and *lung*, dragon.

Telephone   See **Chatterbox** (5).

Television programme   In Germany a smash-hit TV programme is a 'street sweeper' (*Strassenfeger*) because everyone is indoors watching it and the streets are empty of people.

Testicles   (1) In French slang, the family jewels (*bijoux de famille*).

(2) In Spain and the Spanish-speaking world *huevos* (eggs) except Venezuela, where *huevo* is the penis. There is a nasty scene in Oliver Stone's film *Salvador* where some heavies on the point of castrating the American journalist refer to *huevos rancheros*, 'rancher's eggs', or testicles.

(3) The Swahili *makoza* (probably from Arabic) means also ivory amulets or bracelets (which also rattle about) but the word in either meaning was described in 1948 as 'seldom heard'.

(4) The modern Greek *kalabalikia*, testicles, also means a jumbled mass of people or things.

(5) '. . . there was this very precise French butcher and Ann said to him, "Can you tell us what those are", pointing at [some bull's testicles on] the tray, and you know what he said? . . .

'He said, "*Ce sont des frivolités, Madame.*" Isn't that good?' (Julian Barnes, *Before She Met Me*, 1982.)

(6) When eaten, testicles are sometimes called 'oysters'. For example in the United States they are 'Rocky Mountain oysters', not so different from *huevos rancheros*.

(7) The Greek *órchis* has the dual sense 'testicle' and 'orchid', after the resemblance between testicles and tubers. It is related to the Middle Irish *uirrge*, testicles. The same resemblance was noted in England, where in archaic rural slang orchids were once 'bollock-grass'. *Órchis* gives extra zip to 'orchestra', Cockney rhyming slang for testicles (orchestra stalls/balls), as in 'kicked him right in the orchestra'.

The orchid–testicle analogy seems also to underlie the Latin *orchas*, a type of olive. '. . . the *orchitis* is a large kind of olive, so called because the Athenians called it [*órchis moría*] "the sacred olive-berry"' (Varro).

Theatrical terms   The best of these seem to be Spanish. I particularly like *jornada*, act of a play, or a day's journey, and the Spanish collective noun, a *histrionismo*, or a 'histrionics', of theatrical folk. And in Spanish a part in a play, even the title role, is only a *papel*, a paper. Judging from some of the other terms, acting in Spain was once a very rough-and-tumble, even a dangerous, business.

(1) *Audience*: If audiences can irritate the modern actor (Greek, *ipokrítis*) with their popcorn, peanuts, and sweet wrappers they must also have irritated Elizabethan actors (masses of hazelnut shells were found on the site of the Rose Theatre), and the actors of ancient Rome.

In Latin, persons who disturbed a theatrical performance were known as *trittiles*, related to *trit*, which was the sound a bird made when it broke open a grain or a hard seed. *Triticum*, wheat, was so called because it was *tritum*, threshed. If *tritum* is not somewhere at the back of the English 'thresh' (and the *Oxford Dictionary* doesn't put it there), it is certainly preserved in 'triturate' (first recorded usage, 1755), to pulverize, and the French *triturer*, to grind, or to munch.

(2) *Auditorium*: In Latin the *cavea*, cavity or cave, but also an animal's stall, a beehive, and a bird-cage. If the audience were birds, the auditorium was their cage.

(3) *Bit part*: In Spanish, *embolado*, the primary meaning of which, from bullfighting, is a bull that has wooden balls on the tips of its horns, and so is harmless.

(4) *Curtain*: From the Spanish *arrojo* comes *el arroje* – the fearless one – meaning, not a matador or soldier, but the 'man who drops as counterweight to raise the curtain in a theatre'.

(5) *Dresser*: In Japanese kabuki theatre changes of costume and scene frequently take place in full view of the audience. Both the dressers and the stage-hands, to distinguish them from the actors, wear black, and are known as *kurombo*, Negroes.

(6) *Dressing-room*: In Spanish, *camarín*, whose primary meaning is the 'place behind the altar where the images are dressed, and the ornaments destined for that purpose are kept'.

(7) *Fluff*: A fluff in a speech, or a fluffed entrance, is in French a wolf (*loup*).

(8) *Gods, The*: In French the gods in a theatre are 'paradise' (*paradis*) or the 'hen-house' (*poulailler*). And in Spanish, *paraíso*, paradise, or *gallinero*, hen-house or chicken coop. Birds again.

(9) *Pit*: In Russia (1916) a box on the pit tier was *benuár*, from the French *baignoire*, which as well as bath or bath-tub meant (as in the Russian) a ground-floor box behind the pit, presumably because one got so sweaty there.

(10) *Prompter*: In a Spanish theatre *el apuntador* is the prompter; on a ship of the Spanish navy an *apuntador* is a gunner. The prompter, like the gunner, is crouched, hidden in a stall.

(11) *Proscenium*: In a French theatre the proscenium arch is *le manteau d'Arlequin* (Harlequin's cloak). *Arlequín* (harlequin) is how you would ask for Neapolitan ice-cream in a Spanish theatre.

(12) *Rhubarb* is the actor's word for the hubbub of crowd scenes. It is sometimes the word actually used by actors required to make a generalized din in such scenes, and, by extension, it is any incomprehensible speech or line. Rhubarb is from medieval Latin *rheubarbarum*, or 'barbarian Rheum' (Rheum is the name of the rhubarb family of plants) and so contains within itself the Latin word

for those peoples (the barbarians) whose speech the Romans found incomprehensible (see **Walnut (wall?), Welsh**).

Thumbs down   This gesture of rejection derives from the *pollice verso* of the ancient Romans, indicating death to a defeated gladiator. But the Romans turned their thumbs, not down, but up. 'Gérôme's "Pollice Verso" [a painting] expresses, not so much horror at what is being perpetrated, as attraction by the beauty of the spectacle' (Leo Tolstoy, *What Is Art?*, translated by Aylmer Maude, who comments in a footnote to the above: 'In this picture the spectators in the Roman Amphitheatre are turning down their thumbs to show that they wish the vanquished gladiator to be killed.' They should have been turning them up.)

Tibet   The Chinese ransacking of Tibet follows logically enough from the Chinese name for it, *Xizang*, or 'Western Treasure House'.

Tightrope   In Spanish it is *cuerda floja*, 'loose rope'.

Timber   See **Tree, trees** (1) and (2).

Tobacco   (1) Tobacco came to Europe from the Americas in the second half of the sixteenth century. Around 1560, a Spanish doctor called Hernández brought from Mexico some plants which he called *tabaco*, his own 'Spanished' version of one of a number of names for the leaf which travellers found among the native American Indians, and the name which in various forms has triumphed in most of the world's languages. At the same time, the French ambassador to the Portuguese court in Lisbon acquired some tobacco seed originally from Florida, and introduced tobacco into France. The ambassador's name was Jean Nicot, whence the name of the plant's essential oil, 'nicotine'.

Nicot sent the seed to the Grand Prior of France, where for that reason tobacco was known at first as the *herbe du grand-prieur*. Tobacco reached Italy, similarly, from Portugal, introduced by Cardinal Prosper Santa Croce, and known in his honour as *erba Santa Croce*.

Returning to France in 1561, Nicot presented some of the plants to the Queen, Catherine de' Medici. Tobacco in France then became known as 'the Queen's herb' – *herbe de la reine*, or *herbe Medicée*. But the herb of the Medici was thought also to possess medicinal, health-giving qualities, after which it was known, variously, as *erba panacea* or *herba santa*, and in Gerard's *Herball* (1597) it is *Sana sancta Indorum*. The habit of tobacco-smoking quickly established itself in England, but in France, for a long time, it was grown in small quantities for use as a medicinal herb.

Tobacco was sold, not in ounces but in lengths of leaves rolled up like rope, and in England the tobacco 'roll' was the favoured shop-sign among tobacconists. The tapering rolls resembled a sailor's pigtail, or a carrot. There was a variety of tobacco popular in France, sweetened with treacle and called *carotte*, and to this day the sign of the carrot can be seen in French streets to symbolize a tobacconist's. The Russian *rúlya*, borrowed from the German (*Rolle*) means both a roll and a carrot.

(2) For reasons I don't understand (the association, perhaps, of two phenomena both perceived as 'foreign') *tabak* in Papua New Guinea Pidgin also means 'leprosy'.

(3) *Kippe* is German for 'see-saw' and *auf der Kippe stehen* is 'to hang in the balance'. A cigarette hangs in the balance in the mouth and see-saws in the ashtray, and a cigarette end is also *eine Kippe*.

See also **Minum**, **Smoking**.

Tom, Dick, and Harry   The Spanish equivalent is *Fulano, Zutano, y Mengano*. *Don Fulano* is the equivalent of Mr Blank, Joe Soap, Mr So-and-So. The female version of the same is *Doña Fulana*, which is also, familiarly, a prostitute. *Juana* (Jane) is any prostitute in Colombia, and also short for 'Mary Jane', or *marijuana*. *Juan* is a common soldier in Bolivia and Mexico, just as a 'John' is any common Tom, Dick, or Harry in the United States.

Tonsils   The Greek is *amigdalés*, almonds; likewise German, *Mandeln*.

Toothache   See **Worm**

Top hat   In French, *huit-reflets*, or 'eight-reflections'.

Tortuous   *Sneknabaut* ('snaking about'; Papua New Guinea Pidgin).

Traffic jam   In Spain, *ensalada*, salad. Other figurative meanings of *ensalada* are hotch-potch, mix-up (as with French *salade*), or medley. In Venezuela, traffic doesn't make a jam but a biscuit (*galleta del tráfico*).

Tree, trees   (1) A 'lumber' was once a pawnbroker's, in which sense it is said to derive from 'Lombard' (the Lombards were known from the Middle Ages on as bankers and money men generally). But they are said also to have been dealers in old furniture, and 'lumber' in its sense of odds and ends stored in a 'lumber-room' may derive from this or from the pawnbroking connection, or, another possibility, there may be some older root in a word resembling 'encumber', 'cumbersome' (clobber that got in the way). 'Lumber', from the English, gained its sense of rough-cut timber in North America.

(2) The early French Canadians were foresters. They called the forest clearing where they felled trees their 'workshop' (*chantier*), a use which Dunn describes as 'an example of the necessity under which we are sometimes forced to bend the French language to our local needs; this necessity constitutes a right'. A tree that had died in a storm, or of old age, was known as 'a dead body' (*un corps mort*). These are businesslike terms, like *portage* (see **Canada**). Forestry remains the chief source of income, also, for the Austrians, among whom the forest has the businesslike name *das grünes Gold*, 'green gold'.

(3) The Swahili *gongo la mwitu* is the densest part of a forest. Gongo (from *mgongo*, meaning 'backbone' or things resembling a backbone) is most commonly used for the seam in a piece of cloth, but also for a camel's hump or a dense wood or thicket. *Gongo la mwitu* means therefore the backbone, seam, or hump of the forest.

(4) In Colombia, by contrast, the tree-line, the edge and the thinnest part of the forest, is called *la ceja de la selva*, 'the eyebrow of the forest' (see Charles Nicholl, *The Fruit Palace*). In Greek also, *ophrís* means both eyebrow and the crest of a hill. The same metaphor exists in Chinese: Mount Emei, near Chengdu, is Beauty's Eyebrow'.

(5) At the foot of a hill in Pretoria North is the so-called *Wonderboom*, or 'wonder tree', in fact not one tree but several of the species

Ficus pretoriae. An African chief is said to be buried nearby. In 1975 more than a thousand people could shelter in the *Wonderboom*'s shade.

(6) In Jamaica the *Coccoloba krugii*, which similarly branches from its roots, is called when it does so 'big-family' or 'crabwood', in common with a variety of trees thought in one way or another to resemble crabs (the roots growing out of the ground around the tree at the centre like a crab's claws).

(7) '. . . *puszcza*: a Polish word that means a world of trees which have never been felled since the first bands of human beings arrived to hunt . . . The *Puszcza* of Kniszyn, which begins north-east of the Polish city of Białystok, must be ten thousand years old' (Neal Ascherson, 'The Borderlands', *Granta*, 30, 1990).

See also **Regulars**.

Tulip   (1) The English word is from the Turkish *tülbend*, a turban, which a (closed or half closed) tulip resembles.

(2) In Colombia, a tulip is an *escandalosa*, or, literally, a 'scandalous', except that as an adjective *escandaloso* has the meaning 'loud' (of colours). Otherwise in Spanish, the noun *escandalosa* is the topsail of a ship.

Tune   German for a tune one can't get out of one's head is *Ohrwurm* (ear worm).

Turkey (the bird)   In England and the United States it's a turkey, in Turkish it's a *hindi*, in Hindi it's a *perū*, and in Peru it's a *güegüecho*. Even 'turkey' originally named, not the turkey, but the guinea-fowl, a native of Africa, and Yule and Burnell write of a long history of 'strange confusions between the two birds'.

The turkey is thought to have originated almost certainly in America, and in the United States the Thanksgiving Day 'turkey dinner' is a national institution. In a straw poll of languages, however, supposed Indian origins probably get the majority vote. In French it's *coq d'Inde*, or simply *dindon*, in German *Indischer Hahn*, and in Italian *gallo d'India*. In Greece, the last country on earth where one would expect anything to be called a turkey, it is *indiános* (which is also a 'Red Indian'), of which other Greek turkey-words, *diános* and *diána*, are abbreviations (on the model of *dindon*).

Turkish and Arabic (*Daják Hindi*) vote the same way. More specifically the Dutch *Kalkoen* and another German turkey-term, *Calecutischer Hahn*, pinpoint the bird's place of origin as being, like that of 'calico', the Indian city of Calicut, whose name, the eighteenth-century Italian traveller Padre Paolino believed, means 'Castle of the Fowls'.

The Portuguese name is the 'Peru cock' (*galo do Peru*). From Portugal both the turkey itself (via the port of Goa), and the Portuguese name of the turkey, went to India. In most Indian languages it is *perü*, although Hindustani also has *śutra-murgh*, ostrich (literally 'camel-cock') and, from Persian, *fil-murgh*, 'elephant cock', while Tamil prudently names the bird not after a country but after its size, *vãn-kōri*, 'great fowl'.

Yule and Burnell were emphatic (1886) that the turkey didn't originate in India, but they wonder whether the widespread Indian 'peru' name isn't 'very possibly an indication that it came to India, perhaps first to the Spanish settlements in the Archipelago, across the Pacific [i.e. from Peru], as the red pepper known as *chili* did'. That is, they thought that the turkey might have reached India not via an eastern route, from Europe, but via a westward one, from South America.

The Latin American Spanish *güegüecho*, a turkey, means also wattle, or goitre and, as an adjective, silly or stupid or suffering from a goitre, which is held to resemble the folds of flesh at the bird's neck. *Gallipavo*, another Spanish turkey-word, is also a false note in music. Or 'a real turkey'.

See also **Maize**, **Wallflower**.

Turkish delight   In Greek it is simply *loukoúmi* or *rakhátloukoúm*, which roughly translates as 'lounging-about sweet' and from which we get the French *rahat loukoum*, Turkish delight.

Twaddle   The Hindustani *sukhan-takya* (from *sukhan*, word, and *takya*, pillow) means 'pillow-word'. Words with no meaning whatsoever which fill a temporary hiatus while the speaker is trying to think what to say next are 'pillow-words'. Maxwell (1882) advised foreigners thinking themselves fluent in a language against trying to use them.

See also **Theatrical terms** (12).

Twins (1) The Papua New Guinea Pidgin *sangsangana* is about as consanguinary and twinlike a word for twins as one could find.

(2) In Mexico, *cuate* (twin) is also a close friend, boyfriend, or girlfriend.

(3) Twins in Italian (*gemelli*) and in Spanish (*gemelos*) also have the figurative meaning 'cuff-links'.

(4) But Spanish takes the same basic idea further. A *gemelo*, twin, is what the English call only 'a sister ship', while *gemelos de campo* and *gemelos de teatro* are, respectively, binoculars and opera glasses.

(5) *Mancuernillas*, which are cuff-links in Latin America, have the sense of hobbling an animal's or fettering a criminal's legs together. The cuff-links may be said to hobble or to fetter the cuff.

(6) The Russian *dvoika* is a deuce at cards, a pair of horses, and a rowing-boat. Related words mean twins, someone's double (or *Doppelgänger*), two fruits on the same stem (cherries, etc.), or two things belonging together, 'e.g. shirt-buttons', comments Freese. We are back within an ace of cuff-links.

Typhoid   See **Football hooligan**.

Tyre (of car, lorry, etc.)   The Cameroons: *moto fut* (motor foot).
    See also **Alley-way**.

U

U   See pages 59–60.

Underpants   A journalist in Romania found *indispensabili*, for underpants, on his laundry bill.

Urine   See **Ballot box**.

Us and them   Malays describe themselves as *orang di-bawah angin* – people below the wind – and foreigners (Westerners) from far away as *orang di-atas angin* – people above the wind. No one is sure where the distinction derives from, but Maxwell (1882) cites a Turkish text on navigation in the Indian seas, the *Mohgit* (*The Ocean*, AD 1554). 'It enumerates', he writes, 'among others, the monsoons below the wind, that is, of the parts of India situated below the wind, among which are Malacca, Shomotora, Tanassari, Martaban, and Faiku (Pegu).' Maxwell concludes: 'The expression is not of Malay origin, but is a translation into that language of an Arabic phrase.'

   See also **Foreigner**, **Fox**, **'I say . . . !'**, **Tibet**.

Useless   The Papua New Guinea Pidgin word is *faulnabaut* ('falling about'), which also has the special sense 'tangled' when used of ropes, nets, fishing lines, etc., and 'conflicting' when used of testimony or rumour.

Useless words   No word is useless to the person using it, of course, and even the most outstanding wooden halfpennies among words had their uses once. If you are a German worrying that your trousers are about to fall down, then you lack a sense of *Hosenträgersicherheitsgefühl*, which is 'a feeling of security about one's braces'. Nevertheless, every language-culture has its words, like that compound noun, whose very existence seems a mystery to outsiders, and words that may, with time, have become incomprehensible to insiders, too.

The *Listener* magazine once asked readers to submit examples of extremely weird, apparently useless words. Among those offered were the Japanese *tsujigiri* ('trying out a new sword on a chance passer-by'), Spanish *anaranjear* ('to kill a cock by throwing oranges at it'), Gaelic *taghairm* ('inspiration sought by lying in a bullock's hide behind a waterfall'), Old English *mallemaroking* ('carousing by seamen in icebound ships'), ancient Greek *raphanízein* ('to thrust a radish up someone's backside': it was a punishment for adulterers), and Latin *dentilegus* ('one who picks his teeth up after they have been knocked out'). Wrongly, it gave the Eskimo *angekkok* as 'a conjuror for children's parties'. In fact it means magician, shaman, wizard, etc.

The *Listener*'s list can be added to. The Japanese *boronji* translates as 'a person who goes about with his head and face concealed in a basket-hat playing on a flageolet' (Hepburn). I have trouble under-standing the thinking behind some old Eskimo words. *Ikkuserpok*: 'ties one leg of dog to neck'. *Kupiktaurpuk*: 'two having a three-legged race'. The word for 'playing' is *orpiuyartut*, which means literally 'standing on one leg'. *Paomnartok*: 'nervous through seeing many lice'.

V

Vagina (1) The Jamaican *bumbo* is also an alligator.

(2) *Kunazi*, Swahili for the fruit of the Chinese date or jujube tree, 'is sometimes used [in the form *kikunazi*] as an obscene euphemism for part of the female genital organs'.

(3) With differing ideograms for each meaning, the Japanese *chitsu* means both the slip-case of a book and a vagina.

See also page 144–5, and **Box**.

Varicose veins US slang (1950s), 'very close veins'. Jamaican slang, 'breeding veins' (because varicose veins often follow childbirth).

Vein *Rop* in Papua New Guinea Pidgin means vein, vine, rope, artery, and rattan cane. (Rattan from *raut-an*, 'the thing peeled'; *raut* is to peel.) More specifically, a vein is *rop bilong blut* ('rope belong blood').

Very *Tumas* (too much; Papua New Guinea Pidgin in the 1940s; now commonplace in American or Americanized English). Scuchardt: '"very" in Pacific Beach-la-mar [pidgin] is *too much*, and *tumussi* in Sranan Black English [Guyana]'.

Vietnamese See '**I say . . . !**'

Virgin *Kalebassi no broke jeti* (calabash not yet broken; Saramaccan Creole, Guyana, South America).

Virgin Mary, The   *Kwin* (Papua New Guinea Pidgin). Perhaps the Virgin is behind the Pidgin *meri* to mean any woman. People in general are *manmeri*.

See also pages 146–9.

Voice   In US slang (1950s) a voice which wavers from high to low is a 'corduroy voice'. In West Greenland Eskimo, a noun meaning 'one who has a thick voice' and a verb meaning 'speaks as if he has no palate' are derived from *qilángag*, meaning 'puffin'.

W

Waiter The French *garçon* means more commonly 'boy' – its use to mean 'waiter' is a feudal survival. How, after the supposed social levelling of the French Revolution, can a twenty-year-old café customer in Paris address a sixty-year-old waiter as 'boy'? Even though that is not, we hope, the spirit in which he uses the word.

Slaves, or servants, were (or are, as the case may be) referred to in terms meaning 'child', 'boy', or 'girl' in Greek, Latin, and Arabic. Throughout Europe, well into the Middle Ages, servile adults were referred to as children. Thus, for example, the anger of Coriolanus when he is called 'thou boy of tears' by Aufidius – 'Measureless liar, thou hast made my heart / Too great for what contains it. "Boy"? O slave!' – in which Shakespeare seems to be making explicit the equation of 'boy' and 'slave'. It exists not only in *garçon* but also, for example, in Syriac, with *telaye*, boys or children, and *telaya*, slaves or servants. Also, of course, the word 'boy' is (I hesitate to use the past tense) a racial insult in the southern United States.

John Boswell (in *The Kindness of Strangers*) calls the identification of childhood and serfdom 'both a philological subtlety and a social one ... related to the fact that the social roles themselves (slave, serf, servant, etc.) were those of "children" in terms of power and juridical standing, whether the person discharging them was young or old'. On an anecdotal level, we have all known people, like the English *grande dame* I knew once, who refer to the plumber, builder, electrician, and so on, as 'little man', as in, 'I had this little man round to mend the cooker.'

See **Child, children** (2), **Civilians and soldiers**, **Pidgin**.

Wake (funeral wake)   Cameroons: *krai dai* (cry die). When it's an older person's funeral a wake is the rather more cheerful *chop dai* (eat die).

Wallflower (at a party or dance)   German *Schimmel*, mould, Spanish *pavo*, turkey.

Walnut (wall?), Welsh   Varro's editors find no fault with his etymology for the Latin *iuglans*, a walnut, 'because while this nut is like an acorn [*glans*] before it is cleansed of its hull, the inner nut, being best and biggest, is called *iu-glans* from *Iu*-piter and *glans* acorn'. Varro's 'best and biggest' (*optima et maxima*) refers to Jupiter's title, *Optimus Maximus*. In Latin, then, the walnut was conceived of as 'Jupiter's acorn'. What has survived into the modern world, however, is the image of the walnut as foreign, a foreignness hinted at in the English word's root *wal-*. In Russian it is more specifically 'the Greek nut', and in Lithuanian 'the Italian nut'.

The popular etymology (greengrocer's English) for 'walnut' is that it has something to do with walls, and walnuts are often seen on sale under the spelling 'wallnuts'. Etymologists, who must amuse themselves as they may, like to smile at this, even though in John Gerard's *Herball, or Generall Historie of Plantes* (1597) 'wallnut' is with 'wallflower' in the index. 'But for the accident that walnuts are no wall fruit', wrote Müller in the 1860s, 'I have little doubt that by this time schoolmasters would have insisted on spelling the word with two *l*'s, and that many a gardener would have planted his walnut trees against the wall.'

A guide to the true etymology is the German *wälsche Nuss*, or 'foreign nut'. *Wälsche*, the modern *welsch*, means 'Latin, Romance, French, Italian', and is colloquially 'foreign'. It meant originally foreign in the sense of 'barbarian', and is said to have been especially used by the Germans of the Italians: Italy was *Welschland*, and the original German conception of the walnut seems to have been, like the Lithuanian, 'the Italian nut'.

Before *wälsche*, its antecedent *walh* was used by the Germans of their Celtic neighbours. *Walh* is related to an Anglo-Saxon word which some writers transliterate as *vealh* and others as *wealh* (it depends on your view of Anglo-Saxon sound-shifts between 'w' and 'v' before and after the migration to Britain). However the word was pronounced, the invaders used it of the native Britons (the Welsh) and it was probably echoic, referring to the incomprehensibility of Celtic speech. If so, then *wealh/vealh* started off as a mocking sound, like 'blah, blah' or the bleating 'barbar-' of the Latin 'barbarian'. Barbarians, in fact, spoke rhubarb (see **Theatrical terms** (12)). One wonders whether *walh* does not also underlie 'Gaul', the old pre-Frankish name for France, and the French name for Wales, *pays de Galles*.

The Greek equivalent of 'barbarians' was *Aglossoi*, the 'speechless', while the Poles had the same idea about the Germans, whom they called *niemiec*, the 'dumb' people. The Turks got *nimiec* from the Poles and used it of the Austrians. This must have been the word that Coleridge had in mind when he remarked that for all his admiration of the Germans there was, even so, a certain 'nimiety' about them. Cognates of the same word, all meaning 'German', exist in Russian, Bulgarian, Serbo-Croatian, and Slovenian. And the English 'Dutch' (as in 'double Dutch') is from the German *Deutsch* for 'German'.

But back to *vealh*, or *wealh*, the barbarian British, or Welsh. Müller writes that it 'is supposed to be the same as the Sanskrit *mlekkha*, and, if so, it meant originally a person who talks indistinctly'. *Mlekkha* has also been identified with 'Beluchi': a strange area of probable common ground between Beluchistan and the principality of Wales, whose very name is an Anglo-Saxon insult.

Also insulting was the now-defunct nickname for the Jamaican 'Jabbering Crow' (*Corvus jamaicensis*). It was called 'the Welshman' because, according to Edward Long (in his *History of Jamaica*, 1774) 'with their strange, noisy gabble of guttural sounds ... [they] are thought to have much the confused vociferation of a party of Welsh folks'.

'Walnut', then, is related to 'Wales' but not to 'wall'. At the same time, one hesitates to rule 'wall' altogether out of the picture. It is from the West Saxon *weall*, corresponding, the *Oxford Dictionary* informs us, to Old Frisian, Old Saxon, Middle and modern Low German, and Middle Dutch *wal*, and including also in its genealogy the Latin *vallum*, rampart, originally fencing, from *vallus*, stake. It is perhaps originally from *vallum*: it is thought that the Anglo-Saxons were alone among the Germanic tribes in borrowing from Latin.

Quite a different family tree then, and yet one good reason for walls is to keep foreigners out, and foreigners are the people in the next *valley*. It would take a brave etymologist to state categorically that there was never any connection whatsoever between *weall*, wall, and *vealh/wealh*, foreigner or barbarian.

See also **Adam's apple**, **Nutmeg**.

For more on 'foreigners', see **Foreigner**, '**I say . . . !**', and **Pidgin**.

Walrus Eskimo has at least six different words for the walrus, ranging from *nutara* (a newborn walrus) to *timertik* (a fully grown male walrus).

See also **Branch**.

Waltz See **Whirlpool** (2).

Washer-up In French, someone who does the washing-up in a restaurant or hotel is *un plongeur* or *une plongeuse*. The primary meaning of *plongeur* is 'diver', and specifically the diver-bird, which gives us the droll image of a full-time washer-up as someone who repeatedly sticks his head in the water.

Water I like the following US slang terms for water: 'dog's soup', 'sky juice', 'windmill cocktail'.

Waterfall Before it was renamed by Dr Livingstone (in late 1855) the Victoria Falls in what is today Zimbabwe were called *mosi oa tunya*, 'the smoke that thunders'. Dr Livingstone, in Ruskinesque vein, wrote in his diary after seeing the great waterfall, 'On sights as beautiful as this Angels in their flight must have gazed', and today, in memory of his diary-entry, the sightseeing flight over the Falls is billed as 'The Flight of Angels'.

See also **Canada**.

Water-lily A white water-lily in French is a 'water moon' (*lune d'eau*).

Waxwing   In German-speaking Switzerland the waxwing is the *Sterbevogel*, the 'death-bird', a name reflecting the old superstition that the sighting of large numbers of waxwings in a particular year was an omen of war, disease, or freezing weather.

Wheatear   People will believe just about anything, and it was once believed that the eggs of the wheatear were hatched by toads. Perhaps this belief underlies the bird's name in County Kerry, 'cunning little old man under the stone'. In Oxfordshire, it was sometimes known as the 'horse-match' because it flew alongside horse-drawn carriages as though trying to race them.

Whirlpool   (1) In Greek, *máti tís thálassas*, the sea's eye.
    (2) Also in Greek, *stróvilos* is whirlpool, whirlwind, turbine, a spinning-top, a waltz, and a pine-cone. The verb *stróvilizo* is to whirl around, or to waltz.

White   The power of whiteness over the imagination is the subject of the chapter in Melville's *Moby-Dick* entitled 'The Whiteness of the Whale'. In its third paragraph, which must be one of the longest sentences in literature, Melville lists examples from a variety of cultures of whiteness as emblematic of virtue, innocence, beauty, goodness, honour, and the division of 'the human race itself, giving the white man ideal mastership over every dusky tribe'.

But the paragraph, or sentence, ends: '. . . yet for all these accumulated associations, with whatever is sweet, and honorable, and sublime, there yet lurks an elusive something in the innermost idea of this hue, which strikes more of panic to the soul than that redness which affrights in blood'. And the chapter closes with the reflection that 'the palsied universe lies before us a leper', and the image of the 'infidel' (or the man who has ceased to believe in God), who 'gazes himself blind at the monumental white shroud that wraps all the prospect around him'.

In Russian, the adjective 'white' is frequently used to denote excellence. The Russian for white, *byély*, is also found in words and phrases for delirium tremens, a hut with a chimney, a cataract in the eye, foam, and a dandy (someone who's afraid to wash his hands).

See also **Great White Shark**, **White man**.

White man (1) The West Indian *backra*, *buckra*, or *bockra* for 'white man' is sometimes said to derive from the English 'buccaneer'. In Belize, it was ingeniously suggested to me that it came from the white man's complaint, after exposing himself to the sun, 'My *back* is *raw*.' Both are attractive explanations, but the one that must be preferred is that it is from the African (Ibo and Efik) *mbakara*, for white man ('he who controls and governs'). As an adjective it has the attributive senses of 'white' ('Backra rum' is 'white rum'), 'introduced by the white man' (thus the Bible is 'the Backra book'), 'belonging to the white man' (England is 'Backra country') and, most intriguingly, the possessive 'my' (thus, for example, 'bockra boots' means 'my boots').

(2) In Canadian Eskimo, white men are *kabluna* (literally, 'big eyebrow').

See also **Belong** for another association of the white man with an alien sense of property.

Wife A Japanese calls his own wife *uichinomono*, 'the one inside', exactly corresponding to the Cockney "'er indoors' for wife popularized in the TV series *Minder*. Someone else's wife is *okusan*, 'inner' or 'innermost person'. *Oku* conveys the sense of depth measurement in physical space, and it carries the suggestion of a wife as the person at the back of the house (in the kitchen?); even, perhaps, of a wife as the person who stands 'behind' her husband.

Wife-swapping The Eskimo *areodjarekput* means 'to exchange wives for a few days only'.

Windcheater See **Canada**.

Wishbone See **Lavatory, lavatory seat** (2).

Wolf French: a flaw (in timber, etc.) is a 'wolf', as is a black velvet mask worn at a masked ball (*loup*); someone who is known to everyone is *connu comme le loup blanc* ('known like the white wolf'). The Estonian for wolf, *määrkas's*, means also 'dirty little child, mudlark'. Nineteenth-century French slang for a sailor was *un loup de* *mer* (a sea-wolf). 'Curiously, it was once said that this ferocious creature feared the sea crab and the shrimp' (Newall).

See also **Dusk**, **Indian file**, **Loneliness**, **Puff-ball**, **Theatrical terms** (7).

Worm   Worms are associated with toothache. There is an Old German rhyme: 'Pear tree, I complain to thee; / Three worms sting me.' In Orkney, likewise, toothache was called 'the worm'.

See also **Tune**.

Wren

The wren was traditionally king of the birds. In Latin it is *regulus* (little king), in French *roi des oiseaux* (king of the birds), in Swedish *kungsvogel* (king's bird), in German *Zaunkönig* (hedge king) and *Schneekönig* (snow king). There are similar names in other languages . . . In Scotland . . . the wren is called 'the Lady of Heaven's hen' . . . French peasants called the bird *poulette de Dieu* (God's little chicken), which was supposed to have been in the stable at Bethlehem when Christ was born and to have covered Him with moss and feathers . . . In Breton legend, the wren brought fire from heaven and lost its feathers in the process. Guernsey tradition asserts that it carried water to the island from the mainland.

(Newall)

Writer   See **Office, In the** (squid).

X

X The Spanish *equis*, the name of the letter X, is used as as elsewhere as the coefficient of an indeterminate number, but in Latin America it thrives also in the expression *estar en la equis* ('to be in the X'), meaning to be all skin and bones or, in a familiar and financial sense, to be broke.

See also **Xmas**.

Xmas

Some Jews prefer to use the abbreviated form 'Xmas' so as to avoid writing the word 'Christmas'. Oddly enough, the use of Xmas for Christmas is not a Jewish innovation, nor is its use confined to Jews. The abbreviation was popularized by the print media to conserve space. Some Christians object to the use of Xmas, considering it a sign of disrespect and an attempt by non-believers to rid Christmas of its central meaning. However, Christian scholars have explained that use of the abbreviation should not be thought of as an affront to Christians because 'X' is the first letter of the Greek word *Xristos*.

(Alfred J. Kolatch, *The Second Jewish Book of Why*)

According to the *Oxford Dictionary*, 'Xmas' dates from 1551, and was earlier also X'tmas, Xstmas.

Y

Yellowhammer

In Welsh the word for yellowhammer means servant of the snake, for it was variously supposed to inform snakes if enemies were about, and to hatch them in its nest. This belief was linked with the wavy, serpentine markings upon its eggs. On the principle that like cures like, a Welsh folk remedy for jaundice was to hold a yellowhammer in front of the sufferer's face. A Danish variant of this advised the patient to eat three birds, feathers and all.

(Newall)

Yes (1) Canadian Eskimo for 'Yes, it is indeed so' is *ahamarik* (which is literally 'a fullgrown yes').

(2) In French one says *si* in positive response to a negative question ('*Tu ne vas pas?*' '*Si.*'), and *oui* in positive response to a positive one ('*Tu vas?*' '*Oui.*'). The same distinction, doubtless under Norman influence, once existed in English. In Chaucer, 'Yes' is the positive response to a negative question, corresponding to *si*: the equivalent of *oui* is always 'Yea'.

(3) German jocular *jein* – a blend of *ja* and *nein* – means just that, 'Yes and no'.

Yulan Gem-plant, Chinese, *yu*, a gem, plus *lan*, plant. A Chinese species of magnolia, *Magnolia conspicua*. I include this as another example of jewels and growing/budding metaphors (see page 50).

Z

Z As with 'h' in Northern Ireland, the pronunciation of 'z' is used as a rough-and-ready nationality test in North America. Canadians say 'zed', while in the United States it is 'zee'.

Zebra 'The ancestral father of the Kikuyus had ten wives, the youngest and most beautiful being called Zebra, or, in the Kikuyu language, Wambui. But she is never counted, it being ill-omened according to local tradition to count the last of anything. Wambui remains to this day an exceedingly popular name among Kikuyu girls.' (Newall)

Zebra crossing The English scores strongly over the prosaic French *passage clouté* (nailed passage). A friend's daughter, studying French, thought that *clouté* (nailed) must be the French for 'zebra'.

Zero See **Lavatory, lavatory seat** (3).

Zincalo, Zingano, Zingaro Romany for a Gypsy, or the name by which the Gypsies call themselves. It derives, says Borrow, from the Sanskrit sangkara, or *sankara*, meaning made-up. A Gypsy, therefore, is literally 'a person of mixed blood, one who springs from various races, a made-up person'. Yule and Burnell doubt this explanation, believing it less likely that the Gypsies carried the name *zingari* with them from the East than that they acquired it on reaching the West. They prefer an etymology encompassing the Persian *changī*, meaning harper. If *zingaro* is of Indian origin, they think it more probably comes from *chingaree*: 'They are an ancient tribe of Thugs, and take their wives and children on their expeditions.' The *Oxford Dictionary* gives the Greek '*Athinganoi*, an oriental people'.

Zip-fastener   (1) A colloquial word for a zip in German is *Schmiss*, which also means cut, gash, duelling scar. Closed, a zip resembles a stitched-up scar.

(2) The Spanish *cremallera* is the 'rack-and-pinion' of a mountain railway, and, in everyday contexts, a zipper. The railway track resembles a zip, the vehicle on it the zip-pull. *Schmiss* and *cremallera* combine in the scar-imagery of this snatch of dialogue (from Carl Hiaasen, *Tourist Season*):

> 'Let me see your stitches.'
> Keyes turned to one side and lifted his right arm.
> 'Oh boy,' said Jenna, whistling.
> 'Nasty, huh?'
> 'Looks like a railroad track.'

(3) In Italian, 'lightning fastener' (*chiusura lampo*). I once heard a Vatican official challenged on the radio to produce a Latin equivalent for 'zip'. He simply translated (without acknowledgement) *chiusura lampo*.

BIBLIOGRAPHY

(The authors and titles of other books are cited in the main text. The *Oxford Dictionary*, so referred to throughout, is *The Shorter Oxford English Dictionary* in the revised edition of 1973, with occasional excursions to the London Library to consult *The Oxford English Dictionary*, second edition, 1989.)

Beaujean, A., *Dictionnaire de la Langue Française Abrégé du Dictionnaire de É. Littré*, Paris, Librairie Hachette, 9th edn, 1895.

Beeton, D. R., and Dorner, Helen, *A Dictionary of English Usage in Southern Africa*, Cape Town, Oxford University Press, 1975.

Betteridge, H. T., *Cassell's German–English English–German Dictionary*, London, Cassell, 1978.

Bloomfield, Leonard, *An Introduction to the Study of Language*, London, G. Bell and Sons/New York, Henry Holt, 1914.

Bodmer, Frederick, *The Loom of Language*, London, Allen & Unwin, 1943.

Borrow, George, *Romano Lavo-Lil, Word Book of the Romany or, English Gypsy Language*, London, John Murray, 1905 (first published 1873).

Bowra, C. M., *From Virgil to Milton*, London, Macmillan, 1945.

Branford, Jean, *A Dictionary of South African English* (new enlarged edn), Cape Town, Oxford University Press, 1980.

Braudel, Fernand, *Capitalism and Material Life, 1400–1800*, London, Weidenfeld & Nicolson, 1973 (first published in France, 1967).

Burton, William, *A General History of Porcelain*, London, Cassell, 1921.

Caillois, Roger, *La Pieuvre: Essai sur la Logique de l'Imaginaire*, Paris, La Table Ronde, 1973.

Cassidy, F. G., and Le Page, R. B., *A Dictionary of Jamaican English*, Cambridge University Press, 1980.

Crawfurd, J., *Grammar and Dictionary of the Malay Language*, London, 1852.

Cumberledge, Geoffrey, *A Standard Swahili–English Dictionary*, London, The Inter-Territorial Language Committee for the East African Dependencies/Oxford University Press, 1948.

Cuyás, Arturo, *Appleton's New Spanish–English and English–Spanish Dictionary*, New York, Appleton, 1908.

Dal, Vladimir, *Tolkovy Slovar Zhivago Velikoruskago Yazyka* (Explanatory Dictionary of the Living Great Russian Language), 4 vols., Moscow, GIINS, 1955 (reprint of the 2nd enlarged edn, St Petersburg & Moscow, M. O. Volf, 1880–82).

Delphinis, Morgan, *Caribbean and African Languages, Social History, Language, Literature, and Education*, London, Karia, 1985.

Freese, J. H., *A New Pocket Dictionary of the English and Russian Languages*, London, Kegan Paul, Trench, Trubner, 1916.

Golovinsky, M., *New English–Russian and Russian–English Dictionary*, Paris, Garnier Frères, (1926).

Hale, Horatio, *A Manual of the Oregon Trade Language, or 'Chinook Jargon'*, London, Whittaker, 1890.

Haugen, Einar (editor-in-chief), *Norwegian–English Dictionary*, Madison, University of Wisconsin Press, 1965.

Hepburn, J. C., *A Japanese–English and English–Japanese Dictionary*, 7th edn, Tokyo/London, Z. P. Maruya/Kelly & Walsh/Trubner, 1903.

Hionides, Harry T., *Collins Pocket Greek Dictionary*, London & Glasgow, Collins, 1983.

Isidore of Seville, in: *American Philosophical Society Transactions*, NS, v. 54 ii, 1964, Introduction and commentary by William D. Sharpe, MD.

Jespersen, Otto, *Language, Its Nature, Development, and Origin*, London, Allen & Unwin, 1922.

Lee, Henry, *The Octopus: or The Devil Fish of Fiction and of Fact*, London, Chapman & Hall, 1875.

Litchfield, Frederick, *Pottery and Porcelain, A Guide to Collectors*, London, A. S. Black, 1925.

Littré, Émile, *Dictionnaire de la Langue Française*, Paris, 1873– (various editions: see, for example, Beaujean above).

Mansion, J. E., *Harrap's New Shorter French and English Dictionary*, London, Harrap, 1978.

Marchant, J. R. V., and Charles, J. F., *Cassell's Latin Dictionary*, London, Cassell.

Maxwell, W. E., *A Manual of the Malay Language*, London, 1911.

Müller, F. Max, *Lectures on the Science of Language*, London/New York, Longmans, Green, 1890.

Murphy, Captain John T., *The Book of Pidgin English*, Brisbane, W. R. Smith & Paterson, 3rd edn, 1949.

Nance, R. M., *A New Cornish–English Dictionary*, St Ives, James Lanham, 1938.

Nansen, Fridtjof, *Eskimo Life* (trans. William Archer), London, Longmans, Green, 1893.

Newall, Venetia, *Discovering the Folklore of Birds and Beasts*, Tring (Herts), Shire, 1971.

Ovid, *The Metamorphoses* (trans. Henry T. Riley), London, George Bell and Sons, 1902.

Peck, Rev. Edmund J. (ed. Rev. W. G. Walton), *Eskimo–English Dictionary* (compiled from Erdman's Eskimo–German edition, 1864), Hamilton, Ont., The Church of the Ascension Thank-Offering Mission Fund (Hamilton), 1925.

Pei, Mario, *The Story of Language*, London, Allen & Unwin, 1952.

Pliny, *Natural History*, vol. 2 (trans. and annot. John Bostock and Henry T. Riley), London, Henry G. Bohn, 1855.

Pliny, *Natural History. A Selection from Philemon Holland's Translation* (ed. J. Newsome), Oxford, Clarendon Press, 1964.

Pring, J. T., *The Oxford Dictionary of Modern Greek*, Oxford, Clarendon Press, 1986.

Quine, W. V., *Quiddities, An Intermittently Philosophical Dictionary*, Cambridge, Mass. / London, The Belknap Press of Harvard University Press, 1987.

Rebora, Piero (with the assistance of Dr Francis M. Guercio and Arthur L. Hayward), *Cassell's Italian–English English–Italian Dictionary*, London, Cassell, 1958.

Reynolds, Barbara, *The Concise Cambridge Italian Dictionary*, London, Penguin, 1975.

Robert, Paul, *Dictionnaire Alphabétique et Analogique de la Langue*

Française, Paris, Société du Nouveau Littré, 6 vols., 1957, 1962 (and other years, depending on volume). See also the later, single-volume edition, *Le Petit Robert*, Paris, 1967.

Scuchardt, Hugo, *The Ethnography of Variation. Selected Writings on Pidgins and Creoles* (ed. and trans. T. L. Markey), Ann Arbor, Mich., Karoma, 1979.

Selzer, Richard Alan, MD, 'The physician as writer', *Bull. Med. Libr. Ass.* (US), 78(1), January 1990.

Sillar, F. C., and Meyler, R. M., *The Symbolic Pig. An Anthology of Pigs in Literature and Art*, Edinburgh / London, Oliver & Boyd, 1961.

Smith, Colin, in collaboration with Manuel Bermejo Marcos and Eugenio Chang-Rodríguez, *Collins Spanish–English English–Spanish Dictionary*, London & Glasgow, Collins, 1971.

Smyth, W. H., *Sailor's Word-Book*, London, 1867.

Symbolic Pig, The. See Sillar and Meyler, above.

Taylor, James L., *A Portuguese–English Dictionary*, London, Harrap, 1959.

Thiebert, Arthur, *English–Eskimo Dictionary*, Ottawa, Research Center of Amerindian Anthropology, University of Ottawa, Canada, 1954.

Todd, Loreto, *Modern Englishes: Pidgins and Creoles*, Basil Blackwell (Oxford) in association with André Deutsch (London), 1984.

Varro, *On the Latin Language* (with an English translation by Professor Roland G. Kent of the University of Pennsylvania), Cambridge, Mass., Harvard University Press / London, Heinemann, 1951.

Warner, Marina, *Alone of All Her Sex: The Myth and the Cult of the Virgin Mary*, London, Weidenfeld & Nicolson, 1976.

Wasson, V. P., and R. G., *Mushrooms, Russia, and History*, New York, Pantheon Books (privately printed in an edition of 512 copies), 1957. In this book the husband-and-wife team is referred to simply as 'Wasson'.

Wedgwood, Hensleigh, *On the Origin of Language*, London, Trubner, 1866.

Yule, Colonel Henry, and Burnell, Arthur Coke, *Hobson-Jobson, Being a Glossary of Anglo-Indian Colloquial Words and Phrases, and of Kindred Terms; Etymological, Historical, Geographical, and Discursive*, London, John Murray, 1886.